Modern Wiring Diagrams And Descriptions: A Handbook Of Practical Diagrams And Information For Electrical Construction Work, Showing At A Glance All That Ordinary Electrical Workers Need And Nothing That They Do Not Need

Victor Hugo Tousley, Henry Charles Horstmann

Nabu Public Domain Reprints:

You are holding a reproduction of an original work published before 1923 that is in the public domain in the United States of America, and possibly other countries. You may freely copy and distribute this work as no entity (individual or corporate) has a copyright on the body of the work. This book may contain prior copyright references, and library stamps (as most of these works were scanned from library copies). These have been scanned and retained as part of the historical artifact.

This book may have occasional imperfections such as missing or blurred pages, poor pictures, errant marks, etc. that were either part of the original artifact, or were introduced by the scanning process. We believe this work is culturally important, and despite the imperfections, have elected to bring it back into print as part of our continuing commitment to the preservation of printed works worldwide. We appreciate your understanding of the imperfections in the preservation process, and hope you enjoy this valuable book.

STOKE-ON-TRENT LIBRARIES	
01679 0352	
Amazon	6.9.10

Copyright **1918**, 1914, 1911, 1906 and 1903

By

HORSTMANN & TOUSLEY

TABLE OF CONTENTS

CHAPTER I.
Call Bell Circuits, Bells, Dynamo Connections . . Page 7

CHAPTER II.
Annunciator Circuits 21

CHAPTER III.
Fire and Burglar Alarms 28

CHAPTER IV.
Telephone and Telegraph Circuits 43

CHAPTER V.
Electric Gas Lighting 61

CHAPTER VI.
Primary and Secondary Batteries 66

CHAPTER VII.
Connecting Up, Locating Trouble 76

CHAPTER VIII.
Miscellaneous 86

CHAPTER IX.
Electric Lighting 97

CHAPTER X.
Arc Lamps, Nernst Lamp, Cooper Hewitt Lamp . . 116

CHAPTER XI.
Recording Wattmeters 125

TABLE OF CONTENTS

CHAPTER XII.
Direct Current Motors 131

CHAPTER XIII.
Automobiles, Charging Stations, Gas Engines . . 159

CHAPTER XIV.
Direct and Alternating Current Generators, Compensators, Arc Lamp Control for Motion Picture Work 167

CHAPTER XV.
Alternating Current Motors, Transformers . . . 196

CHAPTER XVI.
Armatures 233

CHAPTER XVII.
Switchboards, Ground Detectors 236

CHAPTER XVIII.
Storage Battery Connections 250

CHAPTER XIX.
Testing 259

CHAPTER XX.
Light 273

CHAPTER XXI.
Wiring Tables 277

CHAPTER XXII.
Electric Signs, Flashers, Display Lighting . . . 285

MODERN
WIRING DIAGRAMS AND DESCRIPTIONS.

CHAPTER I.

CALL BELL CIRCUITS.—BELLS.—DYNAMO CONNECTIONS.

Figure 1 shows a simple bell circuit with extra wires for a door opener to be operated from the vicin-

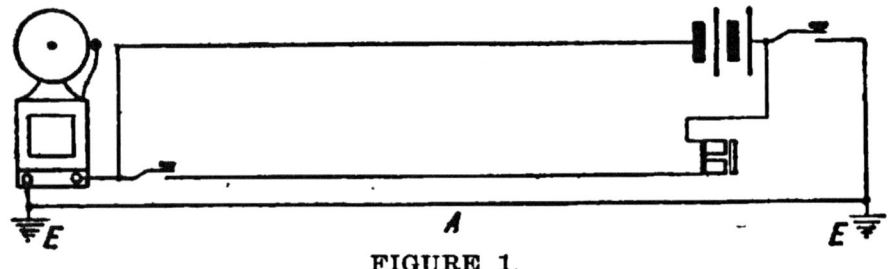
FIGURE 1.

ity of the bell. In this diagram the wire A may be left out and two ground connections used as shown at E.

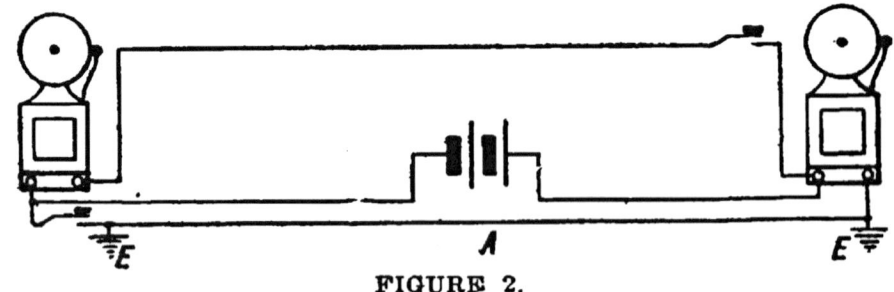
FIGURE 2.

Figure 2 shows a method of wiring usually employed where it is desired that parties at either end may call and also receive an answering ring as an indication that the signal has been heard.

Figure 3 shows another method of wiring to accomplish the same purpose as the foregoing figure. In this case the bells are in series. This method requires greater battery power and one of the bells must also be arranged to act single stroke.

Two ordinary circuit breaking bells will not act well in series as for instance the one having the stiffer spring or slightly weaker magnet would always lag

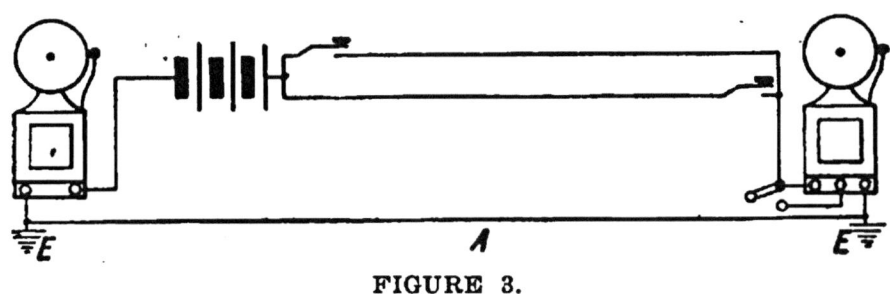

FIGURE 3.

behind the other never coming to a full stroke. The advantage of this arrangement is that it enables the caller to know (by the ringing of his own bell) that the one at the other end is ringing. If the single stroke bell is located at the employer's end and the circuit breaking bell at the attendant's end the employer may know absolutely that the bell at the other end rings when the one at his station does, since it is the attendant's bell which breaks the circuit and causes the one at his own desk to ring. At one station (which may be taken as the attendant's) there is shown a 3-way switch by which the attendant may change his bell from vibrating to single stroke. This will enable him to arrange so that the bell may attract general attention or that it may be noticed only by one near it.

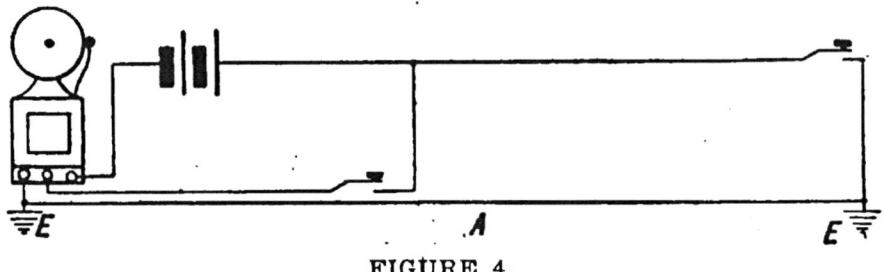
FIGURE 4.

Figure 4 shows one bell arranged to be rung from two stations. From one of the stations it will act single stroke and the ringing will indicate which station is calling.

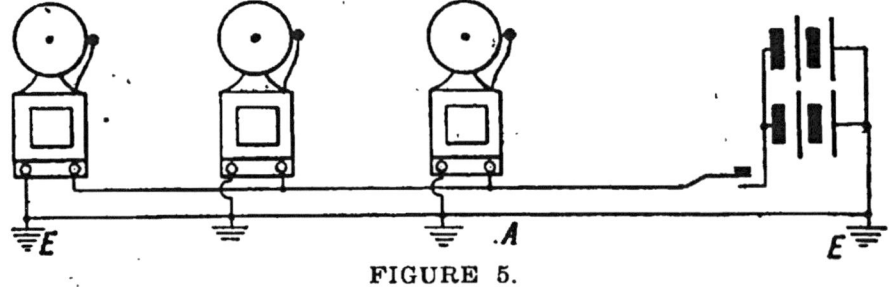
FIGURE 5.

Figure 5 shows a number of bells arranged to be rung from one push button. With this method it is essential that the battery be of low internal resistance and of ample current capacity. This result may be obtained by grouping the cells as shown in the figure; it is, however, preferable to use large cells singly rather than smaller ones in multiple.

Figure 6 shows connections by which either of the right hand pushes will ring the single bell near battery, while from the station at battery the other two bells may be rung with one push button.

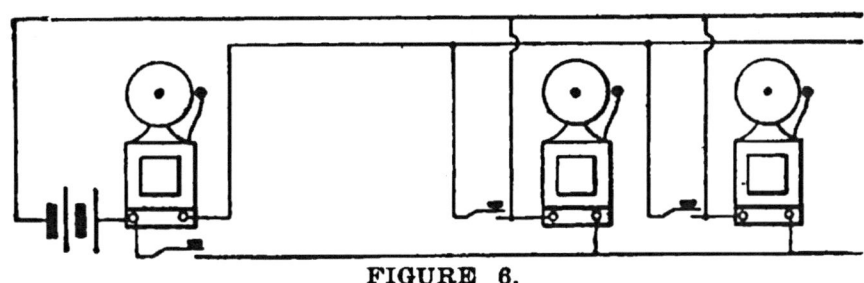
FIGURE 6.

Figure 7 shows two bells arranged with one wire and grounds so that parties at either end may call. This method is economical in regard to wire but requires a battery and 3-way push at each end. The push buttons must normally keep the line closed from bell to bell, leaving the battery circuits open. When a push button is pressed the battery at that end rings the bell at the other.

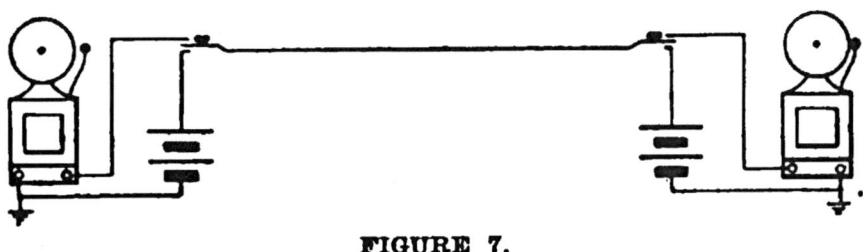
FIGURE 7.

Figure 8 shows a bell so connected that it may be controlled from either of two stations. If both switches are set to the same wire the bell rings. If

CALL BELL CIRCUITS

either switch is moved to the other wire the bell stops. The advantage of this method lies in the fact that the bell may be left to ring continuously or not as desired. At one station the wiring is arranged

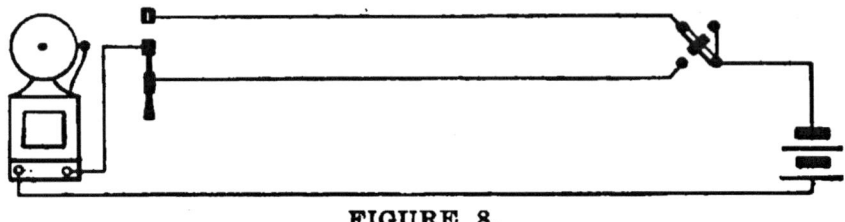

FIGURE 8.

for a double throw knife switch and at the other end for a 3-way snap switch.

Figure 9 shows an arrangement of switches which enables one to turn the bells on or off at any one of any number of stations. These bells are in series and

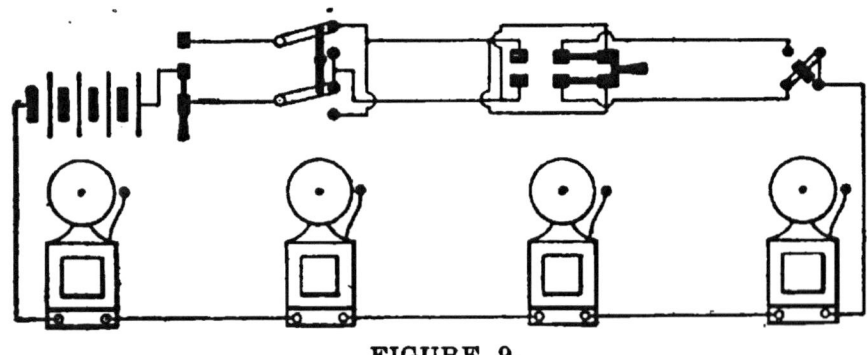

FIGURE 9.

may be left to ring continuously or not as desired. In this diagram throw-over knife switches, snap switches and specially designed switches are shown to illustrate the different ways of attaining the same object.

Figure 10 shows two bells connected by means of the switch S so that either may be used alone or both

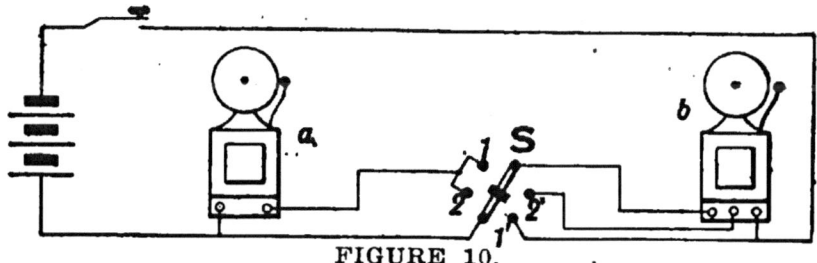
FIGURE 10.

together. With the switch as shown *b* will ring alone. If the switch is turned to 2 and 2′ both bells

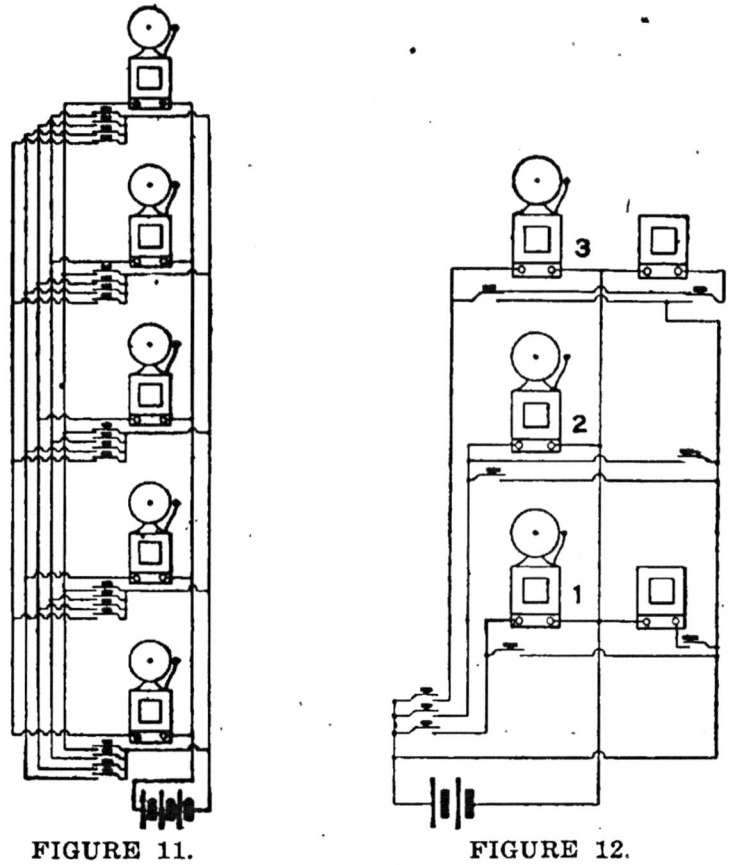
FIGURE 11.   FIGURE 12.

will be in series, one acting single stroke. With the switch connecting 1 and 1′ *a* will ring alone.

CALL BELL CIRCUITS

Figure 11 shows the manner of wiring commonly used in connection with speaking tube systems. It may also be used with interior telephones. Any station is able to call and may also be called from any other station. Only one battery is used and from one of its poles one wire connects to all of the push buttons. From the other pole another wire passes to one binding post of each bell. From the other binding post of each bell wires are then run to the corresponding push buttons at each of the other stations.

Figure 12 shows an arrangement of wiring often used in connection with flat buildings. One set of push buttons is arranged at the main entrance on first floor usually together with letter boxes and speaking tubes. Another set of push buttons may also be placed one at the front door of each flat. This enables the bell to be rung either from main entrance or from entrance to flat. In addition to these, three different connections are shown in the three flats. In flat 1 a buzzer has been added and is connected to ring from rear door. In flat 2 the same bell rings from main hall, front door and rear entrance. In this case small signs requesting parties to ring a certain number of times will be found very useful at front and rear doors. In flat 3, buzzer and bell will ring from main entrance; the buzzer alone will ring from rear entrance and the bell alone

14   WIRING DIAGRAMS

from front entrance. Three-way pushes are used for front and rear door.

Figure 13 shows the plan of a differential bell. The two coils are wound to oppose one another, so that when current is flowing through both there will be no magnetism. When current is applied at first it flows through one coil only; this attracts the armature, which in turn closes the circuit through the other coil. Both coils now balance, and the armature is released, thus producing the same vibrations as in an ordinary bell.

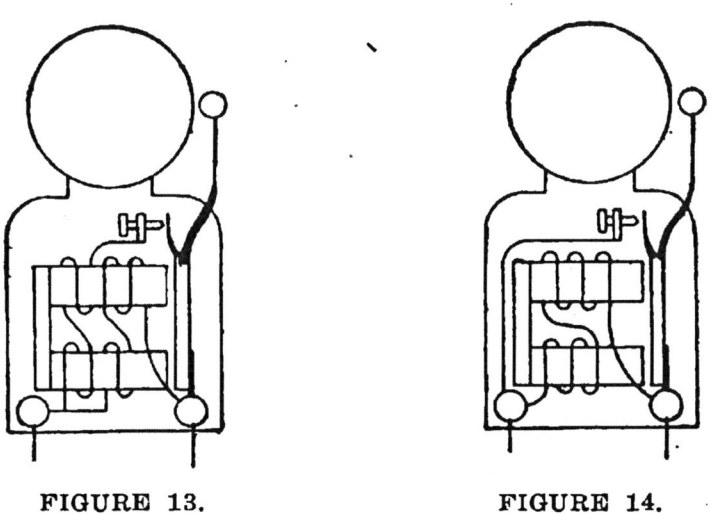

FIGURE 13.   FIGURE 14.

Figure 14 shows a short circuit bell. The current in its circuit is never broken, but, as the magnets attract the armature, the spring in connection with it closes the shunt circuit and this deprives the coil of current, thus destroying its magnetism and releasing its armature. This, and also the differen-

CALL BELL CIRCUITS 15

tial bell, will operate with less sparking than an ordinary vibrating bell, and both are useful on circuits of higher voltage. The short-circuit bell should be used only on circuits where other resistances prevent any great rise in current. On an ordinary battery circuit it would not be useful.

Figure 15 shows a bell arranged to act either single stroke or vibrating. For temporary purposes a bell may be made to act single stroke by simply adjusting the vibrator spring so that it does not open the circuit.

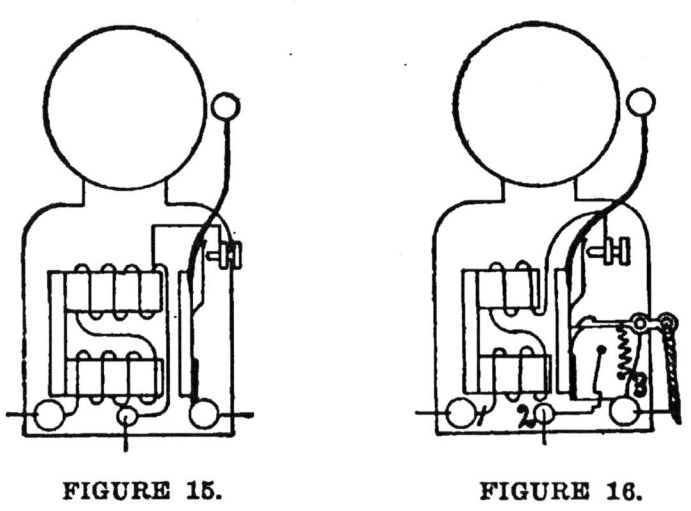

FIGURE 15.   FIGURE 16.

Figure 16 shows a bell with continuous ringing attachment. As the armature is attracted the lever falls and completes the circuit through binding post 2. From this post a wire leads to the battery and completes the circuit through post 1. This attachment may be added to any of the other bells. The bell will continue to ring until the little lever is placed in its normal position.

Figure 17 shows the arrangement of a polarized bell. This bell may be used in connection with alternating currents, and is the type generally used in telephone work. This type of bell may also be used with continuous currents when provisions for reversing are made; and in this way can be made to act as a single stroke bell, each reversal of current causing one stroke.

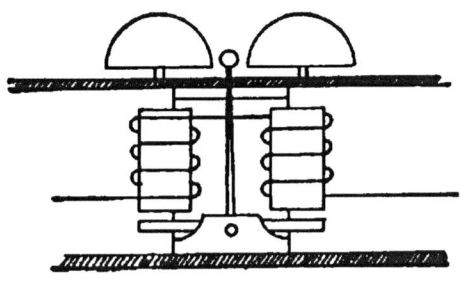

FIGURE 17.

It is often desirable to operate bells from electric light circuits, either direct or through suitable storage batteries. For this purpose incandescent lamps may be placed in series with the bell system, and by choosing lamps of the proper candle power and voltage any necessary current may be obtained. There are also special resistances designed for this purpose which may take the place of lamps shown in diagram or may be placed one with each bell. The main objection to lamps as shown in the diagrams would

CALL BELL CIRCUITS

be encountered when several bells in a system are to be used at the same time; since only a certain amount of current can pass through the lamps, only one bell at a time can be arranged to work properly. This trouble can be avoided by placing a lamp or resistance in series with each bell and leaving out those shown in diagrams. One lamp on one side of the circuit is sufficient to insure proper operation, but it is advisable to use one on each side, as shown in the figure, to prevent serious damage which might be caused by grounds if one side only contained resistance.

If dynamo current is to be brought into connection with bells, the wiring and insulation should be fully equal to that required for incandescent wiring. Push-buttons should be mounted on fireproof bases and no inflammable material should be used either within or about the bells.

When the ordinary incandescent lamp is used for resistance, it must be borne in mind that the resistance of the lamp when cold is very much greater than when hot or burning; varying in the ordinary 110 volt 16 c. p. lamp from 900 ohms cold to 220 ohms hot. If the lamp is to be used in a circuit where the current is low the cold resistance must be figured, but if the current approaches that at which the lamp burns the hot resistance must be figured, otherwise the rise in current when the lamp heats might damage the instruments in the circuit. To overcome this, special lamps are made to be used on circuits where the current is low.

In Figure 18 an arrangement is shown by which the battery is automatically disconnected when the

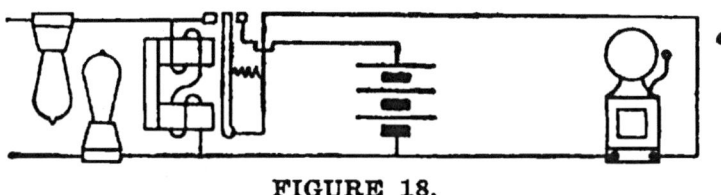

FIGURE 18.

dynamo is in operation. The magnet when energized attracts its armature, thus breaking the battery circuit and completing the dynamo connections to the bell system. When the dynamo current ceases a spring draws the armature back again, closing the battery circuit.

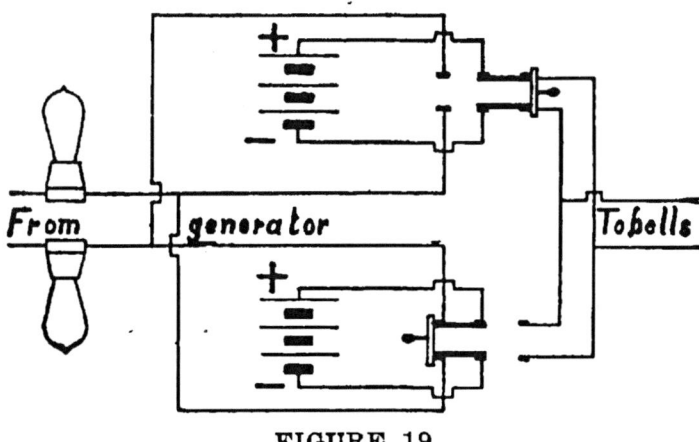

FIGURE 19.

Figure 19 shows two batteries, each provided with a throw-over switch. While one is operating the bells the other is charging. The dynamo current

CALL BELL CIRCUITS

never comes in contact with the bell wiring and no extra insulation is necessary. The + pole of the dynamo must connect to + pole of battery always, in order to charge.

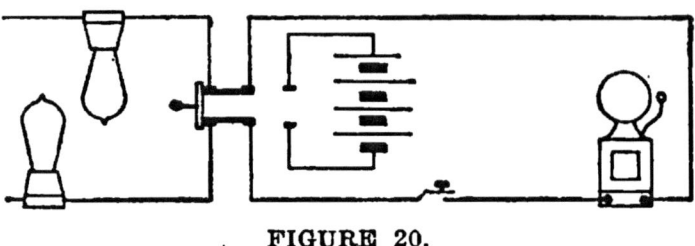

FIGURE 20.

Figure 20 shows dynamo connections direct to the bells and a primary battery provided to operate bells when dynamo is at rest.

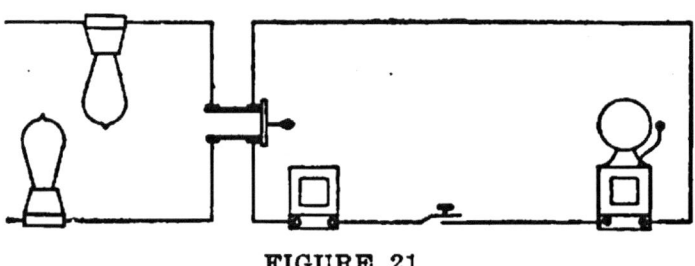

FIGURE 21.

Figure 21 also shows direct dynamo connection to the bell wiring. In this diagram a master circuit breaker in the form of a buzzer or bell is introduced into the circuit, and the bells throughout the building may be arranged single stroke. The sparking is always more destructive with high potential, and often causes much trouble with ordinary cheap bells; therefore this circuit breaker should be of high grade and located convenient to engineer or janitor, so it may be kept in order. This circuit breaker should also be selected with reference to the bells used, as it must not vibrate faster than the natural vibration of the bells.

CHAPTER II.

ANNUNCIATOR CIRCUITS.

Figures 22, 23 and 24 show diagrammatical representations of ordinary annunciators. In Figure 22 two annunciators are shown, one to be located in the kitchen or hall and the other perhaps in the servant's bedroom. By means of the switches 1, 2, 3, the push buttons are connected to either one of the annunciators as may be desired. The bell connected with each annunciator has a continuous ringing attachment shown by the extra wire attached to the middle bind-

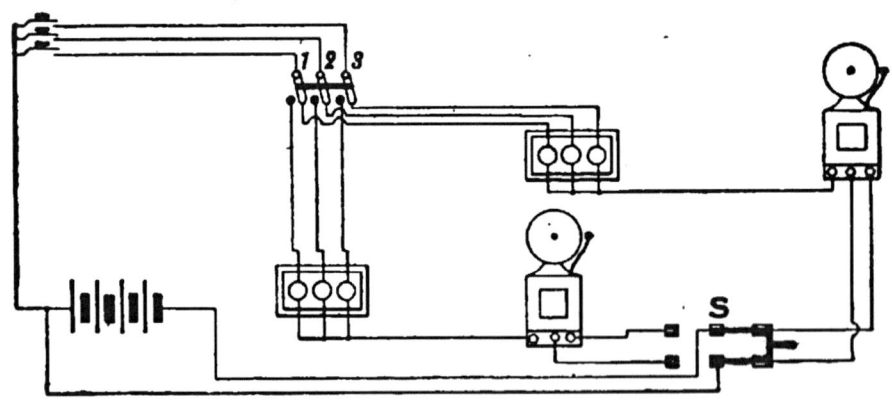

FIGURE 22.

ing post. The overthrow switch S is not absolutely necessary but is quite desirable as a safeguard; it sometimes happens that the continuous ringing attachment falls, and without this switch the bell would ring and run battery down, even though the annunciator were disconnected by the switches 1, 2, 3.

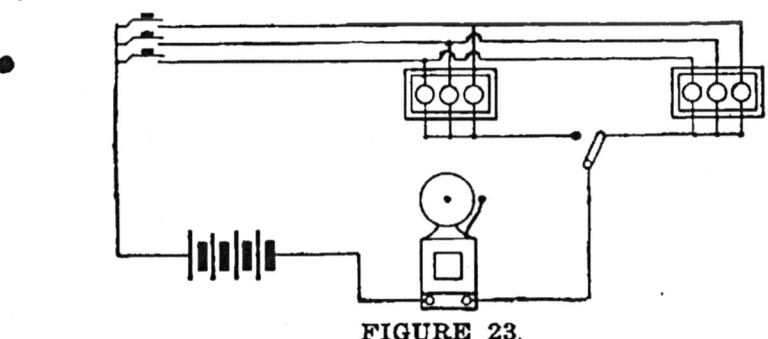
FIGURE 23.

Figure 23 shows a method of connecting two annunciators which should be avoided. With just the right battery strength and accurate adjustment of drops it may work fairly well for a time, but sooner

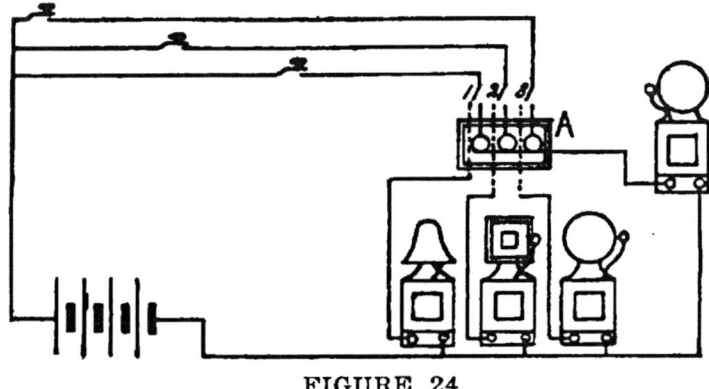
FIGURE 24.

or later it will result in confusion. By tracing out the circuits it will be seen that from any push there are several paths which the current may take although one is more direct and has less resistance than the others.

ANNUNCIATOR CIRCUITS

Figure 24 shows an annunciator to which have been added the switches 1, 2, 3, and also the wires leading to the three bells shown below it. The switches are mechanically connected so that all may be operated at once. These switches serve to disconnect the annunciator magnets and at the same time to connect the three bells with the push buttons. With the switches set to the magnets, the current from any push button passes through the corresponding magnet and through the single bell at the right. With the switches set to the wires leading to the bells the current passes through the corresponding bell without

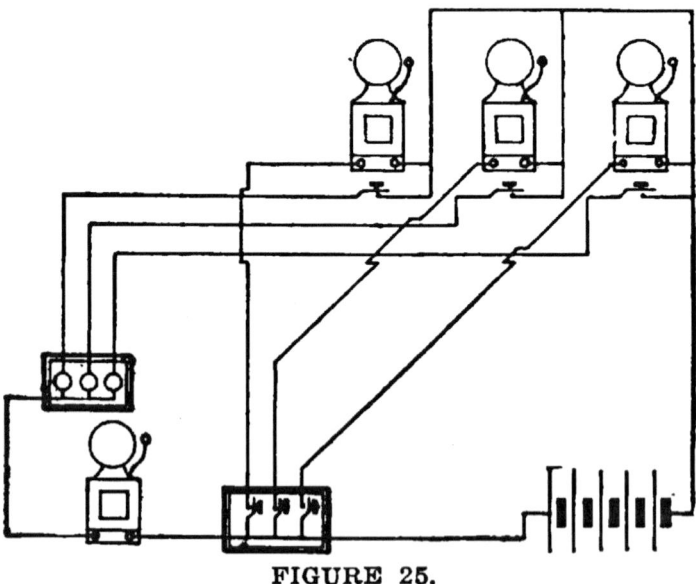

FIGURE 25.

disturbing the single bell. The three bells shown together are of different sound and the ring will indicate location of the caller without the necessity of looking at the annunciator. This may be useful in many residences where the room in which the annunciator is located is not always occupied.

Figure 25 shows a return call annunciator system as it is frequently used in hotels, where it is necessary that a guest may call the office as well as be called from the office. This system requires one battery and two leading wires for each room, one leading wire passing from each room to the annunciator, while another passes from each push to one of the bells located in rooms.

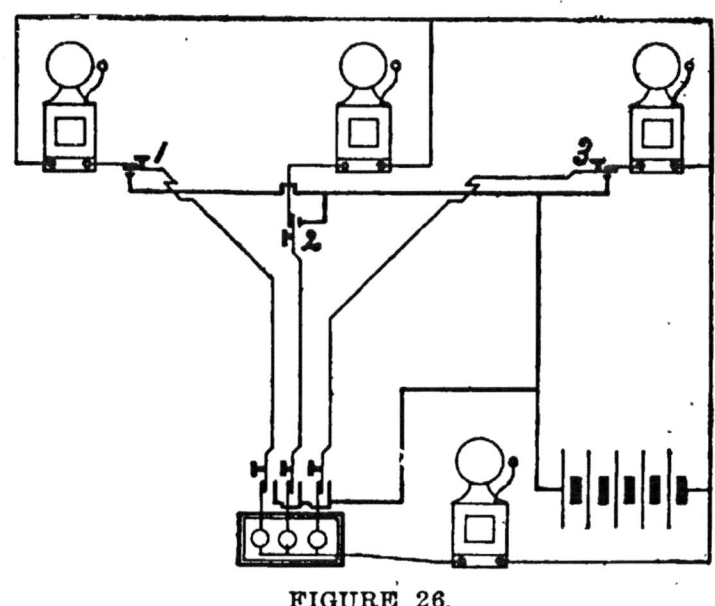

FIGURE 26.

Figure 26 shows another system of annunciator wiring for the same purpose as Figure 25. This system requires only one leading wire from each room, but two general battery wires. One battery wire leads to each bell and to the annunciator, while

ANNUNCIATOR CIRCUITS

the other leads to one point of each push button. Three-way push-buttons are used in the rooms and at the annunciator. Pressing any of the buttons 1, 2, 3, will operate the annunciator, while pressing any of the buttons at the annunciator will ring the bell in the corresponding room.

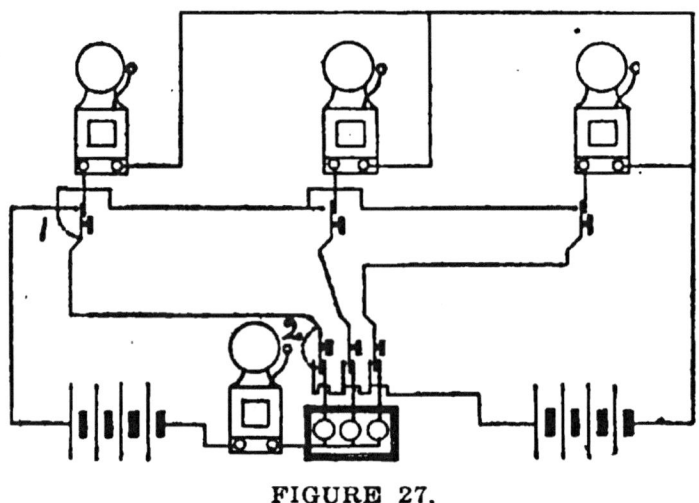

FIGURE 27.

Figure 27 shows diagrammatically the wiring used in the Partrick, Carter & Wilkins annunciator system, which is quite extensively used. Two general battery wires are necessary, and also one wire from each room to the corresponding drop on the annunciator. Two three-way pushes, one at the annunciator and one in each room, are also necessary. These push-buttons are mounted on bells and on annunciator respectively, making the whole arrangement very compact. With reference to each other, the polarities of the two sets of batteries must be as shown. If it were otherwise both batteries, acting in series, would ring all of the bells and attract all of the annunciator needles whenever the two push-buttons on the same wire were pushed at the same time. This will, however, very seldom occur. By means of the dotted lines at 1 and 2 the circuits thus formed can be readily traced.

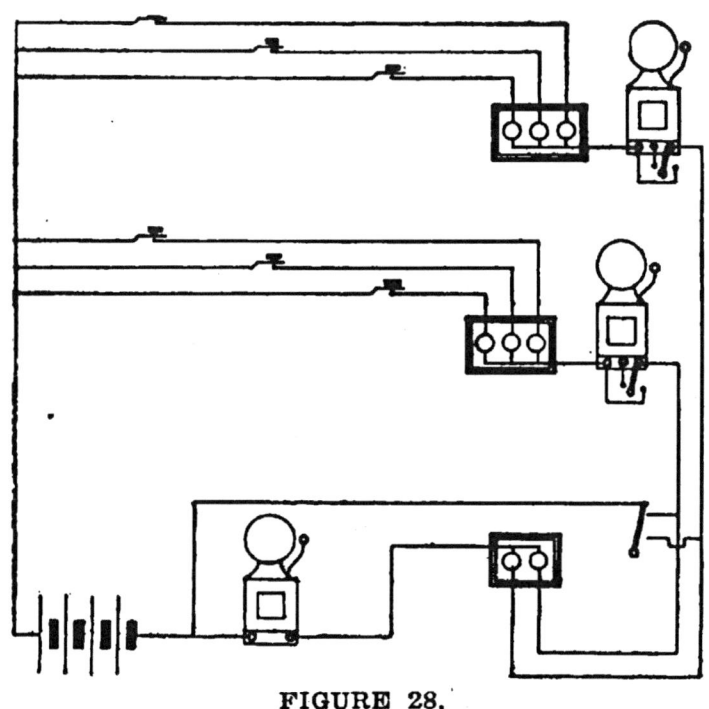

FIGURE 28.

The annunciator magnets used in this system are made so as to partially retain their magnetism after the current ceases to flow, in order to hold the indicator until an attendant releases it. The magnets are magnetized in a certain direction before the annunciator is sent out, and it is advisable to connect the battery so that this magnetism is not reversed.

ANNUNCIATOR CIRCUITS

The binding post on annunciator to which the zinc pole of battery should be connected is plainly indicated on each instrument.

It must not be understood that the P., C. & W. annunciators can be used with this method of wiring only; in fact, either of the methods shown in Figures 25 or 26 are applicable to it, Figure 25 being preferred where it is likely that at some time telephones may be connected with it.

Figure 28 shows an arrangement of annunciators which is quite economical in hotels or restaurants, where there is a great variation in business at different hours. Each floor has an annunciator which indicates the room sending a call, and each of these annunciators is in series with one drop of another annunciator located at the main office and which indicates the floor from which the call came. The bells located with annunciators on the different floors are each provided with a switch, by which any one of them may be made to act single stroke or be cut out altogether. During busy hours an attendant is kept on each floor and the bells are set to act independently, while the annunciator and bells at the main office are cut out altogether by the switch shown. During slack hours the bells on the different floors may be cut out and an attendant stationed at the main office only. The figure shows switches by which the bells may be cut out.

CHAPTER III.

FIRE AND BURGLAR ALARMS.

Figure 29 shows a number of annunciators arranged to act as a manual fire alarm. When any one of the switches S is closed it causes a bell to ring on each floor, and each annunciator indicates from which floor the alarm came. Independent batteries are provided for each floor to insure greater reliability, as one battery failing will disable one floor only. The batteries must all be arranged as shown in diagram, so that all will send current in the same direction.

Figure 30 shows the building system of the Consolidated Fire Alarm Telegraph Company, of New York, and the description here given is condensed from a memorandum furnished by this company to the Underwriters' Bureau of Fire Engineering, and which forms part of Electrical Signal Report No. 14.

The house wiring used with this system consists entirely of two parallel circuits led throughout the building in close proximity. At suitable intervals, as required by the local insurance boards, thermostats, c, and manual switches, D, are installed. The current flows continuously through both circuits, including the magnets A and B. The magnet A while energized holds at rest a transmitting device which, when released, automatically causes a fire signal to be sent in.

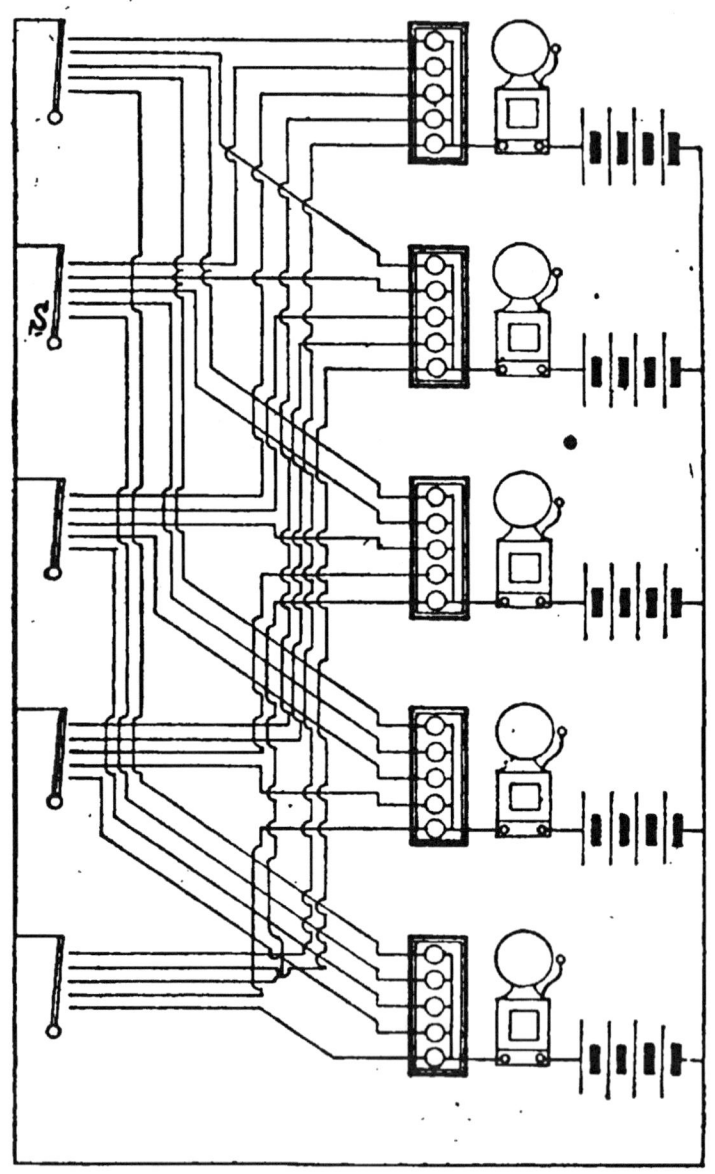

FIGURE 29.

In order to send in a fire signal, it is necessary that both coils of magnet A be de-energized; this will occur only when both lines are broken, either through the melting of a fuse in each line, or by means of

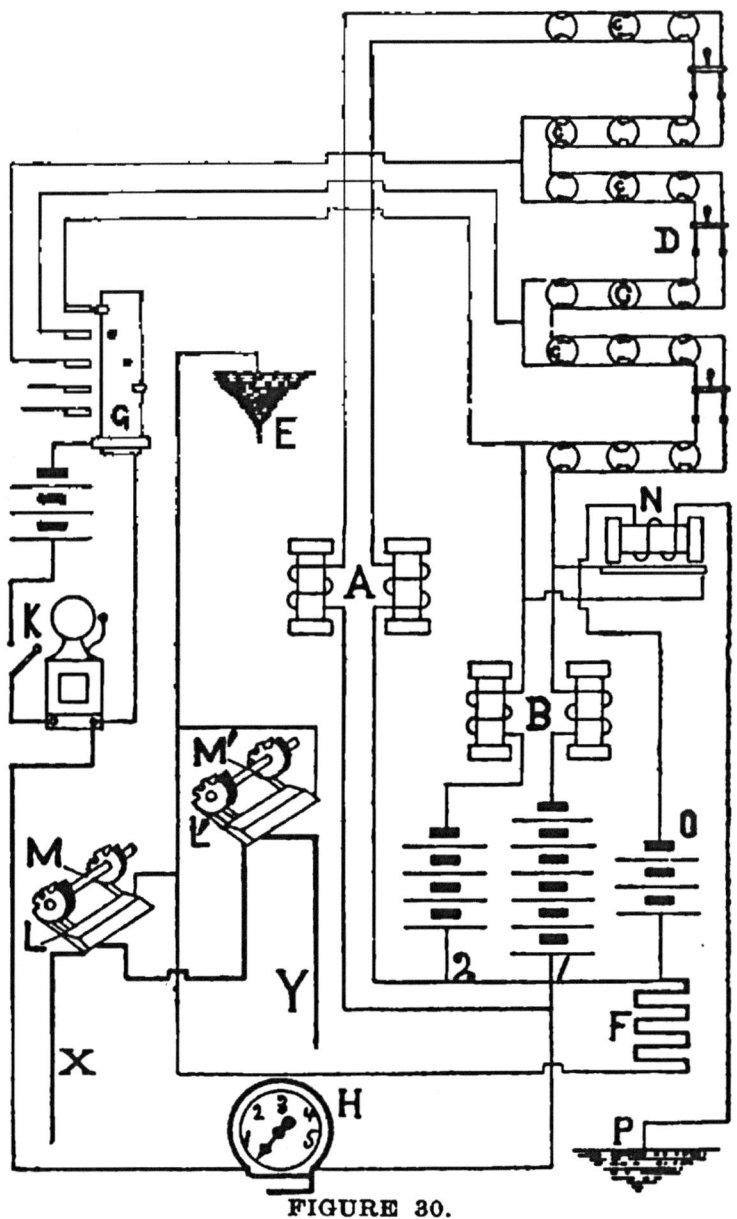

FIGURE 30.

one of the manual switches. The two coils of magnet B are wound in opposite directions, and hence there is no magnetism while current flows equally in both lines. Should, however, any variation in current strength occur in either of the lines the balance is at once destroyed, and the armature being now attracted releases a transmitting device which sends in a trouble alarm. In order that any possible electrical defect may disturb the balance of the magnet B and send in a trouble alarm, the battery in one of the lines is of higher voltage than the other. The resistance of the magnets and lines vary in the same proportion, so that normally the current in both lines is equal. Part of the transmitting devices are shown at M and M'. The double contact springs L and L' normally keep the outside circuit X-Y closed. The springs M and M' are provided to connect the ground E by means of projections on the contact wheels, whenever the double contact springs close on any of the other projections. In this way, by means of the ground, signals are transmitted, even though the circuit X-Y be broken somewhere.

In view of the importance of the grounds E and P, they are placed under constant test by means of the battery O, which maintains current from E to P through the relay N. If this current fails, the armature of N short-circuits the main wires, causing a trouble call to be sent in. Whenever a fire alarm occurs the transmitting device revolves the cylinder G. This cylinder, by means of raised teeth, engages the contact springs of wires led to it from the different floors, and in this way controls the magnet in the annunciator H, which moves the pointer forward one step for each impulse received. When a point beyond the broken line is reached, the impulses cease and the pointer stops, indicating the location of the fire. The cylinder G is so arranged that the local ringing circuit is closed only when a fire alarm is sent in.

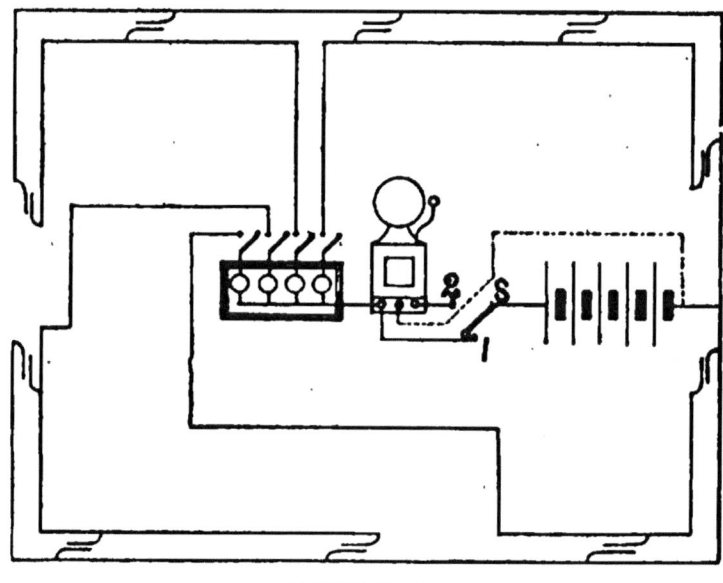

FIGURE 31.

Figure 31 shows an annunciator arranged as a burglar alarm. When used for this purpose it is usual to have the bell arranged to ring continuously when once started. It is also necessary to arrange for what is known as the silent test. For this purpose each circuit leaving the annunciator is provided with a switch by which it may be disconnected during the

FIRE AND BURGLAR ALARMS

day to avoid giving an alarm whenever a door or window is opened. When ready to close the house at night the switch S is turned to connect at 1; each circuit is then thrown in singly, and if any door or window has been left open the drop will indicate it without ringing the bell. When all is in order the switch is turned to 2, thus completing the circuit

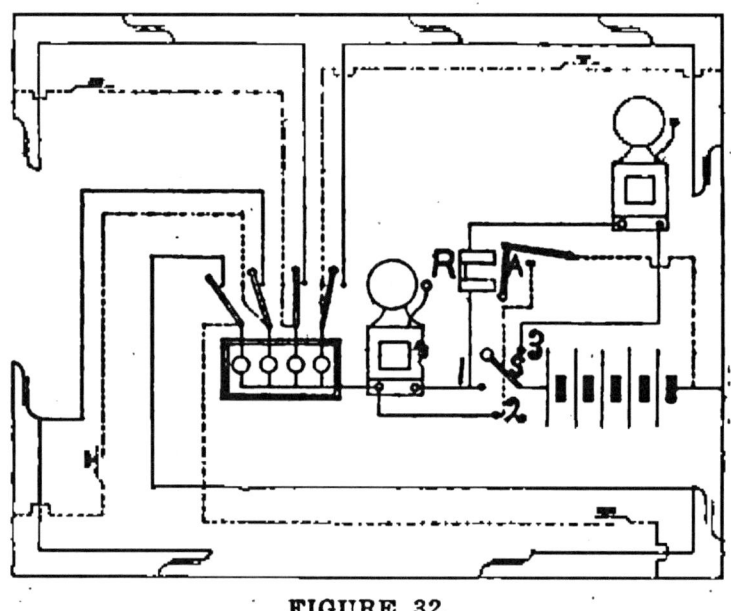

FIGURE 32.

through the bell. The dotted lines show the wiring for the continuous ringing attachment as shown in Figure 16, Chapter I.

With burglar alarm systems it is quite usual to connect the wiring through a suitably arranged clock, which can be made to connect or disconnect the wiring at certain hours. Provision may also be made by which the current, when releasing the annunciator drop, also releases a weight or spring, allowing them to operate a mechanical bell.

Figure 32 shows the same annunciator and bell arranged to act as a combination burglar alarm and house annunciator. The same provision for silent test has been made as in Figure 31. The solid lines show the wiring for window and door springs, while the dotted lines indicate wiring to push buttons. By means of the four switches shown on the annunciator, the window and door circuits may be shut off during the day, leaving only the push buttons connected. The push buttons are always in circuit, so that an alarm may be turned in at any time.

In this figure an extra bell is shown, which may be connected in series with the annunciator bell by moving the switch S to point 3. In this case the current entering through any drop of the annunciator will pass through both bells and the magnet R to point 3, switch S and the battery. Current passing through R attracts the armature A, allowing the switch to drop, thus closing the battery circuit through both bells, causing them to ring continuously. The extra wiring for this purpose is shown in dotted lines.

Figure 33 shows an attachment for constant ringing which is known as Callows. This consists of a magnet provided with two coils as shown. When the button is pressed current passes around coil 1, and this attracts the armature A, which is also in electrical connection with the battery. A part of the current

FIRE AND BURGLAR ALARMS 35

now passes along the armature to the wire leading to the bell, and at the junction X it divides, one-half passing through the bell and the other around coil 2 of the magnet. The current passing around coil 2

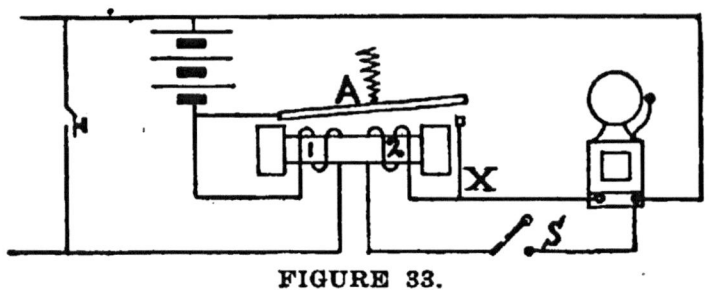

FIGURE 33.

keeps the armature in position while the current in the bell is interrupted. If the switch S is open the bell will ring only while the button is pressed. With this attachment the switch controlling the constant ringing may be at any distance from the bell.

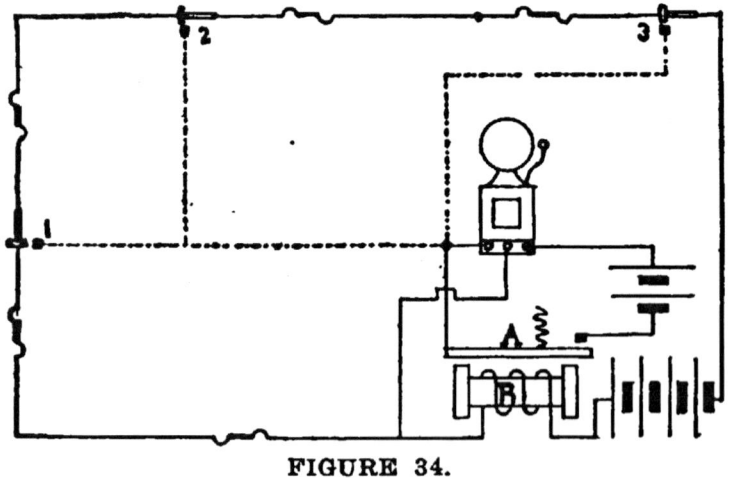

FIGURE 34.

Figure 34 shows a closed circuit burglar alarm. Current is always flowing along the main line. This current, by means of relay R, keeps the local bell circuit open. Whenever the main circuit is opened anywhere the relay armature A flies back, closing the local circuit and causing the bell to ring. This figure also shows combination wiring, whereby the bell may be used single stroke for calling. Switches are provided at 1, 2 and 3, and arranged so that connection is made with the circuit shown in dotted lines before that in the full lines is broken. While current passes along the wires shown in full lines it passes through the relay only. When one of the buttons makes connection with any of the wires shown in dotted lines, the current passes through the bell and relay. The bell is arranged single stroke for calling, but will ring vibrating when the relay closes the local circuit.

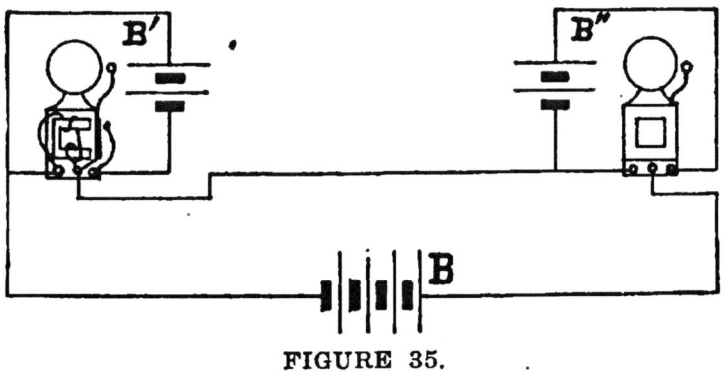

FIGURE 35.

Figure 35 shows a simple closed circuit burglar alarm. In this case the current passes continuously through the bell magnets and keeps the bell armatures attracted. In this way the local circuits B', B" are kept open as long as current from the closed circuit battery B flows through the magnets. Whenever the main wires are opened both bells will ring continuously. Short-circuiting the main wires will also cause one or both bells to ring, according to location of the short circuit. This is a very simple and useful arrangement, and may be extended to any number of bells in a building.

If crow foot batteries are to be used in connection with this system the bells must be specially wound; the ordinary bell has not a sufficient number of turns of wire to operate properly with the small currents obtainable from these batteries.

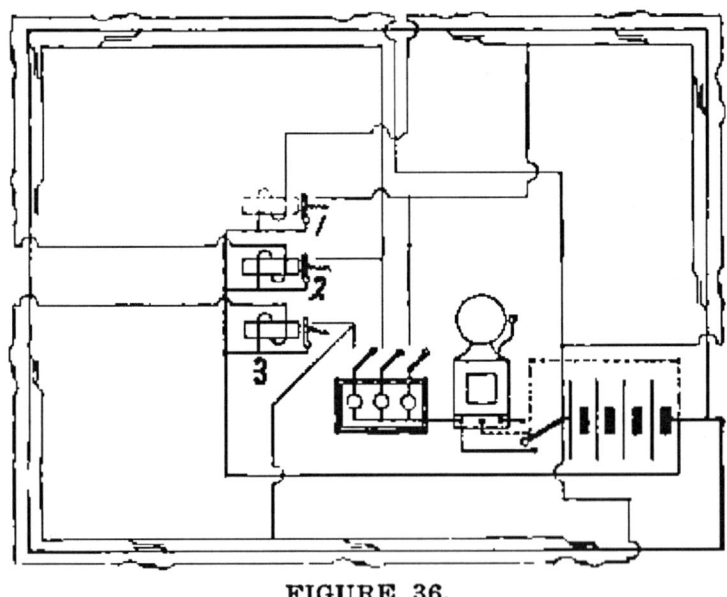

FIGURE 36.

Figure 36 shows a burglar alarm system using both open and closed circuits. Both circuits are run to each opening. The wiring is the same as in Figure

31, and the three closed circuits passing through the three relays, 1, 2, 3, have been added. While current passes through these relays their armatures are attracted; if any circuit is opened the corresponding armature flies back and closes the circuit through the corresponding drop on the annunciator. This system requires a closed circuit battery, and, when certain kinds of cells are used, provision must be made to keep the battery at work if the annunciator is disconnected for any great length of time. As here shown, the battery will always be at work unless a window or door in each section is open.

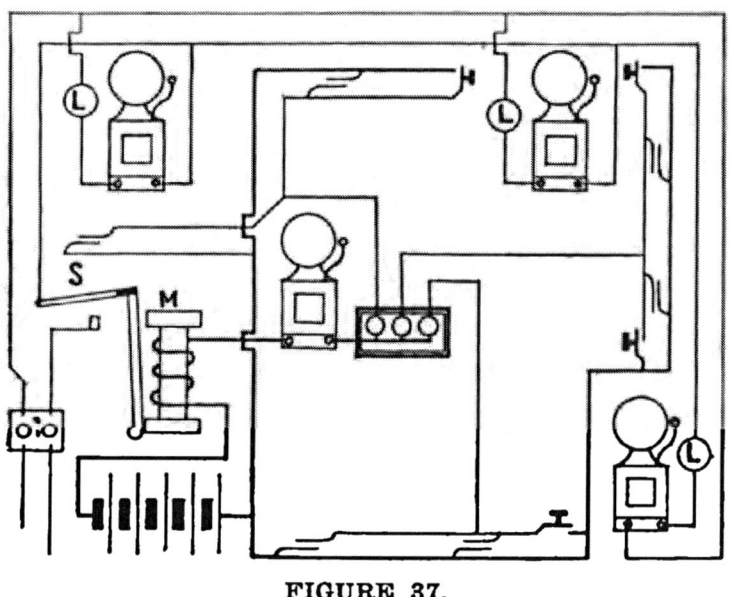

FIGURE 37.

Figure 37 shows an annunciator as it may be used either as a fire or burglar alarm. By means of the magnet M, an electric circuit is closed whenever contact is made by one of the push buttons or contact springs. With each electric light, L, an electric bell is placed, and whenever the alarm is set off bells will ring in the different sections and a general illumination will take place. The bells used for this purpose should be of the type shown in Figures 13 or 14, Chapter I, and should be carefully installed, so there may be no grounding or bad contacts.

The electric light circuit here shown may be added to any of the closed or open circuit burglar alarm systems described by simply arranging a magnet like M, which, by attracting or releasing its armature, allows the switch S to fall and close the electric light circuit. Any burglar alarm annunciator may also be used as a fire alarm if suitable thermostats are connected with the wiring, arranged to open or close the circuit when the temperature rises above a certain point.

Figure 38 shows a system of burglar alarm wiring which can be used when some special object is to be protected. This object may be a safe, vault or room, and may be located any distance from the alarm station.

In the diagram C is a coil of any chosen resistance, which is to be placed inside the object to be protected. By tracing the circuits it will be seen that current from battery B, which is a closed circuit battery, flows through this coil and through a closed circuit

burglar alarm spring G, thence through magnet R'
back to battery.

Another circuit running from the same battery
goes through magnets R" and M, back to battery.
When current is flowing from battery B the armature
E is held in a balanced position midway between R'
and R" (this is facilitated by means of springs as
shown), and the armature A is attracted. This holds

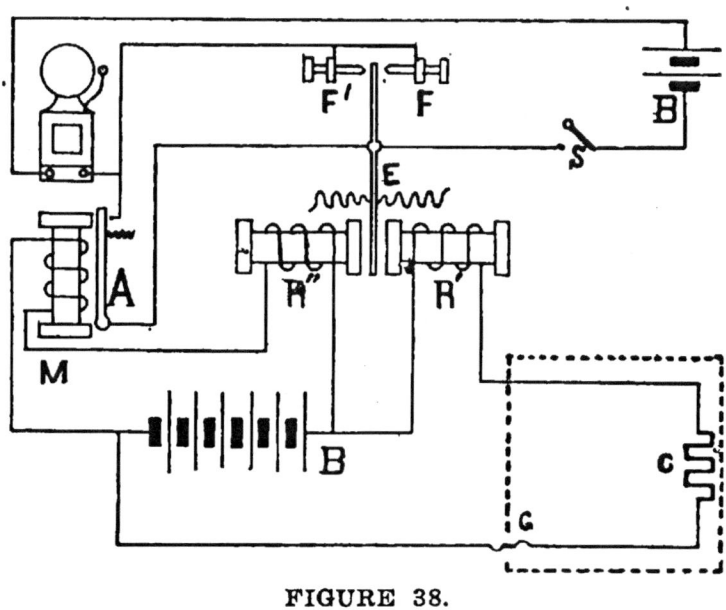

FIGURE 38.

the local bell circuit open. If the line running to C
is opened, the current through R' ceases, and it becomes demagnetized. The armature is then attracted
by magnet R" and the bell circuit is closed at F. If
the line running to C is short-circuited, the increased
current in R' attracts the armature and the bell circuit is closed at F'. If for any reason the battery B

FIRE AND BURGLAR ALARMS 41

gives out, the magnet M is demagnetized and the armature A closes the bell circuit. When alarm is not in use the switch S is thrown over, opening the alarm circuit. This device was designed and patented by G. B. Lehy, of Medford, Mass.

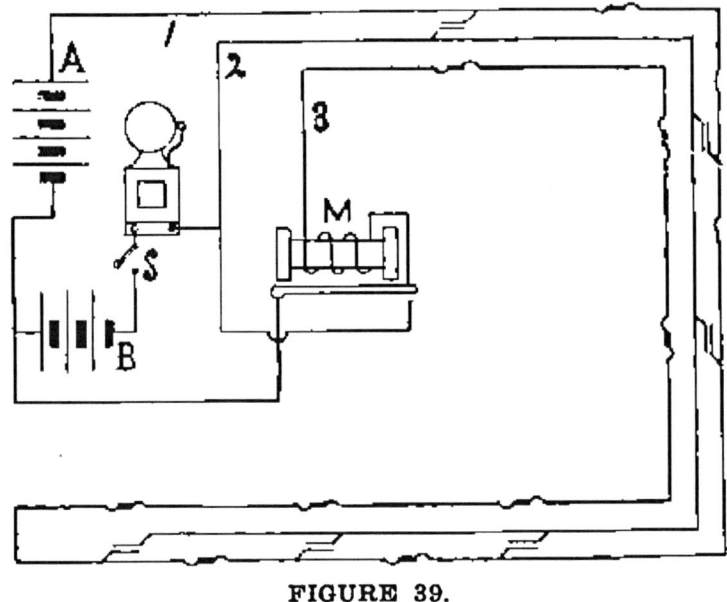

FIGURE 39.

Figure 39 shows the wiring of a burglar alarm in which both closed and open circuits are used. Current from the closed circuit battery A flows continually through wires 1 and 3 and the magnet M. If this circuit is broken the armature of M falls and closes the bell circuit; this rings the bell by means of the open circuit battery B, and keeps it ringing continuously. If any of the springs between 1 and 2 are brought together, both batteries will work through the bell in series.

In systems of this kind the wires may be twisted or braided into cables, and it will be very difficult to determine which wires must be short-circuited or cut in order to make the alarm ineffective. The switch S is provided to cut the alarm bell in or out of use as desired.

This arrangement is taken from Max Linder's book on "Haus Telegraphie," and was devised by O. Schoeppe, of Germany.

CHAPTER IV.

TELEPHONE AND TELEGRAPH CIRCUITS.

Figure 40 shows diagrammatically the connections of an ordinary telephone instrument when in use. While the receiver R hangs on the hook, the line circuit is complete through the polarized bell and magneto generator to ground. This is the connection when the instrument is not in use. T is the transmitter, and it is in series with a small induction coil and

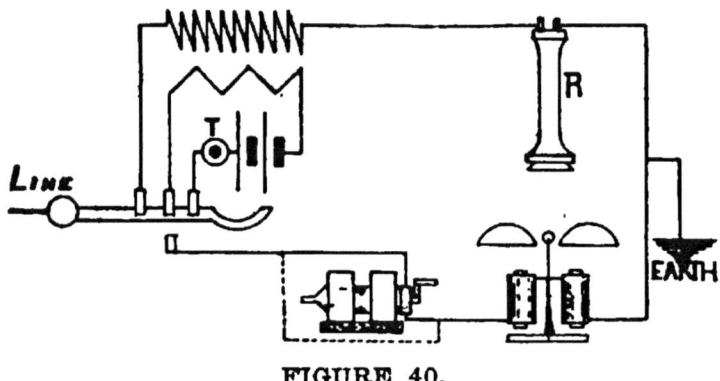

FIGURE 40.

battery, which is connected with the local circuit as shown; the local battery circuit being open when the telephone is not in use. The magneto generator is usually provided with a shunt circuit, which allows the calling currents from other stations to pass around it and ring the bell. The generator is so arranged that this circuit is automatically opened when the handle is turned.

Figure 41 shows the connections of the bridging bell system. In this system the bells are all in multiple and always in circuit. The resistance of the bell magnets is very high and the self induction quite great. This gives them sufficient impedance to pre-

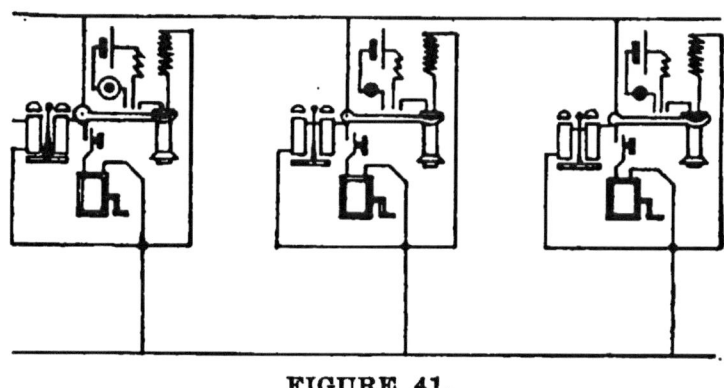

FIGURE 41.

vent telephonic currents from passing, but does not prevent the lower frequency currents of the magneto from ringing the bells. The magneto generator must be of sufficient capacity to ring all of the bells at the same time. This system requires some code of signals, since all the bells ring whenever any station is called.

Figure 42 shows a telephone line with the stations arranged in series. With the instruments here shown no induction coil is used, the talking batteries and transmitters being arranged directly in series with the telephone instruments. A signalling battery is required at each station, and also a 3-way push. Whenever this push is pressed at any station all of the bells will ring. The number of stations that may be ar-

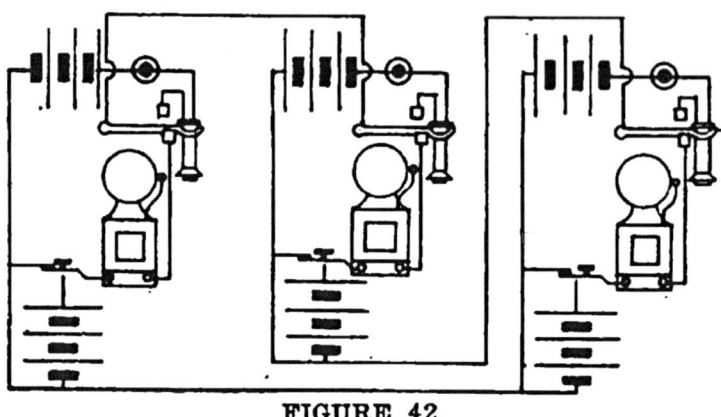

FIGURE 42.

ranged on a line of this kind is very limited, since the talking currents must pass through the bell magnets of all stations except those talking.

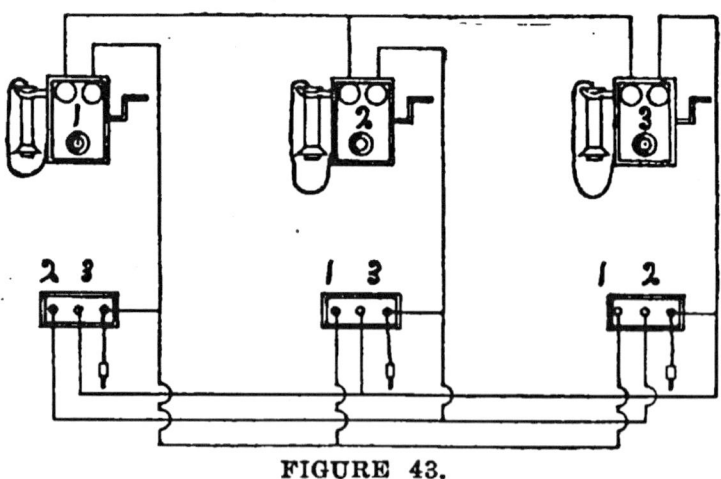

FIGURE 43.

In Figure 43 an intercommunicating system is shown using magneto generators for calling. Each of the stations 1, 2 and 3 contains the arrangement shown in Figure 40. To call any station the plug is inserted in the jack which connects with the wire leading direct to the station wanted. On turning the generator the bells will ring, and upon taking up the receivers the line is ready for talking.

Figure 44 shows an intercommunicating system using one common battery for signalling and individual talking batteries at each station. As in Figure

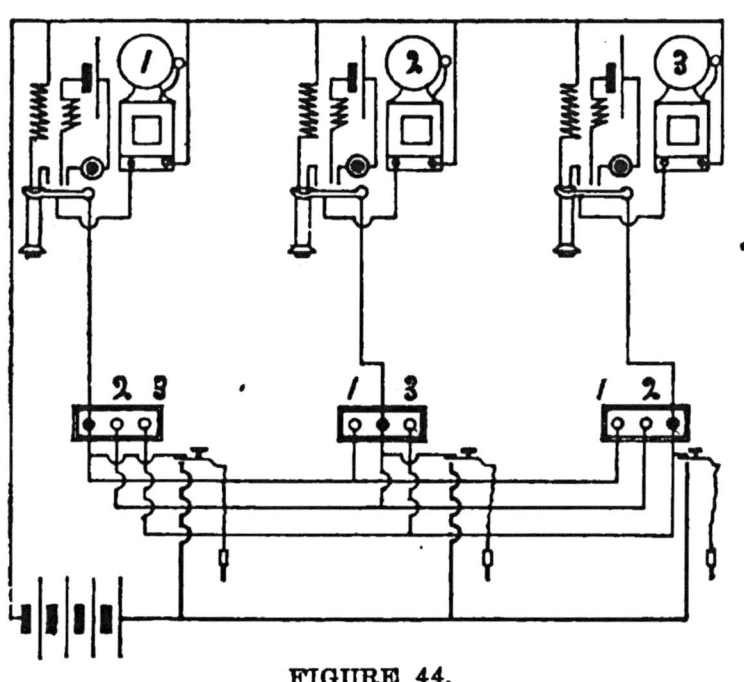

FIGURE 44.

43, the plug is inserted in the proper jack, and upon pressing the 3-way push the bell at the corresponding station will ring. The bell at the calling station will not ring.

TELEPHONE CIRCUITS

With all systems such as these the plugs are likely, through carelessness, to be left in the jacks, and more or less confusion may result. To obviate this, special devices are made, to take the place of plugs shown here, and which automatically make the proper connections when the receiver is replaced.

Figure 45 shows an ordinary annunciator system adapted for the use of telephones. Each station can communicate with the office only. A is the annuncia-

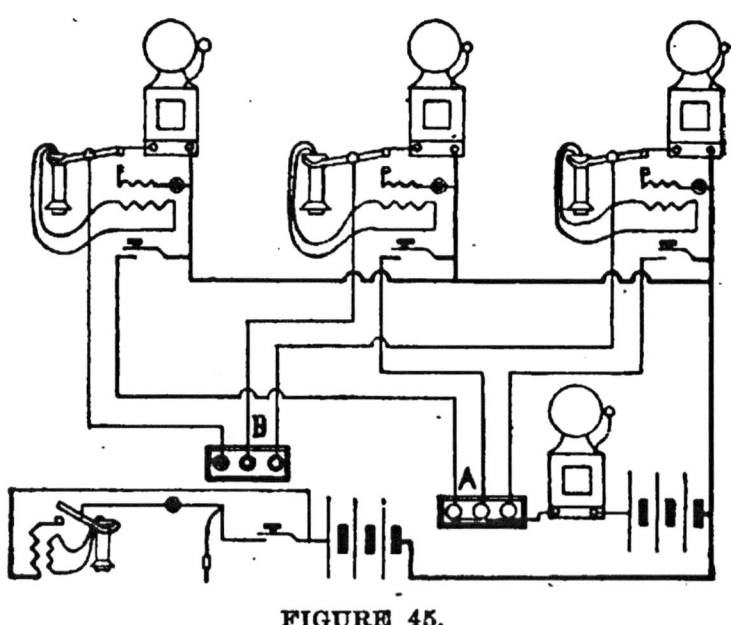

FIGURE 45.

tor receiving the signals from the different stations. By plugging in at the proper wire in B, and pressing the button any station may be called. When the button is released the line is ready for talking if the receivers are removed from their hooks. As here shown, one common talking battery is used, and another battery is used for signalling.

In Figure 46 an adaptation for telephones of the annunciator system given in Figure 26 is shown. Whenever the plug is inserted in any of the jacks at B, it breaks the wire at this point, thus forming an independent circuit through the station called and the

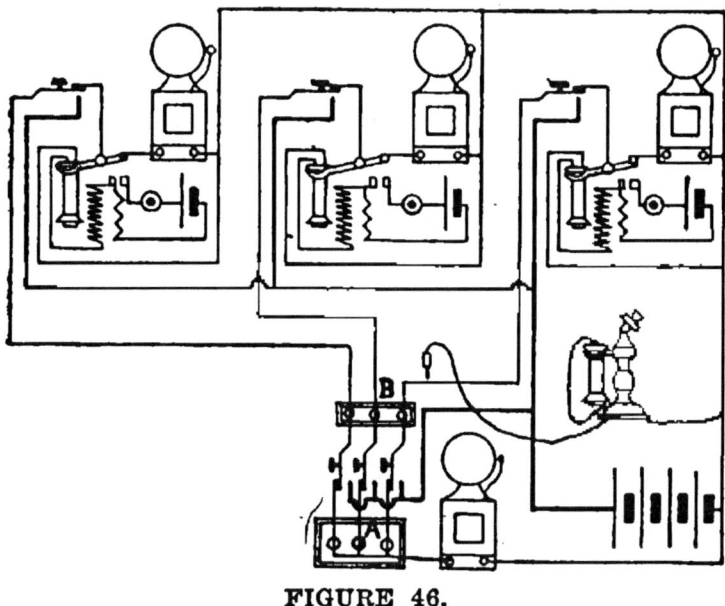

FIGURE 46.

office instrument. With this system there is shown one common signalling battery for all stations and a talking battery at each station.

It has not been thought necessary to give more than the foregoing diagrams in connection with telephones, as anything approaching a full exposition of the many different methods of connecting them would alone fill a volume. The foregoing diagrams are sufficient to illustrate the methods usually employed in house wiring. For a fuller treatment, and for illustrations of exchange practice, the reader is referred to the more pretentious works dealing with telephone practice only.

As telephone receivers are very sensitive, it is essential that the wires connecting them should not be run very close to other wires carrying currents of electricity. To avoid cross talk and other disturbing influences, the lines should be arranged so that both sides are of equal length and resistance. Arrangements should be such that no electro-magnets are left in circuit when the line is used for talking. It is also advisable to cross wires or twist them together; this will help neutralize inductive influences. In factories and kindred places where there is much vibration, the telephone instruments may be suspended from springs.

Figure 47 shows the connections of an ordinary long distance telegraph line with relays R and sounders S. The relays are used, because in long distance lines it has been found unprofitable to maintain currents sufficiently strong to control the heavy armatures necessary on sounders to make the signals audible. For this reason the relays are equipped with very light armatures, and control a local circuit which operates the sounder. One-half the battery is placed at each end of the line; this lessens the trouble from leakage. Each station is also equipped with a lightning arrester connected to ground, as shown, and a switch closing around the key. This applies to intermediate stations as well as end stations, and intermediate stations are also equipped with a switch, by

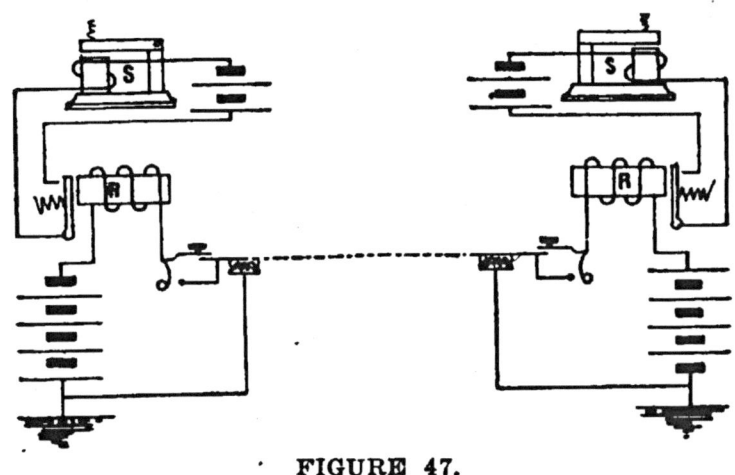

FIGURE 47.

which they may be entirely cut out or connected to ground on either side, in case of a broken line or other trouble.

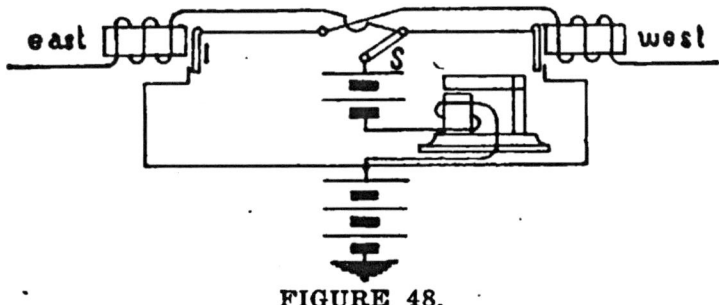

FIGURE 48.

In Figure 48 a very simple form of repeater is shown, which is due to Edison. It can be very readily set up, and requires no additional apparatus except

TELEGRAPH CIRCUITS

a 3-way switch shown in diagram. With the switch S, as shown, the current from the eastern line passes through both batteries to ground and keeps the armature I attracted. At the same time current from the west passes through the armature I and the main battery to ground. When the eastern circuit is opened, armature I is released and opens the western circuit, thus repeating into it. With the switch turned to the other point, the western circuit will repeat into the eastern.

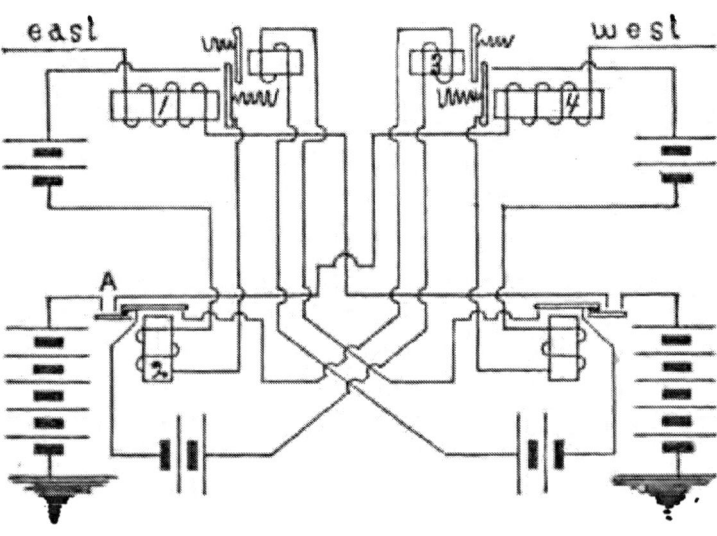

FIGURE 49.

In Figure 49 another form of repeater, known as Milliken's, is shown. This does not require the changing of any switch to make one circuit repeat into the other, but is entirely automatic. The current coming from the east normally keeps the armature of magnet 1 attracted; this armature controls the circuit of magnet 2. If, now, the current in the eastern circuit is interrupted, the armature of 1 flies back, opening the local circuit of magnet 2; this in turn releases its armature and breaks the western circuit at A. The breaking of this circuit would result in releasing the armature of 4, but at the same instant the armature of 2 opens the western circuit it also opens the extra circuit controlling the magnet 3. This releases the pendant armature, which is drawn by its spring against the armature of 4 and prevents its opening the circuit. The west end station is an exact duplicate of the eastern, and when sending from that side the operation is repeated in a similar manner.

THE TELAUTOGRAPH.

An elementary diagram of the connections of the telautograph is given in Figure 49a and the complete connections showing switches, etc., in Figure 49b.

The message to be transmitted is written upon the platen P, Figure 49b, by a pencil occupying the position shown as a black dot. The movement of the pencil, by means of light rods, moves the arms A, A', sometimes pulling one and pushing the other. These arms move over resistances and thereby vary the current strength in two lines which lead to the receiver shown in upper half of the figure. In the receiver each of the two magnets M, M', are fitted with plungers which are free to move up and down. These plungers are drawn upward by springs and sucked into the cores of the mag-

TELEGRAPH CIRCUITS 53

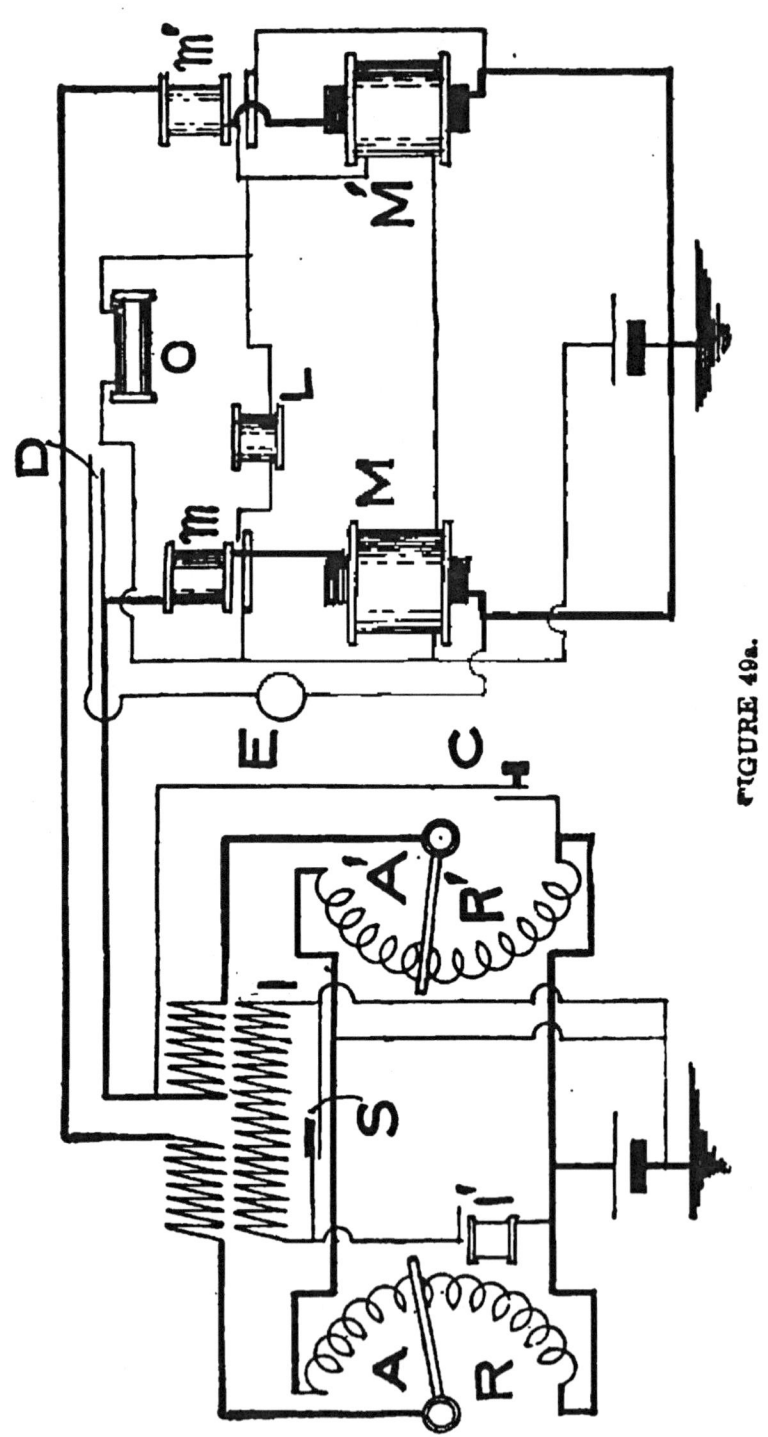

FIGURE 49a.

nets by currents passing through the coils of the plungers. The magnets themselves are separately excited.

These plungers connect to two arms similar in principle to those of the transmitter and the nature of the connection is such that every motion of the pencil upon the platen P is reproduced by a similar pencil or pen designated by a black dot in the receiver. Thus the message written upon the transmitter platen is reproduced with great fidelity upon the platen of the receiver.

The manner in which this is accomplished can best be explained by reference to the elementary diagram Figure 49a. When the instrument is in action current flows from the battery shown with the transmitter at the left, along the wires drawn as heavy lines, passing through the main magnets M, M', and the auxiliary magnets m, m'. The actual work of writing is done entirely by the currents passing over these wires. It will be seen that the arms A, A', as they move over the resistances cutting out or in resistance and also acting as shunts to each other, produce great variations in the current strength in the two transmitting lines. These changing currents affect the magnets M, M', correspondingly and reproduce the writing.

In the transmitter is also included an induction coil I and its secondaries, together with an interrupter I'. The alternating currents produced by these coils are

TELEGRAPH CIRCUITS

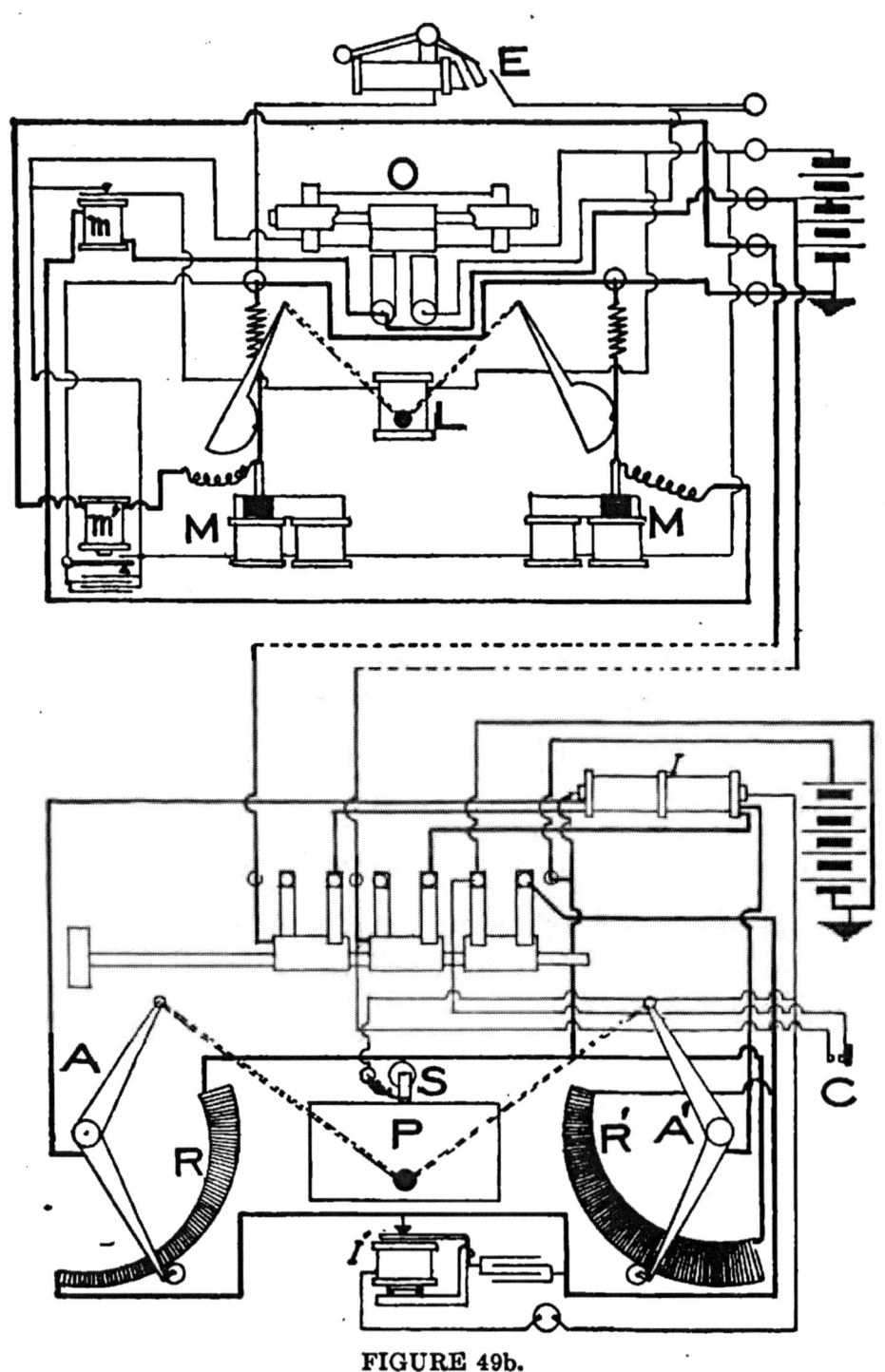

FIGURE 49b.

superimposed upon the continuous currents in the main circuit.

S is a small switch so connected that it is closed when the instrument is not writing. Pressure of the writing pencil upon the platen opens this switch and thereby strengthens the alternating currents. This increase in current strength operates the relay m in the receiver and causes it to open the circuit through the pen lifting magnet L. This releases the pen so that it becomes free to move in accordance with the arms of the receiver. The arrangements are also (by vibration of armature of m) such that the alternating currents keep the pen in a slightly vibratory state and thus reduce friction to a minimum. When the pressure is withdrawn from the platen the alternating currents become too feeble to interfere with the continuous, the relay m again closes the circuit through the penlifter and the pen is raised.

The object of m' in the receiver is to control the battery and the local circuits in the receiver. When its armature is attracted, the circuit through L, M, M', and O are closed.

O is an electromagnetic device which shifts the paper when the circuit is broken at the end of a line. When no current is on the line, O keeps the contacts D closed. This places the bell E in parallel with M and m, and as these are of higher resistance than the bell, the latter rings whenever the push-button C is pressed. This is used merely for signalling.

X-RAY CIRCUIT.

A diagram of the wiring and instruments often used in connection with X-ray tubes is given in Fig. 49c. The tube itself is shown at T connected to the secondary of a strong induction coil. At the terminals of this secondary winding of the induction coil an adjustable spark gap G is provided. This is used to protect the tube against excess voltage. This gap properly adjusted will act as a shunt and the excessive current will jump the air between the spark points rather than pass through the tube.

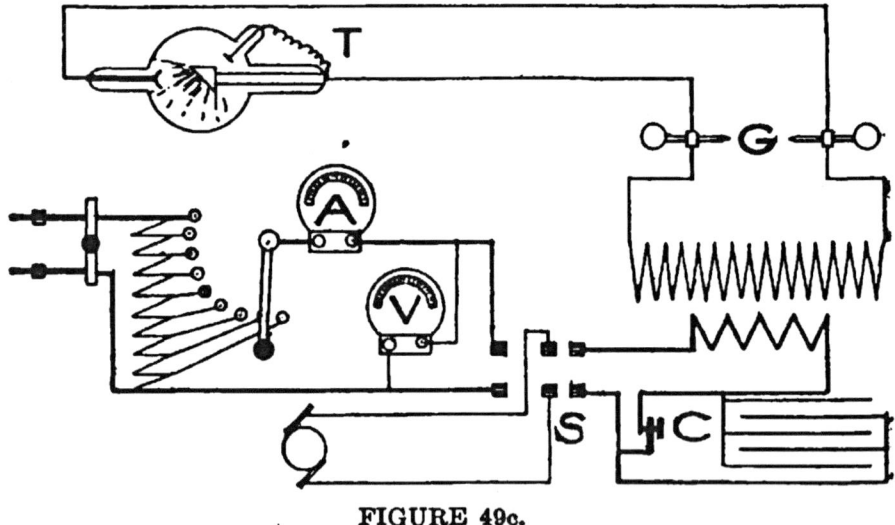

FIGURE 49c.

The exact nature of the light emitted depends somewhat upon the degree of vacuum maintained in the tube.

As a general rule tubes of low vacuum take more current, emit more light, and the light is of greater actinic power.

The light emitted from a high vacuum tube, however, is more penetrating, that is, will pass through greater opaqueness than the other.

To obtain the best results in all cases, it is therefore advisable to have on hand a stock of tubes suitable for different kinds of work.

The color of the light also varies somewhat with the nature of glass used.

In order to properly operate the tube it is necessary to send a very rapidly interrupted current of electricity at a very high voltage through it. This is done by means of a good induction coil which differs from the common form only in the nature of the interrupter.

In the ordinary induction coil in which no particular attention is paid to the exact nature of the make and break, secondary currents are induced at time of make and also of break.

An induced current is produced in the secondary whenever lines of force are increased or decreased in the winding or iron core. These secondary currents flow in one direction while the lines of force are increasing and in the opposite while they are decreasing. The value of the induced E. M. F. is in proportion to the rate of change of the lines of force. That is to say, if the current is increased from 0 to 10 amperes in 1 second it will induce secondary currents with 10 times the E. M. F. as if it were increased the same amount in the time of 10 seconds.

In the X-ray tube it is essential that the currents be practically all in the same direction and therefore one of the induced currents must be as far as possible eliminated. The E. M. F. induced at time of break of the primary current is much greater than that at make because the circuit may be very suddenly (practically instantaneously) opened, while the make current rises comparatively slow to its full value. The break E. M. F. is therefore much greater than the make and it is the one that is used to produce the light.

The greater the difference between the two the more desirable it is for if the make E. M. F. can be kept low enough it will not send current through the tube.

The sparking which occurs at time of break of circuit is the only element that prevents instantaneous break of current, and to reduce it as much as possible, for the double purpose of preventing destructive action and increasing the suddenness of the break the condenser C is provided. Part of the current at time of break instead of continuing in the form of a spark rushes into the condenser to be discharged when the make occurs.

There are three distinct methods of interrupting the current in use. One of these is the well known method employed with ordinary induction coils or vibrating bells.

The second method is that of causing the interruptions to be made through a small motor which operates either a plunger or a disc with projections so arranged that they enter and leave a mercury contact with great rapidity. A motor is also sometimes employed to throw a jet of mercury against a succession of contacts mounted on the inner periphery of a suitable jar.

The third method is known as the electrolytic. This is an arrangement very similar to a battery. The positive pole of the circuit is connected to one of the poles of the break (which is platinum) and the other pole of the break is a lead plate. Diluted sulphuric acid is also used. As current passes through this cell bubbles are formed on the platinum and these stop the current flow by their resistance. They immediately pass away and the current begins to flow again. The interruptions produced in this way are much more rapid than those of any other method and this method can also take care of much stronger currents. These breaks are simple and easily kept in order. Always make the platinum the positive pole, if otherwise it will soon be destroyed.

It is important to arrange that current cannot be turned on to the induction coil unless the interrupters are in action or ready to act. For this reason where motor drive interrupters are used the switch S may be arranged to close the motor circuit before the circuit to the coil is closed.

By means of the shunt resistance connected as shown any desirable voltage is obtainable from a 110 volt circuit. Start with low voltage and work up to desired voltage.

If an alternating current is to be used it must be rectified by motor generator or some other means.

CHAPTER V.

ELECTRIC GAS-LIGHTING.

Figure 50 shows the wiring of a complete metallic return gas-lighting system. I is the spark coil, which is absolutely essential. This spark coil has a relay attachment, R, which closes the bell circuit whenever the spark coil is energized. Should a ground or short circuit occur on the system, the bell will immediately

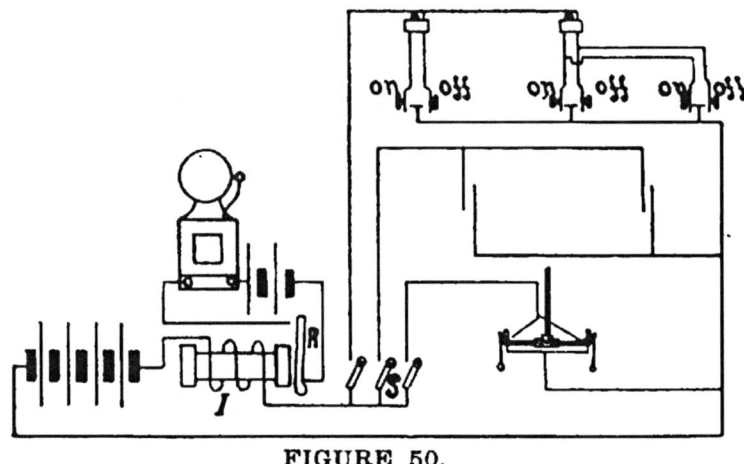

FIGURE 50.

call attention to it. By means of the switches S the system is divided into a number of circuits, and, by disconnecting the circuits, one at a time, the one out of order may be readily found.

For so-called automatic burners it is necessary to run two wires to each burner; and push buttons controlling one burner may be placed in different parts of the building, as shown at top of figure. With pendants the gas can be controlled at the fixture only. Automatic burners are not very safe, as there is always a liability of gas leaking.

If a cheaper installation than the above is desired, the relay, bell, and switches S may be omitted, and the whole installation arranged as one circuit. The gas piping can also take the place of the return wire. Instead of employing a separate battery to operate the tell-tale bell, two cells of the main battery may be used; as the cells so used, however, give out much earlier than the others, it is not considered good practice to do so.

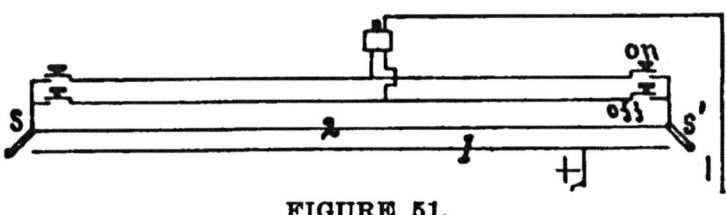

FIGURE 51.

Figure 51 shows a method which allows of two parties controlling one gas jet; the gas not being turned out until both parties are through with it. S and S' are two switches which can make connection with the current carrying wire 1. By turning the switch S or S' to this wire and pressing the proper button, the gas may be lit by either party. The first party to retire will press the off button, and finding no current will, after releasing the button, throw the

ELECTRIC GAS-LIGHTING

switch S or S' to the wire 1. This will give current to No. 2, and when the other party presses the proper button the gas will be turned off. This method presupposes that the switch S or S' is returned to its normal position after being used.

Figure 52 shows a system of gas lighting with an induction coil. A spark of high potential is produced which can jump many small air gaps arranged above gas jets in series. With the switch one circuit at a time is ignited. In systems of this kind about 15

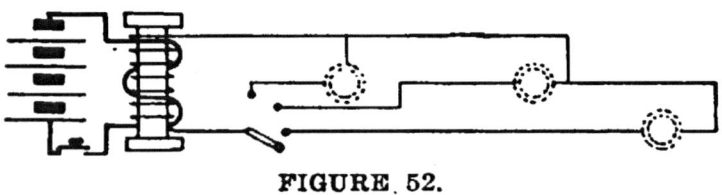

FIGURE 52.

burners are allowed to a 1 inch spark coil; *i. e.*, a coil giving a spark 1 inch in length. If possible, gas jets should be arranged so close together that they will light from one another. In such a case only a few of them need be equipped with spark contacts. Very high insulation is essential with this system, and there may be but little use for it in these days of electric lighting.

In Figure 53 are shown the connections used in the Edwards condenser system. Here all of the burners are wired in multiple and each is equipped with a small condenser. This system is mentioned in Mr. H. S. Norrie's work on gas lighting, and is said to be successful. A suitable induction coil is used, and it need not have a very great spark capacity, and

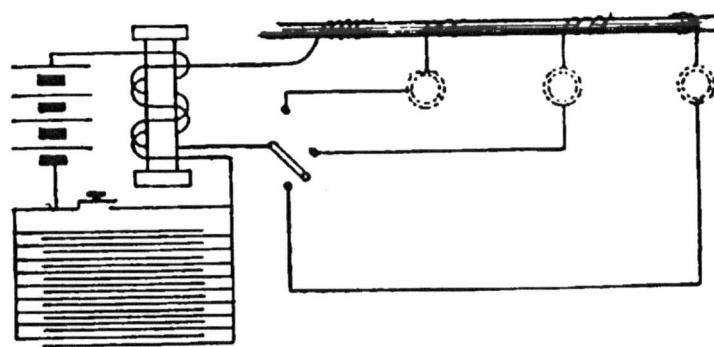

FIGURE 53.

there is much less danger of a breakdown in the insulation.

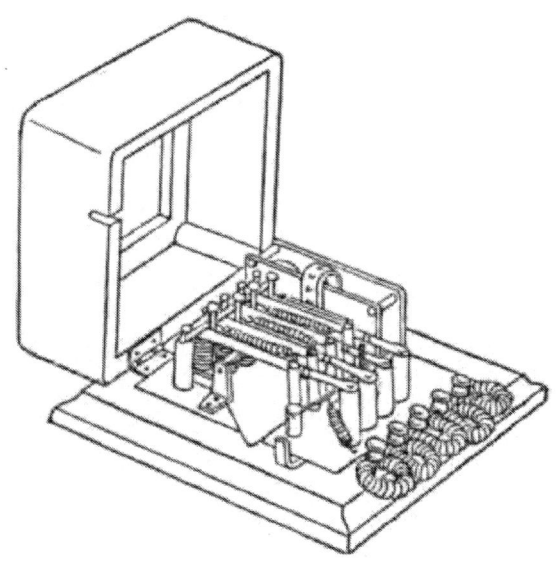

FIGURE 54.

Frictional gas lighting machines may also be used, and they are connected similar to Figures 52 and 53,

ELECTRIC GAS-LIGHTING

one terminal leading to ground or common return wire, and the other to the switch.

As grounds and short circuits on gas lighting systems are quite common, several forms of automatic cutouts have been devised. One of these is shown in Figure 54. The battery wire passes through a magnet which controls clockwork connected with a long pinion shaft. This clockwork is started and continues in operation while current is passing through these magnet coils. If the current lasts only an instant there will be but very little movement; while, if through a short circuit or ground the current is kept on for any great length of time, the clockwork will open the circuit.

CHAPTER VI.

PRIMARY AND SECONDARY BATTERIES.

The Figures 55 to 58 show different ways in which batteries may be grouped. Figure 55 shows the usual manner. In this way the highest E. M. F. is ob-

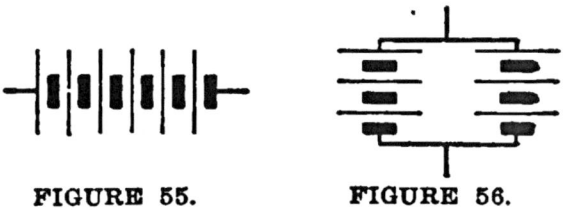

FIGURE 55.   FIGURE 56.

tained, and also the best results in all cases where the line resistance exceeds the battery resistance. It must be borne in mind that the battery has an internal resistance independent of that of the line, and this in-

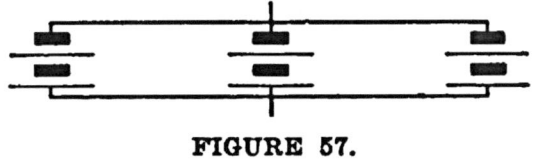

FIGURE 57.

ternal resistance will modify the current quite as much as any other resistance. The battery resistance varies inversely as the surface of the plates exposed in the liquid, and directly as their distance apart.

Taking into consideration this law, we can readily see that six cells placed in multiple, as in Figure 56, will have but one-fourth the resistance of those in Figure 55. In Figure 55 the resistance of six cells is $6 \times R$; in Figure 56 it is $\dfrac{3 \times R}{2}$; in Figure 57 it is $\dfrac{2 \times R}{3}$; and in Figure 58 it is $\dfrac{R}{6}$. Also in any arrangement of cells the internal resistance of the battery equals $\dfrac{X \times R}{N}$ where X stands for the number of cells in series; R for the resistance of one cell and N for the number of groups in parallel.

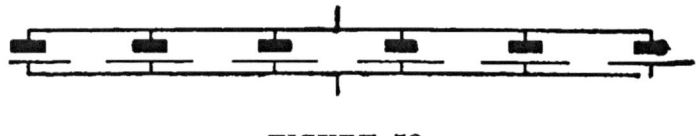

FIGURE 58.

The total E. M. F. of any battery equals $N \times E$, where N stands for the number of cells in series and E for the E. M. F. of one cell. The E. M. F. of any cell is independent of its size, and while no current is flowing is independent of its internal resistance. When current is flowing, however, the drop in E. M. F. is equal to the current $\times$ the internal resistance. As the internal resistance of all primary cells is quite high, this fact must not be overlooked whenever large currents are to be used.

As a general rule cells should be so grouped that their internal resistance is nearest equal to that of the line and instruments through which they are to work.

Where very high resistance lines are worked, as in telegraphy, for instance, the internal resistance of the battery is of little consequence, since an addition of 100 ohms resistance to a circuit of several thousand ohms would hardly be noticeable. For circuits of low resistance, such as gas lighting, it is, however, an item which must not be overlooked. The resistance of an average gas lighting circuit does not exceed a few ohms, and to place into such a circuit a battery having ten or twenty ohms resistance would obviously be poor practice. Where large currents are used it is advisable to use large cells. Placing small cells in multiple has many disadvantages, and great care must be taken that all cells are of the same E. M. F., and they should also be of the same make.

There are two general classes of primary batteries, each suited to a different class of work.

For all intermittent work an open circuit battery should be chosen. Cells of this kind will last a very long time on open circuit without deterioration, but must never be left on short circuit or used for continuous work.

Perhaps the best known of all open circuit batteries is the Leclanche cell, and the instructions here given will apply most specifically to it, but can be followed in general with all open circuit cells.

Never use more sal ammoniac than will be readily dissolved; about six ounces will be sufficient for ordinary use. It is preferable to make a saturated solution of sal ammoniac, and after filtering it through cloth or cotton wool, add about 10 per cent. of water.

Do not fill jars more than three-fourths full of solution, and keep them in a cool place, well inclosed, to prevent evaporation.

Never allow your battery to freeze.

Keep all exposed parts covered with paraffine and see that all connections are clean and tight.

Do not allow the battery to be short-circuited or run down. If this has occurred let it remain on open circuit for a few hours; it will often pick up.

If the solution appears milky it is an indication that more sal ammoniac is required. It will also be beneficial to remove the carbon and let it dry out thoroughly before using again.

Impure zincs which do not eat away evenly facilitate the formation of crystals, which greatly increase the resistance, and if not removed will destroy the action of the battery.

Dry batteries for general use are made up of the same materials as open circuit batteries, the main difference being that the material is applied in the form of a paste. They are used quite extensively for portable work. When run down some of them may be recharged by sending a current of two or three amperes through them for a few hours.

If they are dried out so that current will not flow through them an opening may be made in the shell and the cell then soaked in a solution of sal ammoniac. This will facilitate charging. The opening should be sealed again to prevent evaporation. As the shells of the cells usually consist of the zinc element, it is well to see that they are covered, or at least that two cells do not touch.

The primary battery commonly used for closed circuit work, or continuous work, is the so-called "crowfoot" or gravity battery. The copper element rests on the bottom of the glass jar. The jar is filled with clean water and enough sulphate of copper (blue vitriol) is added to give a blue tint to about one-half of the water. The blue line should be maintained about midway between the copper and the zinc, which is suspended from the top of the jar, and is usually made in the shape of a crow's foot.

When this battery is first set up it should be short-circuited for several hours, and it must be kept in action, as it deteriorates rapidly when left on open circuit.

While this battery remains in action the specific gravity of the upper solution increases. This solution should be maintained at about 25 degrees hydrometer test. If it falls below this the battery should be short-circuited for a little while. If it goes beyond this, some of the solution must be removed and the rest diluted with clear water. The resistance is much increased by dense sulphate of zinc solution. The zinc oxide which sometimes forms on the zinc may be removed with a brush and water.

The gravity cell has a high internal resistance, and is suitable only where a continuous current flow of small quantity is desired. This cell and also the Leclanche exist in many modified forms. Enough has been said to enable anyone to select a suitable battery, and detailed instructions will be found with all batteries where such instructions are necessary.

SECONDARY BATTERIES.

Storage, or secondary batteries, as they are often called, are quite extensively used in latter day practice. It is beyond the scope of this treatise to give anything but a few working directions covering general operation. Detailed instructions applicable to the different types will accompany most cells when purchased.

The E. M. F. of secondary batteries will average a little over 2 volts. On discharging, the E. M. F. should not be allowed to fall below 1.8 volts.

The charging should proceed slowly, and should never be carried beyond 2.5 volts.

The charging E. M. F. should not exceed that of the battery more than 5 per cent.

Cells should not be discharged more than two-thirds of their capacity. They should never stand uncharged.

In battery rooms all exposed metal work should be painted as a protection against acid fumes.

Wooden floors should also be protected against acid.

If charging is continued after the active material has been used up, oxygen and hydrogen gas will be given off.

Pure sulphuric acid should be used, and this should be diluted with distilled water. Pour the acid into the water slowly. Never pour water into acid, as much heat is generated.

Whenever necessary, replenish evaporation with distilled water and mix well, as otherwise the water will float on top.

Two methods of measuring the internal resistance of batteries are shown in Figures 59 and 60. In Figure 59 A represents an ammeter and V a voltmeter. Instruments for this purpose must be chosen suitable to measure the small currents and E. M. F. likely to be used, and must have a scale sufficiently large to admit of reading fractions of volts and amperes. To make the test, first close the circuit through the voltmeter. This gives us the E. M. F. of the whole battery, and may be called E. Next close the circuit through the ammeter and note the current reading; also at the same time note the reduced reading of the voltmeter and call this E'. The internal resistance of the battery is equal to $\frac{E-E'}{A}$, where A is the number of amperes flowing through the ammeter, and the other two symbols as above. The readings must be taken in a very short time, or polarization will modify both current and voltage. If the ammeter used above is of very low resistance, an additional resistance should be placed in circuit with it to prevent excessive current flow.

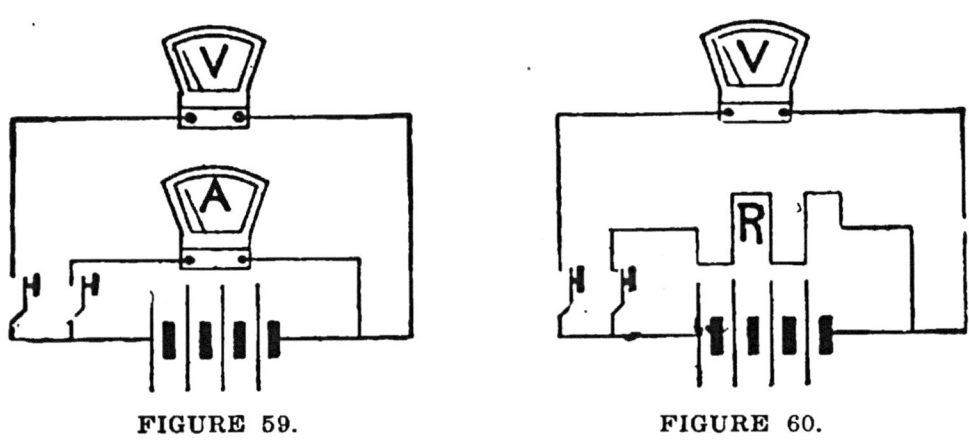

FIGURE 59.   FIGURE 60.

In Figure 60 no ammeter is needed, but the resistance of R must be known. Take the voltmeter reading as in Figure 59 and call it E. Next take the voltmeter reading with current flowing through R and call it E'. The internal resistance of the battery is $\dfrac{E-E'}{\dfrac{E'}{R}}$. In other words, divide E' by R, which gives the current flowing through R; then divide the difference between E and E' by this current. The result will be the battery resistance.

A comparative test as to the value of the different batteries may be made in the following manner: Procure the same number of cells of each kind to be tested. A suitable resistance and a voltmeter with a suitable scale must also be procured, and connections made as in Figure 60. The voltmeter should be of quite high resistance, so the current flowing through it will not materially affect the battery. The resistance should be about equal to the battery resistance. This will allow a current to flow which will gradually polarize any open circuit battery. When all is ready, close the circuit through R, and at regular intervals, of say one minute, note the fall in E. M. F. on the voltmeter until the battery is nearly polarized. Now open R and in the same way take readings at regular intervals, until the battery regains its former E. M. F.; or, if this is too long, for any convenient time.

The figures obtained may be plotted in curves, as shown in Figure 61, where the time is plotted horizontally each division representing one minute, while the drop in E. M. F. is plotted vertically, two divisions representing one-tenth of one volt.

The figure shows the polarization and recovery curves of a Laclede cell having an initial E. M. F. of 1.2 volts, and discharging through a resistance of 3 ohms. During the first minute the E. M. F. fell to .78; during the second to .68; third to .62; fourth to .58; fifth to .55; and at the end of twenty-six minutes it had fallen to .3.

SECONDARY BATTERIES

Upon opening the circuit the E. M. F. rose during the first minute to .47, and during the second to .5; and then in a more gradual and steady manner as indicated by the curve.

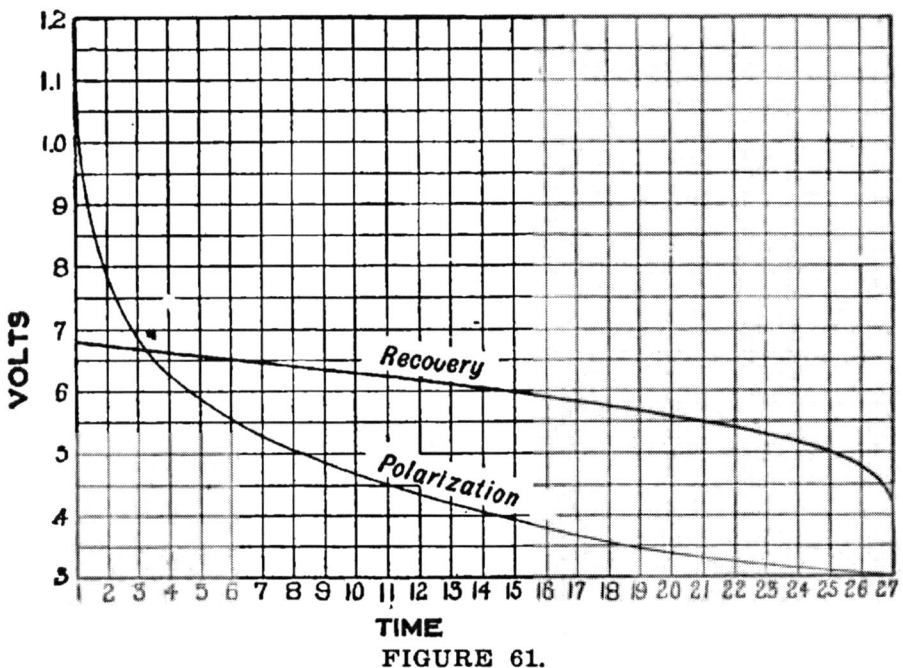

FIGURE 61.

If all batteries are tested with the same resistance and voltmeter, and given the same time, the result must be fairly comparative.

CHAPTER VII.

CONNECTING UP—LOCATING TROUBLE.

Figure 62 shows the rough wiring used to connect an annunciator with a call from each of the floors 1, 2, 3, 4, and also a call from the office to each of those floors. This figure is introduced to illustrate a

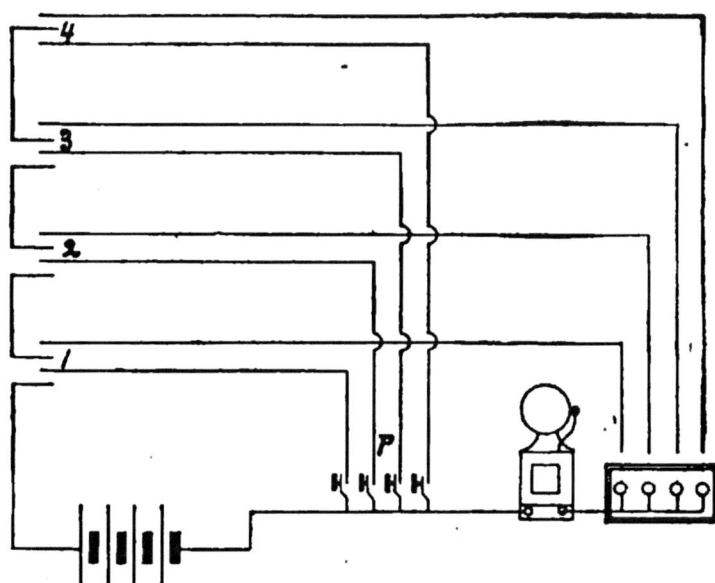

FIGURE 62.

method of testing to find the proper wires to make connections, and it will be assumed that all of the wires are concealed and all are of the same color, so that it is impossible to trace out any part of the wiring. Let it also be assumed that the party who is to connect the system did not install the wiring, and knows nothing about any part except the purpose for which it is installed.

The first step should be to separate the wires at all outlets so there may be no accidental connections which would cause confusion. The next step is to connect the battery to the two battery wires as shown, which will very likely be found without any trouble. Now go to floor 1 and bunch all wires found there, testing each wire to all other wires with a portable bell before connecting. If a ring is obtained it is an indication of a short circuit or wrong connection, which must be located and corrected before proceeding farther. Next proceed to the push buttons, P, and with the test bell find the wire coming from 1; when the bell is connected to the wire coming from 1 and to the battery wire a ring will be obtained. Now take up the annunciator wires and find the wire coming from 1 in the same way.

Having now found one wire which rings with two others, this must be the battery wire, and may be connected to one side of all the pushes, and to the annunciator through the bell. The other two wires may be marked and the connections at 1 removed. After this has been done, connect the two wires coming from 1 each to its proper place, push 1, and drop 1 respectively, and fix the push button so it will keep the circuit closed. Had this been done without first opening the connections on floor 1, a short-circuit would have been the result.

Now return to 1 and find the wire which rings the annunciator, and also the one which rings the test bell without disturbing the annunciator. The one wire used in common for both is the battery wire, and connects to one side of the bell and also to the push for annunciator. The wire leading to push P is to go on the other side of bell, while the one leading to annunciator goes to the other side of push button. The fourth wire must necessarily be the battery wire leading to the floor above, and is to be connected to battery wire coming from floor below.

For these tests a bell to act either single stroke or vibrating is very useful, especially when the annunciator is so far away that the ringing of its bells cannot be heard. A bell of this kind will indicate at once whether the wire through which it rings is connected with the annunciator or the push buttons, since it will ring vibrating in series with the annunciator bell and single stroke in connection with the push button wire.

The foregoing tests represent a great deal of time and labor, much of which may be avoided by using wire of one color for the battery wire and a different color for all the other wires on each floor. For Figure 62 this would require five colors. With wires arranged this way, the steps necessary to con-

LOCATING TROUBLE

nect up the system will be: First connect the battery wires on the different floors so that there will be one continuous wire from the battery to the fourth floor. While doing this note the color of wire used on each floor, so that the annunciator and push button wires may be connected up accordingly. After connecting these and the battery, return to each floor and set up the bell and connect it to the battery wire. Now touch one of the two remaining wires to the bell; if it rings it is the wire coming from the annunciator, and the other is the proper wire to connect to the bell.

Always locate the battery as near as possible to the push buttons. In this way the chance of leakage may be reduced to a minimum, since one wire only is exposed for any considerable length, the other being cut short by the pushes.

When one is alone a bell and battery is a very valuable help in fish work. Insert one piece of wire coming from the battery into the ceiling where it is expected to bring the wire to. Connect the fish wire to the other side of the battery and proceed in the usual way. When the two wires meet the bell will ring.

LOCATING TROUBLE.

While looking for trouble always work according to a fixed plan; haphazard testing and guessing will usually waste time. In all cases the most important thing to ascertain is whether the battery is in working order. If there are several bells and any one of them is working properly, the battery may be set down as all right. If there is no bell in operation, and none at hand, the most convenient way to test the battery is by "tasting"; arrange wires so that both poles come in contact with your tongue. If the battery is in order you will notice a peculiar taste, and a little experience will enable anyone to determine, approximately, whether the current is in proportion to the number of cells employed.

It will be well to avoid "tasting" circuits provided with an unusual number of cells and large magnets or spark coils, as the taste is apt to be very strong, especially if the wires are allowed to meet on the tongue and then break. If no current is obtained at the battery, examine the binding posts and connections; see whether each jar is properly filled and whether any of the zincs have been eaten away, or covered with crystals, which often causes a total cessation of current. If the battery is not found defective in any of the above points it may be entirely run down, either from overwork or a short circuit.

Some idea of the trouble may often be gained by questioning parties interested. If the bells stop suddenly it would indicate a broken line or a short circuit. If any bell were ringing continuously for a long time it would run the battery down. If the battery has been merely run down it will pick up in a short time if left on open circuit. A small galvanometer is very useful and will soon indicate whether a battery is picking up; it may also be used to test each cell separately. In any case, it is best to have the battery in good working order before looking elsewhere for the cause of trouble. If the battery is in order the next step (if there is but one bell) should be to examine the bell and push buttons; see that contact points are in order and that the bell is properly adjusted; also examine the line connections and see that they are clean and tight. A portable battery is very convenient, and with it one can quickly determine whether the bell is in order.

If, after the foregoing, the bell still fails to work, the trouble must be looked for in the line, and it will be well to examine the wires near bell and push buttons, as these wires are handled quite often for various reasons, and will often be found broken quite close to their connections. Splices are also quite often to be found quite close to terminals, as wires are often cut short when installed. When there are several bells and all fail to work, the inference would naturally be that the main battery wires are either broken or short circuited. If the battery is in good working order, one may be certain that no short circuit exists, and an open circuit must therefore be looked for.

From the many foregoing diagrams it will be seen that in all ordinary multiple bell systems, one wire coming from the battery leads to the bells and the other to the push buttons; this does not mean that the bells must all connect to the same wire and the push buttons to the other, since, in Figure 63, the location of any bell and its push button might be exchanged without hindering its operation. In Figure 63, 1 and 2 are the battery wires connecting with bells and buttons as shown. Suppose none of the bells will ring and we have come to the conclusion that one of the battery wires is broken; the best way to locate a break in the main wires is with a test bell, starting from the battery end of the line. At any

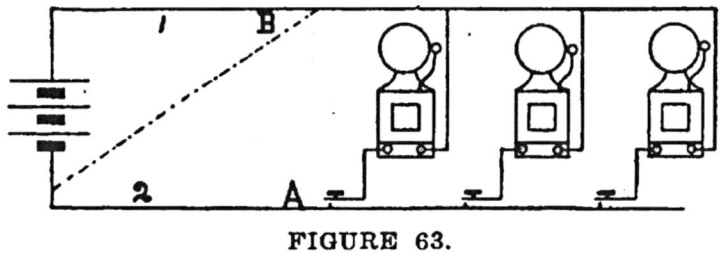

FIGURE 63.

convenient place where both battery wires are accessible, say at A and B, connect the test bell; a ring will show that the line between it and battery is in order, while failure to ring would indicate the break to be between it and the battery. Suppose no ring has been obtained and we now wish to ascertain which one of the main wires is broken; we can do so by running a temporary wire from B back to the battery as shown by the dotted lines. If the wire (1) is not broken between B and the battery, a ring will be obtained when connections are made to the opposite battery pole. If the wire is broken no ring can

LOCATING TROUBLE

be had from either battery pole; but when the temporary wire is connected to the wire and pole of the battery in which the break is, the whole system will be in working order.

If a short circuit exists, say at C and D, Figure 64, one way to locate it is by cutting a bell into the circuit at the battery. If the battery has been run down by the "short," as will likely be, one must either recharge or wait for it to pick up, unless an extra battery is at hand. Having connected the bell near

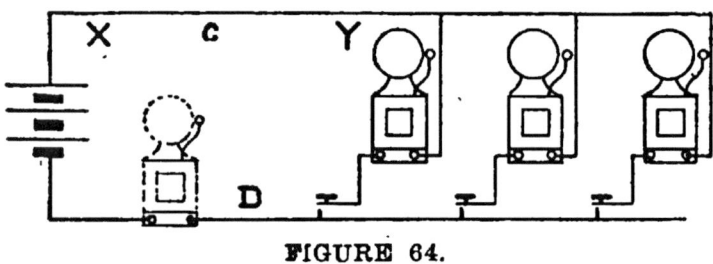

FIGURE 64.

the battery, we can now cut one of the main wires at any available place. If this stops the bell ringing, the short circuit is farther from the battery; if it does not stop the bell the short circuit is between the cut and the bell. If a portable battery is at hand, it and the bell may be carried about and cut into the circuit wherever desired. In this case the regular battery should be disconnected and the battery wires connected together. If the short circuit exists at C and D, as aforesaid, and the battery is cut in at X, a ring will be obtained; while when we get beyond the short circuit and cut in at Y, no ring can be obtained. By making several tests as outlined above, the seat of trouble can be very closely located. The foregoing instructions assume that the wiring is concealed or that a close inspection is very difficult. Short circuits will generally be found where wires cross metal pipes or bars, or where one staple holds two or more wires. Wire lath is also a very prolific cause of short circuits, and it must be borne in mind that two grounds on opposite wires are equal to a short circuit. As a matter of fact if a bell system can be kept clear of grounds, there will be but very little trouble from short circuits.

An easy and also a sufficient test for battery bell systems can be made by means of a strong magneto. Connect the magneto in place of the battery and give it a few sharp turns; if a ring is obtained the insulation between opposite poles is weak. This may be caused by the leak across the surface of a push button or kindred device, or it may be the result of poor general insulation, both poles being slightly grounded. A ground on one side only would not be discovered in the above test.

To test the insulation resistance to ground, connect one wire of the magneto to a convenient water or gas pipe, the former being preferred on account of the poor conductivity often caused by rust or red lead in the joints of the gas pipes; the other wire connects to the whole bell system without the battery. If, on turning the magneto, a ring is obtained, it is an indication of poor insulation resistance, and very likely some of the wiring is located in a damp place or in contact with metal or other grounded material. By disconnecting one of the battery wires one can easily determine on which side of a system a ground may be located. All grounds should be removed, as they are the cause of leaks which run batteries down, and in time may cause a broken wire through electrolytic action. In telephone systems one or more grounds may also seriously interfere with the talking qualities of a line, even if the grounds are all on one side of the circuit.

CHAPTER VIII.

MISCELLANEOUS.

Whenever a current is flowing in a wire it produces lines of force surrounding that wire. If the current in the wire flows away from the observer the lines of force will encircle the wire from left to right, *i. e.*, clockwise. (See Figure 65.) Lines of force always enter a magnet (compass needle) at the south seeking pole and leave it at the north seeking end.

FIGURE 65.

From this it follows that if a compass be held under a wire in which a current is flowing from you the north seeking end of the needle will deflect toward the left; while if the current is flowing toward you it

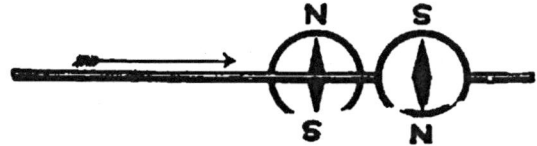

FIGURE 66.

will deflect toward the right. If the compass is held above the wire the deflections will be the reverse of the above, as shown in Figure 66.

Unless an extremely delicate compass be at hand, this method of determining the directions of currents in wires will be confined to comparatively large currents. If there are any magnets in the circuit, and if we know the direction in which they are wound, we can very easily determine the direction of the current, since the relative direction of current and magnetism will be as in Figure 67.

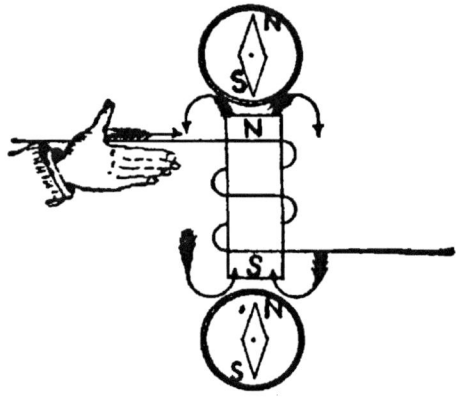

FIGURE 67.

If there is no magnet available, one may be temporarily constructed out of a screwdriver or pocket-knife by taking a few turns of the current carrying wire around it. If no compass is at hand, one can be made from a piece of cork and a steel needle set afloat in a cup of water, the needle being first magnetized.

If the right hand be held above a wire as in Figure 67, in which the current is flowing from you and the winding as shown in the figure, the north pole of the magnet will be as shown. If the direction of winding be reversed, or the direction of the current, the north pole will be at the other end.

All magnets have a retarding effect on alternating or intermittent currents. With an arrangement as shown in Figure 68, a lightning discharge will generally jump the small distance between the points of the lightning arrester rather than pass through the

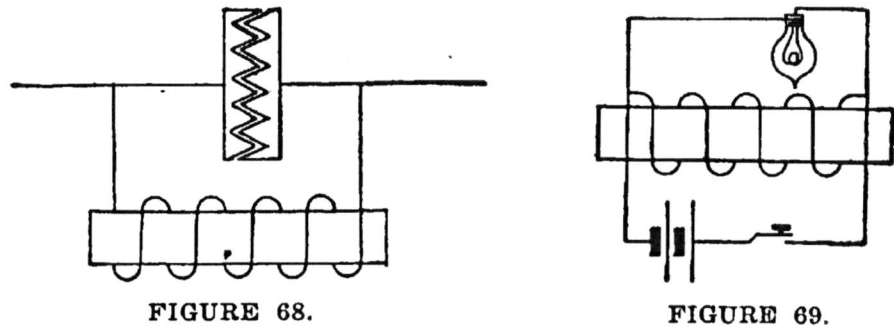

FIGURE 68.   FIGURE 69.

coils of the magnet. When, however, a current has once been started around a magnet it has a strong tendency to continue, and will manifest itself in a long spark if suddenly interrupted, as in a gas-lighting spark coil, for instance. Figure 69 is drawn to illustrate this, and the magnet there shown is of very low resistance compared with the lamp shown in multiple with it. If the battery circuit is closed the magnet will be energized, but no appreciable current will flow through the lamp. If now the battery circuit is suddenly opened, there will be a strong current discharge through the lamp, causing it to flash up for an instant.

MISCELLANEOUS 89

Figure 70 is designed to illustrate some of the differences in electrical currents. The winding of magnet A, if properly proportioned, will be found to be almost impenetrable to rapidly alternating or intermittent currents, while it may offer hardly any resistance to continuous currents. A continuous cur-

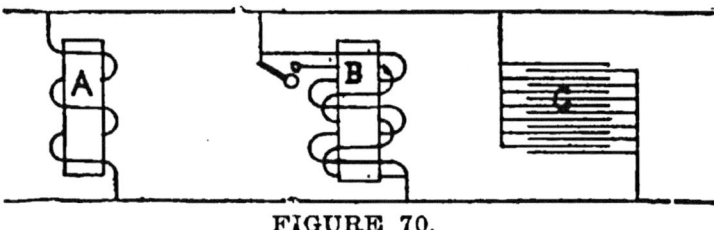
FIGURE 70.

rent working an ordinary bell would be much retarded by it, however, and the bell would work very slow. B has two windings opposed to each other. If one winding only is in circuit it will act similar to A; if

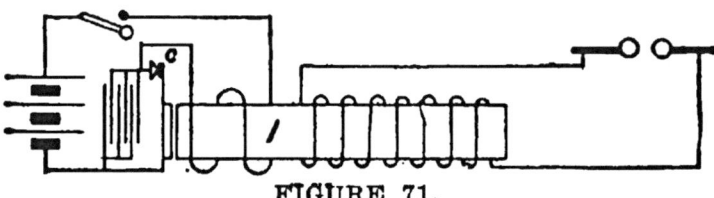
FIGURE 71.

the switch on the second winding is closed there will be but little retardation. The condenser C entirely prevents the passage of continuous currents, but telephonic currents pass readily through, and polarized bells may also be made to ring through it.

Figure 71 shows the plan of an ordinary induction coil. The iron core when energized attracts the interrupter, and this breaks the current at C, as in a vibrating bell. At every make and break in the primary circuit secondary currents are induced in the fine secondary winding. The circuit breaker is bridged by a condenser in order to reduce the sparking to some extent. With cheap coils the condenser is usually omitted.

Two wires carrying current in the same direction will attract each other, while if currents are in opposite directions they will repel each other.

A leak to ground on a positive wire will gradually destroy it; the negative will not be affected much.

An easy method of determining the direction of current consists in letting the current pass through a little water confined in a cup. The current will flow from the positive pole to the wire at which small hydrogen bubbles appear, which is the negative. This method is not applicable to low voltage systems.

The contacts of bells, relays and other devices which produce frequent interruptions in current, should consist of platinum. To determine whether they are platinum or not, drop a little nitric acid on them; this acid will not affect platinum, but will attack German silver and other imitations.

A continuous current will carry an arc much longer than an alternating current. It also produces a chemical action directly in proportion to its amount in amperes.

A magnet in an alternating circuit will greatly reduce the current, and the iron will be heated by the frequent reversals in the direction of magnetism. If the magnet is large and the frequency of the alternations is very great, only a very small amount of current will flow. The magnetism has no such effect on continuous currents. The heat generated in a continuous current magnet is produced by the resistance in the wire only, and the current flow depends on this resistance only. Alternating currents are also greatly retarded and diminished by lead covered wire or wires run in iron pipe. These wires act as condensers and currents are also induced in them. Whenever it is necessary to run wires in this way, both wires should be enclosed in the same sheath or pipe. Continuous currents are not affected in this way except for an instant at make or break.

USEFUL FACTS AND FORMULAS.

In any direct current circuit the current equals the electromotive force divided by the resistance, $I = \dfrac{E}{R}$. One application of this law is indicated in Figure 72, where the voltmeter V is used to measure current. The value of R being known, the current flowing through R is equal to the voltmeter reading, E, divided by R, the resistance.

From the formula $I = \dfrac{E}{R}$ two others are deduced.

In Figure 73, knowing the value of the electromotive

force E, and current I, we can find the resistance R by dividing E by I, $R = \frac{E}{I}$. Knowing the current I and the resistance R, we can find the electromotive force E, by multiplying I with R, $E = IR$.

The volts lost in any circuit equal the resistance of that circuit multiplied by the current.

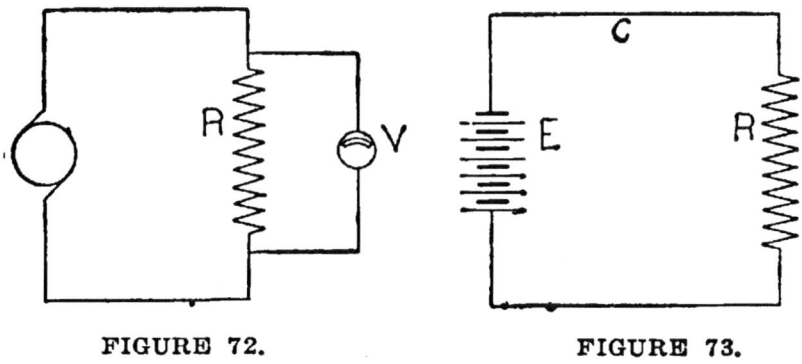

FIGURE 72. FIGURE 73.

Currents of electricity divide among derived circuits in proportion to their conductivities, which is the inverse ratio of their resistances; i. e., the lower resistance takes the most current. The joint resistance of two circuits in parallel is equal to the product of the two resistances divided by their sum.

In Figure 74 $\frac{5 \times 5}{5 + 5} = 2\frac{1}{2}$.

The joint resistance of any number of circuits in parallel if all are equal, may be found by dividing the resistance of one circuit by the total number of circuits. The joint resistance of any number of circuits in parallel, whether they are equal or not, is the reciprocal of the sum of the reciprocals of their resistances. Joint resistance equals

$$\frac{1}{\dfrac{1}{R}+\dfrac{1}{R'}+\dfrac{1}{R''}}$$

where R, R', R", are different resistances. The reciprocal of a number is 1 divided by that number, thus one-tenth is the reciprocal of 10.

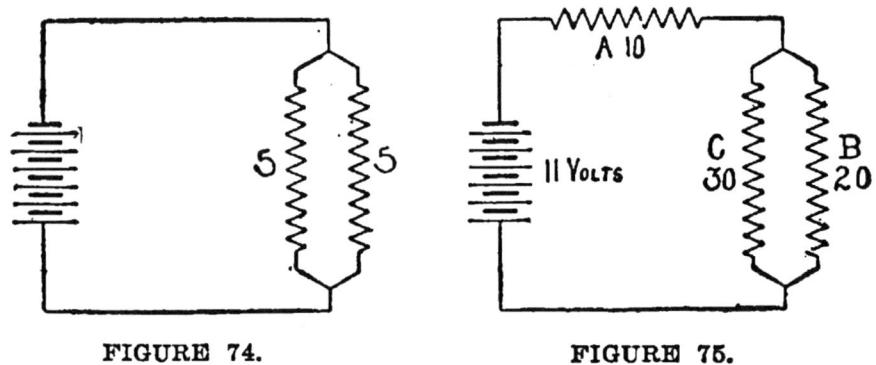

FIGURE 74.   FIGURE 75.

To find the total current, Figure 75, we must first find the joint resistance of 20 and 30, which, according to the above formula, is 12. Next add this to the other resistance 10, in the circuit, and divide the electromotive force 11, by this sum. The result is one-half ampere, of which three-tenths will pass through B and two-tenths through C.

The multiplying power of a shunt is the ratio of the total current flowing in the circuit to that part of it which flows through the ammeter. The shunt required to give a certain multiplying power is found by dividing the resistance to be shunted by the multiplying power desired minus 1. Thus, if the multiplying power desired is ten, we divide by 10 — 1, which is 9. If the resistance to be shunted is 100 ohms, the proper resistance of the shunt is 100 divided by 9, which is 11 1/9 ohms. Nine-tenths of the current will flow through this shunt and 1/10 will flow through the ammeter.

The amount of work done by a current of electricity is measured in watts. To determine the number of watts multiply the square of the current by the resistance, or $W = I^2R$. For instance, the heat generated in a wire is proportional to the square of the current; thus, doubling the current will produce four times as much heat. Other formulas for determining the watts deduced from the above, using Ohm's law, are: $W = IE$, or the current times the electromotive force, $W = E^2/R$, or watts equals the electromotive force squared divided by the resistance. One horse-power equals 746 watts. To reduce to horse-power divide the watts by 746.

The magnetism produced in an iron core is to a certain extent proportional to the number of ampere turns (current times the number of turns of wire) but when the point of saturation is reached, although the magnetizing force is increased, still there will be but little increase in magnetism. Figure 76 illustrates the increase in magnetism in wrought iron and cast iron, the magnetizing force (ampere turns) being represented by the distance measured along the horizontal line and the resulting magnetism by the distance along the vertical line. This is important to bear in mind when adjusting field coils or rheostats on dynamos or motors.

The circumference of a circle is found by multiplying the diameter by 3.1416, or roughly 3 1/7.

The area of a circle is found by multiplying the square of the diameter by .7854, or the square of the radius by 3.1416.

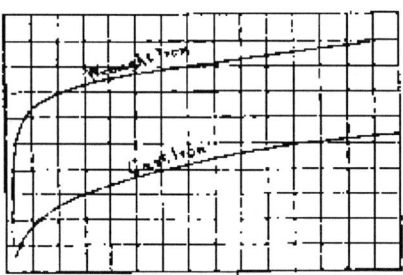

FIGURE 76.

The circular mils in a wire may be found by multiplying the diameter in mils (1000 mils per inch) by itself.

To convert circular mils into square mils multiply by .7854.

To convert square mils into circular mils divide by .7854.

The weight per mile of pure copper wire is $\dfrac{d^2}{62.5}$ where d is given in mils.

The resistance of copper wire increases 21/100 of 1% for each degree rise in Fahrenheit.

The resistance per mile of pure copper wire is about $\frac{54882}{d^2}$, d being in mils.

The weight of iron wire per mile is $\frac{d^2}{72}$ where d is the diameter in mils.

The resistance per mile of galvanized iron wire is about $\frac{360000}{d^2}$, d being in mils; or about seven times that of copper.

The resistance of German silver is about thirteen times that of copper.

CHAPTER IX.

ELECTRIC LIGHTING.

Figure 77 shows what is known as the tree system of electric light distribution. The wires at the lowest floor must be of sufficient capacity to carry the total current. At each floor or succeeding center of distribution the size of mains may be reduced, suitable

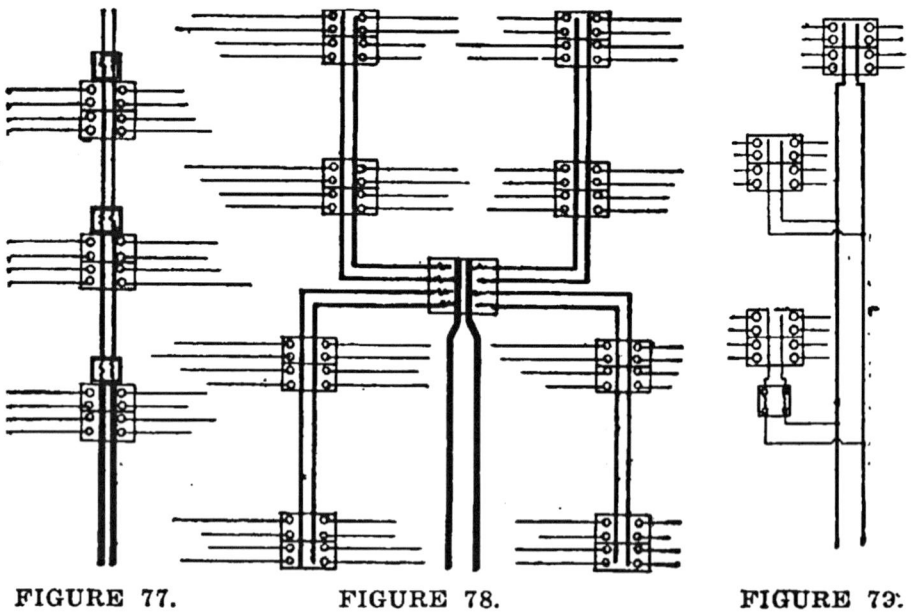

FIGURE 77.   FIGURE 78.   FIGURE 79.

cutouts being provided as shown in the diagram. This system is not to be recommended, as it will result in great difference of potential between those branch circuits nearest the dynamo and those at the extreme end of the system. When the mains are fully loaded, the nearest lamps will either burn too bright or those at a greater distance be dim.

This difficulty is largely overcome by the arrangement shown in Figure 78.

Figure 79 shows a system of distribution which is very often used. The mains are run direct from the dynamo, or street service, to the last center of distribution without changing size of wire. While this system has some of the disadvantages of the tree system in regard to drop, still the losses are greatly reduced owing to the much smaller losses on the mains between those centers farthest away from the source of supply. If the mains are of small size they may be run directly through the branch blocks at the various centers, as shown at the upper part of the figure. If the mains are too large to be run directly through the blocks, either of the methods shown in the lower part of the figure may be used, that shown at the bottom being preferable for, in case of a short circuit, across the contacts on the branch blocks, the smaller fuse will blow, while if the method shown in the center is used the main fuse will blow. This arrangement also allows any center to be disconnected for testing without affecting the remainder of the circuits.

Figure 79a shows how a two wire system may be converted into a three wire. One extra wire will have to be run. If the change over results in doubling the voltage of the system this wire will not require to be

ELECTRIC LIGHTING

as large as the original wires and should be connected to the neutral i. e. should run to all of the cutouts as shown in cut.

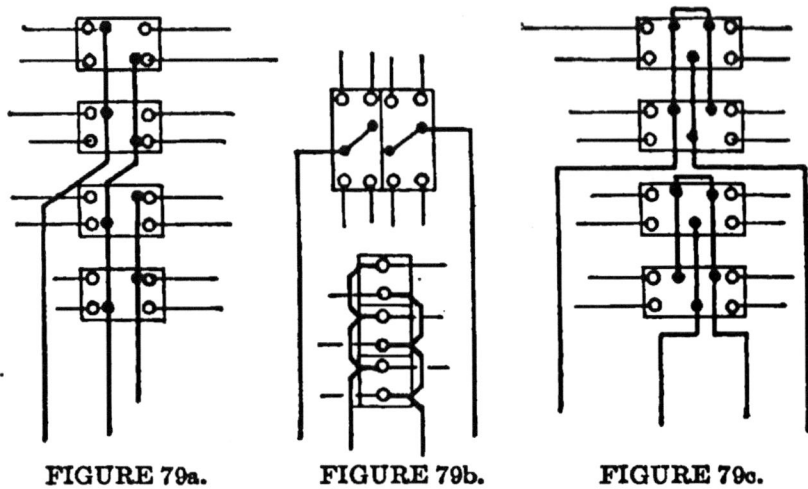

FIGURE 79a.   FIGURE 79b.   FIGURE 79c.

Figure 79b shows method of arranging cutouts so that all branch wires on any side of box are of the same polarity. This is frequently of use in electric signs where large numbers of wires are often bunched.

In Figure 79c a three wire system is shown converted into a two wire. As this usually is accompanied by a

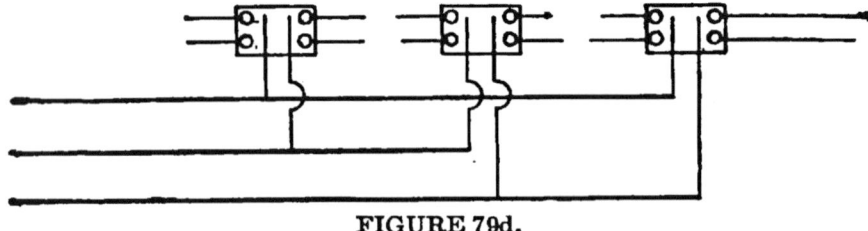

FIGURE 79d.

reduction in voltage and a consequent increase in current for the same number of lights it will likely be necessary to run an additional wire and divide the cutouts as shown.

Figure 79d shows the manner of connecting cutouts to a three phase system where cutouts are scattered along the line. Particular attention must be given to see that lights are as near as possible balanced between the phases.

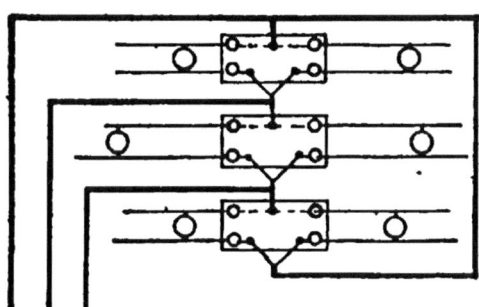 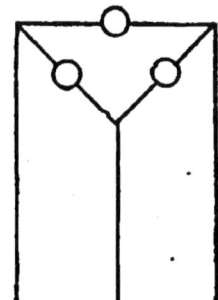

FIGURE 79e.

The delta connection for cutouts grouped together is given in Figure 79e. By tracing out the diagram it can readily be seen that the cutout connections are similar to the connections of the single lamps shown at the right.

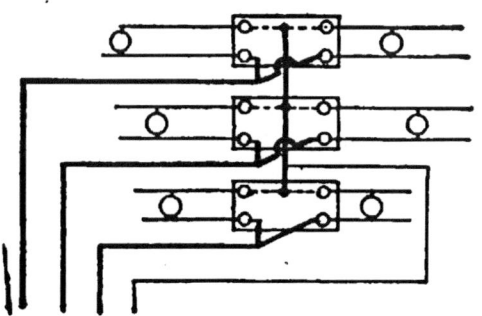 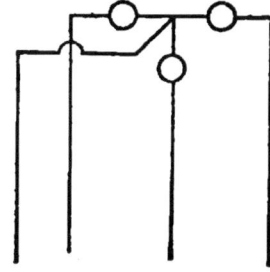

FIGURE 79f.

The voltage of lamps used in connection with this arrangement must be the same as that of the phases.

The star connection of cutouts is given in Figure

ELECTRIC LIGHTING 101

79f. If this connection is used it should have a balancing wire as shown.

The voltage of lamps to be used in connection with this system must be equal to the voltage of the phases divided by 1.73. This method is not generally used.

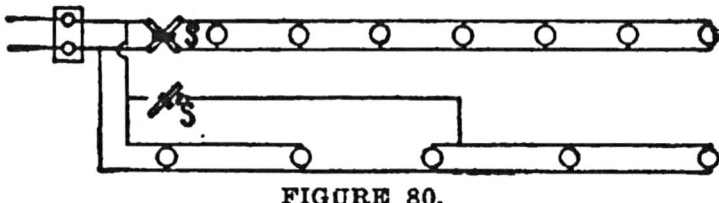

FIGURE 80.

Figure 80 shows a two-wire circuit with seven lights controlled by a double-pole switch, S; three lights controlled by a single-pole switch, S'; and two lights not controlled by any switch.

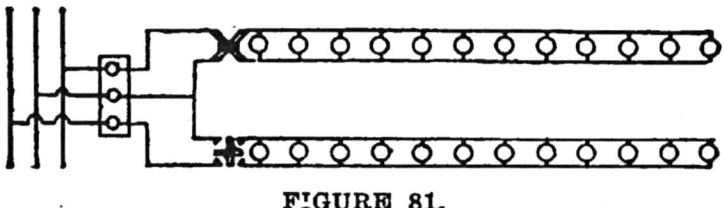

FIGURE 81.

Figures 81 and 82 show three-wire circuits. Figure 81 is arranged with double-pole switches, each switch completely disconnecting the wires controlled by it. In Figure 82 only the two outside wires are broken, the neutral wire remaining intact. When single-pole switches are used in connection with three-wire systems, they should be placed on one of the outside wires, as the neutral wire is nearly always grounded. No switch must ever be connected so as to make it possible to break the neutral wire without also breaking the outside wires at the same instant.

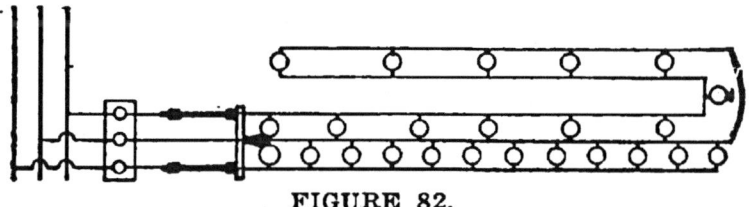

FIGURE 82.

Figure 83 shows a double-pole method of controlling a circuit from two places.

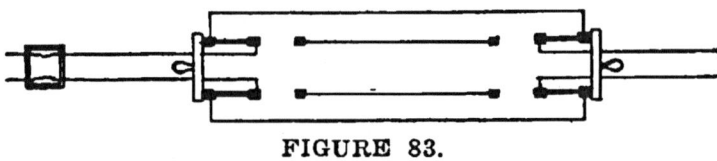

FIGURE 83.

In Figure 84 a similar arrangement is shown acting single-pole and arranged at one end for a throw-over knife switch and at the other for a three-way snap switch.

FIGURE 84.

By Figure 85 the same result is accomplished, and in some cases this method may be more saving of wire than Figure 84; but it cannot be used in connection with direct-current arc lamps, as the polarity may be reversed in turning lamps on and off.

ELECTRIC LIGHTING

Figure 86 shows a method of controlling a circuit from any number of stations. Any number of double-pole switches, as shown in the center, may be cut into

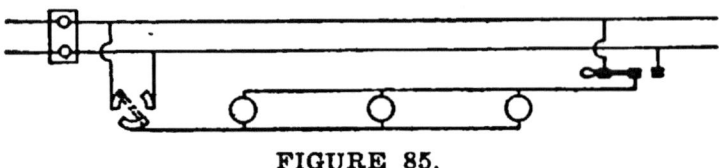

FIGURE 85.

the line. Snap switches as shown in Figure 87 may also be used in place of the throw-over knife switch.

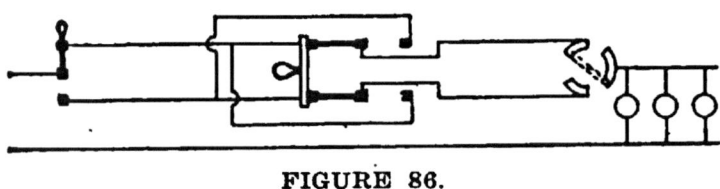

FIGURE 86.

By the system shown in Figure 87, a circuit can also be controlled from any number of places. The single-pole switches remain in the center and other

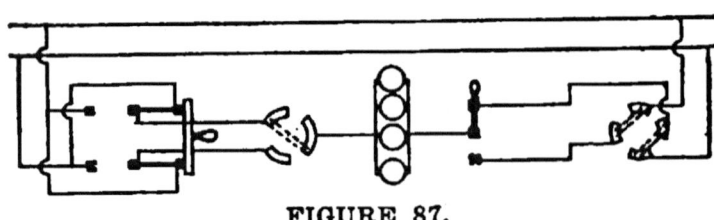

FIGURE 87.

switches are added as required. With this arrangement polarities may also be reversed in turning lamps on and off.

Figure 88 is known as an equal potential loop. This is useful on long lines where there is considerable loss; all lamps receive the same pressure and burn at the same candle-power.

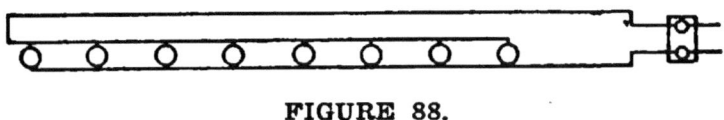

FIGURE 88.

Figure 89 shows a method by which lamps may be used at full candle-power; or, by throwing the switch over, they may be used at half candle-power, two in series.

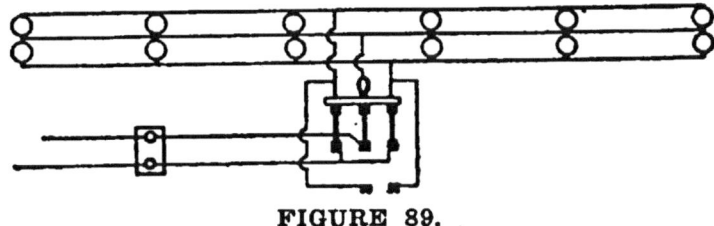

FIGURE 89.

Figure 90 shows one switch arranged to burn either two, four or six lamps. When connected at 1, the two top lights alone will burn; at 2 the four bot-

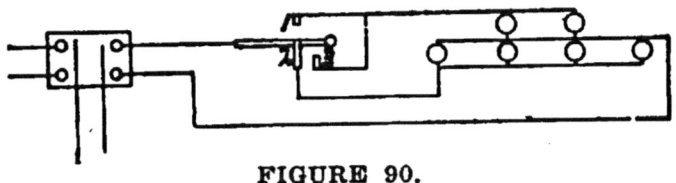

FIGURE 90.

tom lights will burn alone, while by connecting 2 and 3 all six lights will burn.

Figure 91 shows wiring arranged to provide a guest call for hotels or similar places. The bell 2 will ring and the lamp in series with it will burn only as long as the switch at the cutout remains closed. If the double-throw switch is thrown over, the bell 1 will

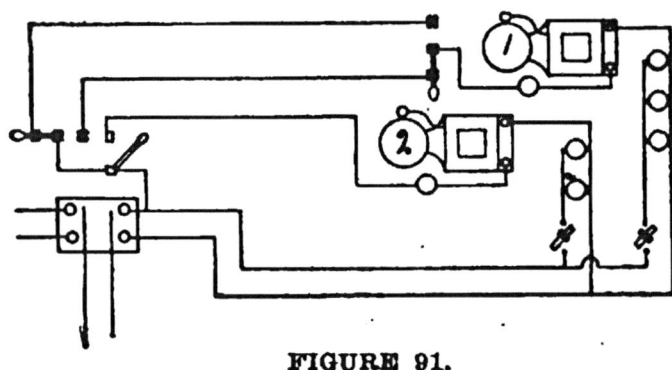

FIGURE 91.

continue to ring and the lamp will burn until the guest throws his switch over, or the party calling returns his to the original position.

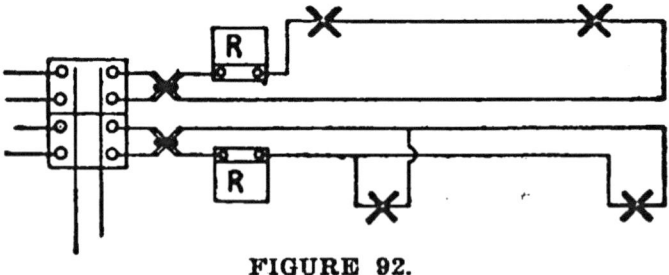

FIGURE 92.

In Figure 92 the wiring for low-tension arc lamps is shown. Such lamps may be wired either in series or in multiple, the wiring being arranged to suit the kind of lamps used. With all lamps of this kind some resistance must be used. With lamps run in multiple it is usually provided with each lamp, and is generally built in with the lamp.

Figure 93 shows a throw-over switch so arranged that only one lamp at a time can be used, one resistance answering for both. All switches used in con-

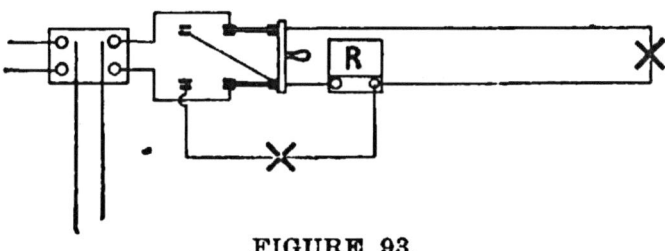

FIGURE 93.

nection with direct-current arc lamps must be arranged so that polarities cannot be changed by them.

Figure 94 shows connections enabling one to burn either the two lamps at the right or those at the left, only two at a time being used. This arrangement requires the use of series lamps.

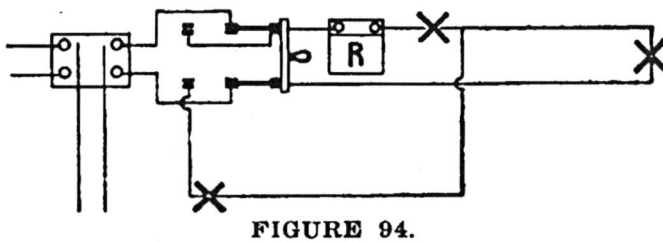

FIGURE 94.

Figure 95 shows a system of wiring which makes it possible to light all of the lamps in a building, not controlled by key sockets, from three different places at any time, even after they have been turned off by the occupants of rooms. In the top part of the figure one double-throw switch and one three-way

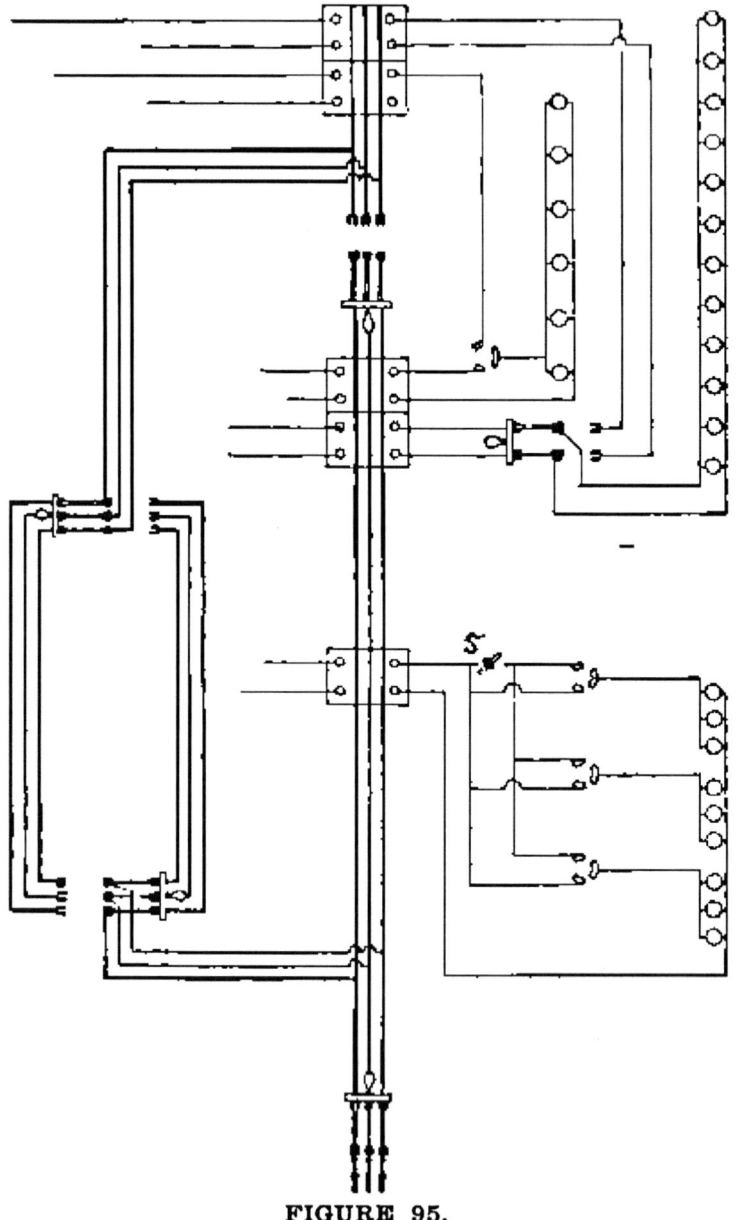

FIGURE 95.

snap switch are shown. Whenever, by either of these switches, the lamps are turned off, the switches make connection with the cutouts above, so that by throwing any one of the three knife-switches the lamps may be lighted again. In the lower part of the figure one circuit is arranged for the same purpose. By closing the single-pole switch S, all of the lights may be turned on at any time, excepting, of course, those that are turned off at the sockets. This arrangement is very useful in case of fire, or any emergency where it is desired to illuminate a whole house quickly.

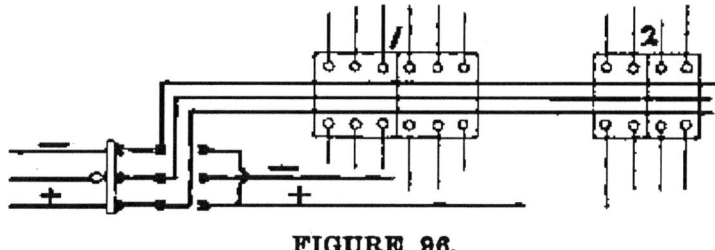

FIGURE 96.

Figure 96 shows the wiring of a convertible system. By means of the three-wire switch, connections may be made to either a two or three-wire supply. With this system the middle or neutral wire should have as much carrying capacity as both outside wires, since when used with a two-wire supply it must carry the full load, while either of the outside wires need carry but half the current. Cutouts of the kind shown in group 1 should not be used in connection with this system. They are not very objectionable in straight three-wire systems, but when used in connection with two-wire systems the middle fuse must be doubled to carry the load. Such cutouts as are shown in group 2 are preferable. Great care is necessary when arc lamps are to be connected to such a system. They can be connected with one side of the neutral only, and this side must be arranged so that polarities are not reversed when the main switch is thrown over.

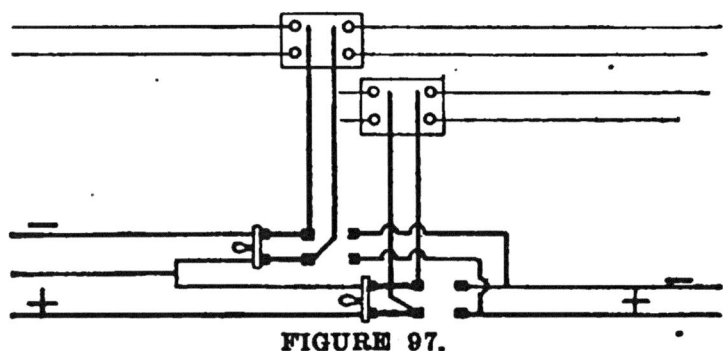
FIGURE 97.

Where arc lamps are used extensively and where it is necessary to balance the load, as on the Edison three-wire system, the wiring used in Fig. 97 may be employed. In place of the two double-pole, double-throw switches, a four-pole, double-throw switch may be used.

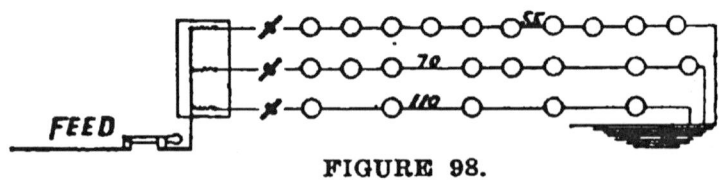
FIGURE 98.

Figure 98 shows incandescent lamps arranged in series. This plan of lighting is generally used in connection with street railway work. The figure shows 550 volt circuits provided with lamps of different voltage. Instead of the ground a return wire may be used.

Figure 99 shows the wiring of a high-tension arc circuit. A group of incandescent lamps is also shown. When incandescent lamps are used in connection with arc lamps as shown there must be enough lamps in each group to take the current used by the arc lamps. The switch S controls the incandescent lamps and also the arc lamps 1, 2, 3 by simply short-circuiting them. The double-pole switch

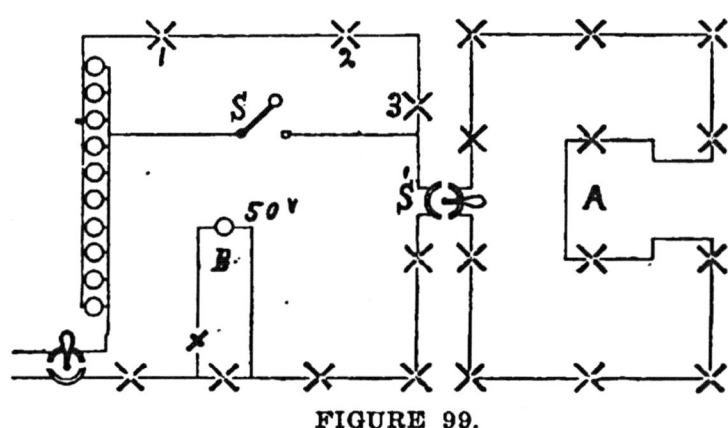

FIGURE 99.

S' controls the group A and is so arranged that when turned off this group is entirely disconnected. This is the only safe way of switching high-tension arcs: where they are merely short-circuited they are nearly as unsafe to handle as when burning. At B one incandescent lamp is shown controlled by a single-pole switch. When this lamp is burning it robs the arc lamp of as much current as it requires, the amount of current depending on the candle-power of the lamp. Incandescent lamps should be used on arc circuits only in an emergency and then only where there is little risk of fire.

Figure 100 shows a diagram of the connections of a theater switchboard. The board is fed by the two sets of mains shown by the arrows on the lower sets of bus bars. The lower set of bus bars feeds the lights in the house, or auditorium, switch 51 controlling the majority of these lights. A set of bus bars running from this switch feeds a number of smaller main switches which control all the lights in the different sections of the house, such as the gallery, balcony, main floor, etc. Bus bars running from these switches feed other switches which control the different groups of lights in the various sections of the house.

The other set of main bus bars at the bottom of the board feeds the lights on the stage, these lights being controlled by four main switches: 24, which controls all the white lights; 35, all the red lights, and 43, all the blue lights, smaller switches being used to control the different colored lights in the foots, borders, strips, etc.

The switches which operate the white lights, 17 to 23 and 26 to 32, are all double-throw, the upper contacts of which are connected to a set of bus bars controlled by the main white switch, 24, while the lower contacts are connected to a set of bus bars independent of this switch. By means of this arrangement part of the lights can be thrown off by the main switch while certain ones are left burning.

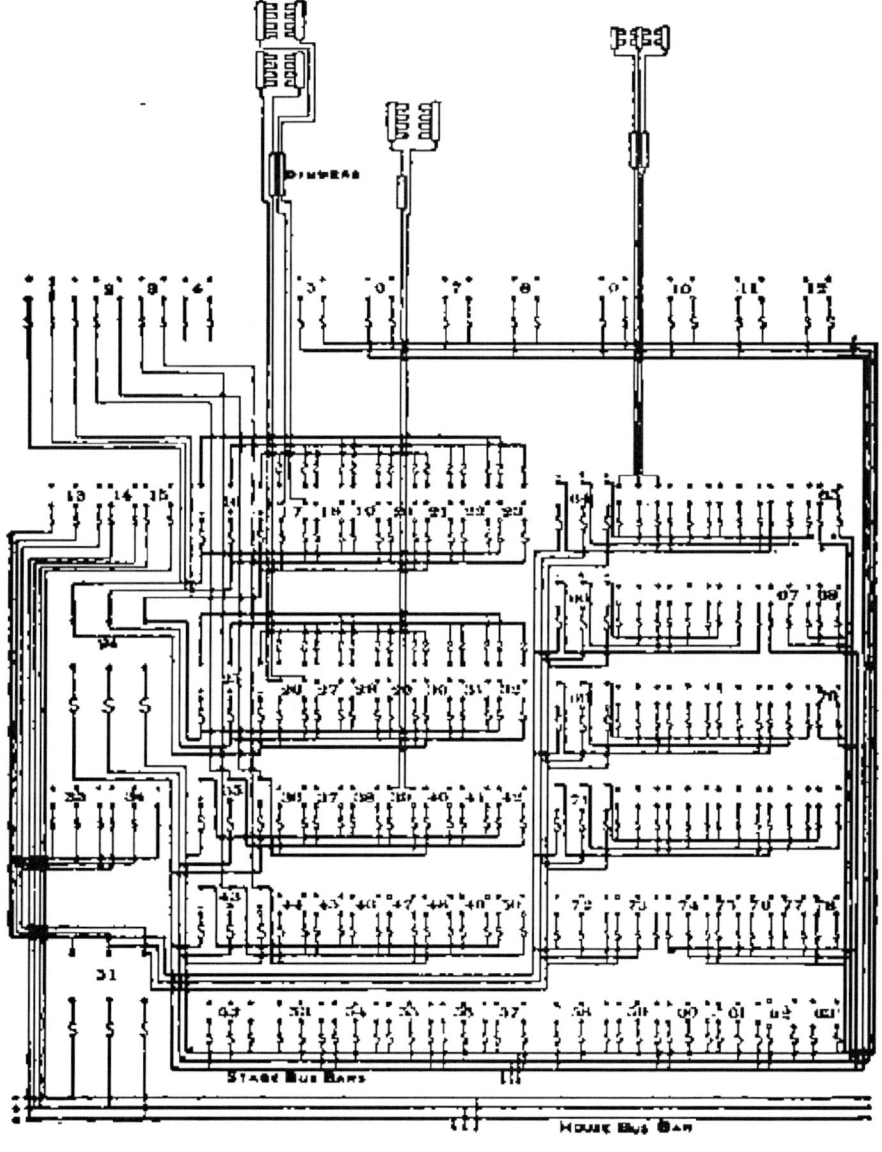

FIGURE 100.

A few of the circuits are shown connected to the dimmers from which they run to the branch circuit cutouts.

1. White Strips.
2. Red Strips.
3. Blue Strips.
4. Switchboard Lights. (Connected to House Bus Bar.)
5. Sub-basement Lights.
6. Basement Lights.
7. Basement Lights.
8. Paint Bridge Motor.
9. Patrol Lights.
10. Air Compressor Motor.
11. Exhaust Air Motor.
12. Exhaust Air Motor.
13. Sunlight Ceiling.
14. Orchestra Lights.
15. Program Lights.
16. Top White Main.
17. Top White Foots.
18. Top White Border, No. 1.
19. Top White Border, No. 2.
20. Top White Border, No. 3.
21. Top White Border, No. 4.
22. Top White Border, No. 5.
23. Top White Proscenium.
24. Main White Switch.
25. Bottom White Main.
26. Bottom White Foots.
27. Bottom White Border, No. 1.
28. Bottom White Border, No. 2.
29. Bottom White Border, No. 3.
30. Bottom White Border, No. 4.
31. Bottom White Border, No. 5.
32. Bottom White Proscenium.
33. Boxes.
34. Boxes.
35. Red Main.
36. Red Foots.
37. Red Border, No. 1.
38. Red Border, No. 2.
39. Red Border, No. 3.
40. Red Border, No. 4.
41. Red Border, No. 5.
42. Red Proscenium.
43. Blue Main.
44. Blue Foots.
45. Blue Border, No. 1.
46. Blue Border, No. 2.
47. Blue Border, No. 3.
48. Blue Border, No. 4.
49. Blue Border, No. 5.
50. Blue Proscenium.
51. Main House Switch.
52. Plug Pockets.
53. 35 ampere Pockets.
54. 35 ampere Pockets.
55. 35 ampere Pockets.
56. 100 ampere Pockets.
57. Curtain Motor.
58. 100 ampere Pockets.
59. Dressing Rooms.
60. 100 ampere Pockets.
61. 200 ampere Pockets.
62. Picture Machine.
63. Picture Machine.
64. Fifth Floor and Gallery.
65. Fans.
66. 4th Floor.
67. Stage Chandelier.
68. Fans.
69. Third Floor.
70. Hoist Motor.
71. First and Second Floors.
72. Balcony Front.
73. Balcony Front.
74. Paint Bridge.
75. Rigging Loft.
76. Fly Floor.
77. Fly Floor.
78. Pump Motor.

Figure 101 shows a diagram of the connections of an elevator signalling device. The diagram is shown for only six floors, but it is evident that it could be extended to any number of floors. At each floor, with the exception of the top and bottom, are two incandescent lamps, the upper lamps (shown by light circles) burn when the elevator car is moving upward, while the lower lamps (shown by black circles) burn when the car is traveling downward. These lamps are connected to a series of contacts, *2, 3, 1', 2'*, etc., which are mounted on a device generally located at the top of the shaft near the elevator machine. A sliding contact, which is operated by means of a screw geared to the elevator drum and so designed that the motion of the elevator car from the top to the bottom of the shaft will move the contact piece over the entire length of bar *a*, makes connection between the contacts *a* and *2, 3, 4, 5, 6*, while the car is moving upward, and between *a'* and *1', 2', 3', 4', 5'*, while the car is moving downward. This movable contact is of such size that connection is made to three or four of the contacts, *2, 3, 4*, etc., at one time. The operation is as follows: Suppose the car is at the bottom of the shaft. The sliding contact piece will connect *a* with contacts *2, 3* and *4*. Current will then flow from the Main to the "up" lamps on the 2d, 3d and 4th floors. As the car moves upward contact is made to points, *3, 4* and *5*, while the contact to the 2d floor is broken. In this way the lamps on three or four floors ahead of the car will

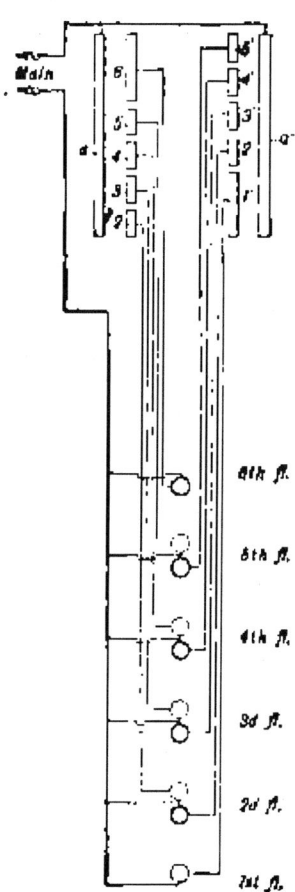

FIGURE 101.

ELECTRIC LIGHTING

burn until the car reaches the top of the shaft. The last contact, 6, is of such size that it will take in the whole movable contact so that while the car is at the top of the shaft the light on the 6th floor only will burn and this light shows that the car is going down. When the car starts to move downward the connection between a and 6 is broken and connection made between a' and $5'$, $4'$ and $3'$, the "down" lamps on the corresponding floors then burning. As the car moves downward the operation previously explained will be repeated except that the "down" lamps will burn.

CHAPTER X.

ARC LAMPS, NERNST LAMP, COOPER HEWITT LAMP.

Figure 102 shows the circuits of the improved Brush arc lamp. This lamp is used on constant-current, direct-current systems. The current enters the

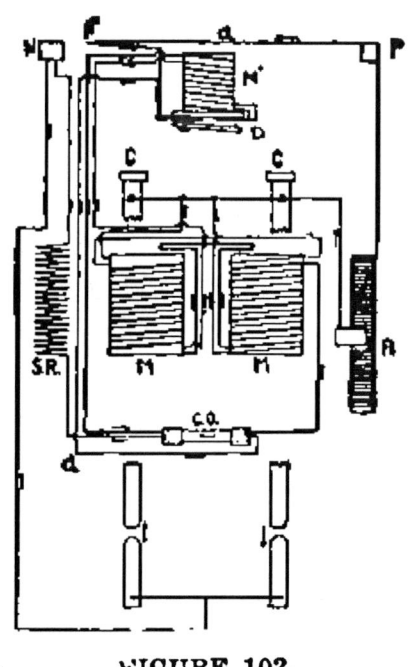

FIGURE 102.

positive binding post P and part of it goes through the resistance R to the carbon rods C, C, then through the carbons to the negative post N. The remainder of the current passes through wire *a* to the cutout block C, O, but, as the cutout is closed at first, the current crosses over through the cutout bar to the starting resistance S, R, and to the negative side of the lamp; a part of this current, however, is shunted at the cutout block through the coarse wire winding of the magnets M, M, and so to the upper carbon rod and carbons and out. The fine wire winding of the magnets M, M, is connected in the opposite direction to the coarse winding, and its attraction is therefore opposite. When the arc increases in length, its resistance increases, and consequently the current in the fine wire is increased. The attraction of the coarse wire winding is therefore partly overcome and the armature begins to fall. As it falls the arc is shortened and the current in the fine wire decreases. The fine wire of the magnets M, M, is connected in series with the winding of the auxiliary magnet M'. This magnet, which also has a supplementary coarse winding, does not raise its armature unless the voltage at the arc increases to 70 volts. The two windings connect at the inside terminal on the lower side of the auxiliary cutout magnet and the current from the fine wire of the main magnets passes through both windings and then to the cutout block and so to the starting resistance and out. If the main current is interrupted (as by the breaking of the carbons) the whole current of the lamp passes through the fine wire circuit. This will energize the auxiliary magnet M' and close a circuit directly across the lamp through the coarse wire on M' to the main cutout and thence to negative terminal. When the main cut-out C, O, operates, the armature of the auxiliary cut-out falls because there is not sufficient current in that circuit to energize the magnet. This lamp is switched off by simply short circuiting it across N, N'.

In all direct current arc lamps care must be taken to see that the current enters at the proper binding post, as the positive carbon burns away about twice as fast as the negative carbon. When a lamp is burning a small cup-shaped formation will be noticed at the arc on the positive carbon and a small projection on the negative carbon. Lamps are generally connected so that the upper carbon is positive, and this hollow formation on the positive will throw the light downward. In this way it can be determined by the way the light is thrown as to whether a lamp is burning right side up or not.

Figure 103 shows the circuits in a constant current arc lamp for use on alternating current systems. When the lamp is switched on current passes through the coarse winding of magnet M and then to the carbon rod and carbons and out at the other terminal. This energizes M and attracts the core A, thus raising the upper carbon and establishing the arc. The magnet M' is wound with a great length of fine wire and opposes magnet M. As the resistance of the arc increases more current is sent around the fine wire winding of M' and the core A and the carbon thus lowered. If for any reason (breaking of the car-

ARC LAMPS

bons, etc.), the resistance at the arc is greatly increased, the core A will be lowered until the two points of the cutout C come in contact when the main current will pass through C and resistance R to the post T'. The resistance of R is in such proportion to M' that just enough current is sent around M' to keep the cutout C closed. By means of the spring S the length of the arc may be adjusted. Tightening the spring increases the arc by requiring a greater amount of current to flow around M' to lower the carbons.

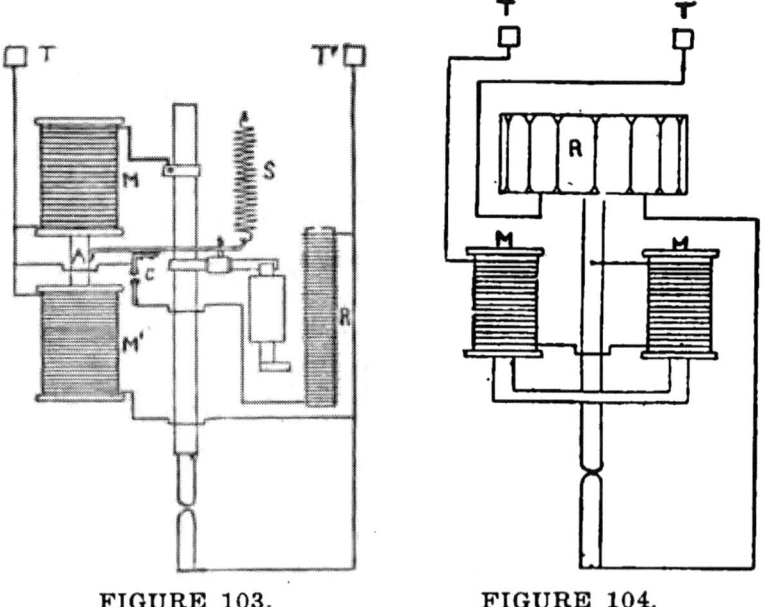

FIGURE 103.   FIGURE 104.

Figure 104 shows the winding of a constant potential, alternating current arc lamp. R is a reactance or choking coil, the purpose of which is to cut down the voltage of the line to that required by the arc. This coil takes the place of the resistance coil in the direct current, constant potential lamp. The current passes from the binding post T to the magnets M, M, and then to the upper carbon, from there to the lower carbon and then through the reactance coil and out at the other terminal. It will be noticed that this lamp has no shunt winding similar to the constant current lamp. This is unnecessary as the voltage at the terminals is practically constant. As the carbons burn away the current through M, M, is decreased, due to the increased resistance of the arc, and the armature is lowered, thus lowering the carbons.

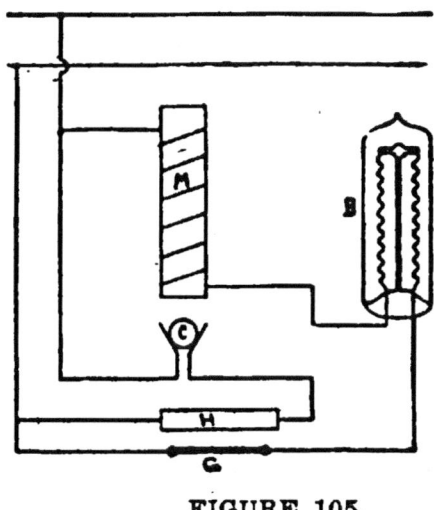

FIGURE 105.

Direct-current, constant-potential arc lamps differ from the constant-current lamps in that no automatic cutouts can be used, and in order to put out the lamp, the circuit must be opened. Constant-current lamps require no extra resistance, while constant-potential lamps cannot be operated without some resistance to steady the current.

Figure 105 shows the diagram of a Nernst lamp. In the diagram, H is the heater, which is made up of a winding of platinum wire on a porcelain tube. The glower G is composed of an oxide which at the ordinary temperature is of very high resistance but when heated lowers in resistance considerably. The ballast B is made up of fine iron wire which increases in resistance as it becomes heated, thus tending to steady the current and keep the voltage over the glower as near constant as possible. When the lamp is started current passes through the heater H, gradually heating it and the glower, which is located directly below it. As the glower is heated current begins to pass through it and the cutout magnet M, until finally it becomes strong enough to attract the cutout C which opens the heater circuit. This circuit will then remain open as long as current is passing through the glower. These lamps are made in several sizes from one to six glower and they consume when burning 88 watts per glower. Each glower is equal in candle-power to three ordinary 16 candle-power incandescent lamps. When the lamp is started more current is used than when the lamp is burning, owing to the fact that the heater coils are in circuit. In the six-glower lamp which takes when burning 2.4 amperes on 220 volts, the starting current rises to about 3.2 amperes. These lamps are at present used only on alternating current systems as the glower becomes blackened in a short time when used on direct-current systems.

Figure 106 shows a diagram of the connections of the Cooper Hewitt mercury vapor lamp. The

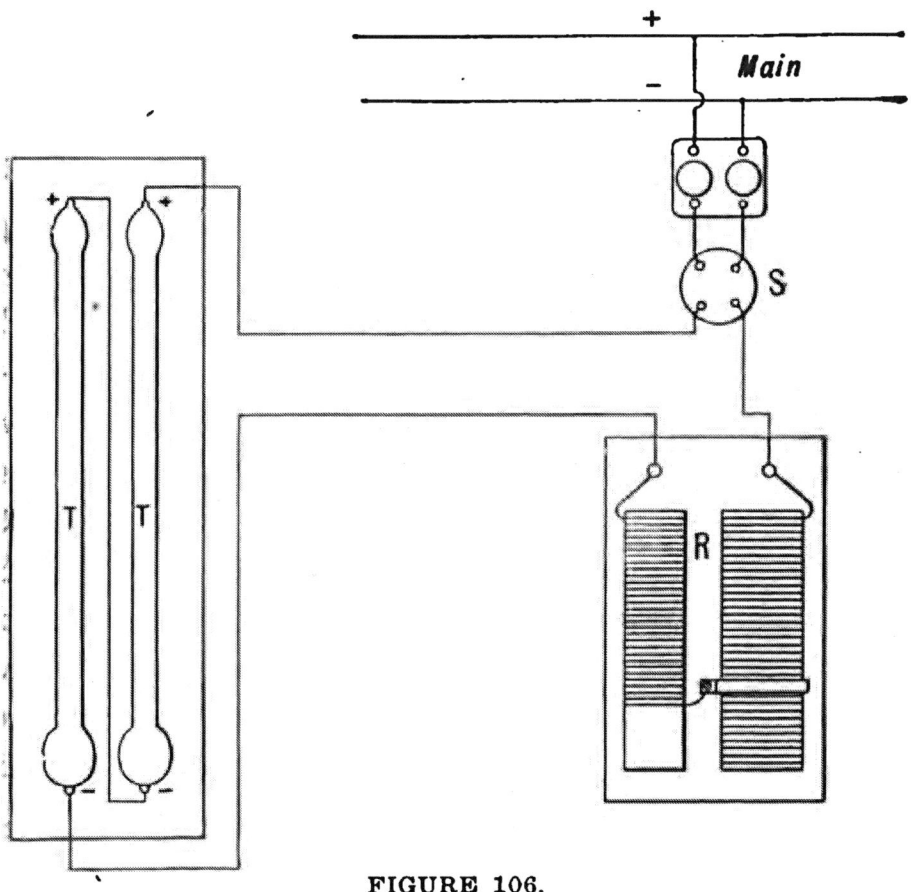

FIGURE 106.

light from this lamp is emitted from the two tubes T, T', which, when current is passing through them, glow with a greenish light. The tubes T, T', are of glass and the air has been extracted from them; they are provided at their upper ends with electrodes inside the tube to which leading in wires are attached and at the lower ends with iron cups which are partially filled with mercury. Either of two different methods are used to start the lamp. In one case a coil of great inductance is used to send a kick of current through the tube between the positive and negative electrodes, thus breaking down the high resistance and allowing current to flow. In the other method after the current is turned on the tubes are tipped until all the mercury in the lower cup flows out into the tube and forms a path to the upper electrode. As the tube is tipped back and the column of mercury leaves the upper electrode light is given off. The connections can be easily traced. Current passing from the positive main flows through the cutout, switch S, to the positive terminal of tube T' then through tube T' to the negative terminal and out to the + of tube T, through this tube and the adjustable resistance R to the negative side of the line. The two tubes and the resistance are simply connected in series through the proper cutout and switch. Great care must be taken to see that current flows through the lamp in the proper direction for, if current is sent through in the wrong direction, even for a few minutes, the tube will be ruined. The type of lamp shown is used for photographic purposes and takes about 3.5 amperes at 110 volts when running normally. At the start the current rises to a little over 100% for a very short time. The ordinary lamp consisting of a single tube is rated at about 750 C. P. After the lamps have been in use for some time (about 1600 hours), the inside of the lamp becomes coated with a brownish substance and small globules of mercury will adhere to the sides. The tubes then have to be replaced. For photographic purposes this lamp taking 3.5 amperes compares very favorably with a 10 ampere arc lamp.

CHAPTER XI.

RECORDING WATTMETERS.

Figure 107 shows the circuits in the two-wire Thomson recording wattmeter. One of the mains is connected through the winding M, M, which forms the fields of a motor. The armature of this motor is connected across the mains in series with a resistance R and the shunt field S. This shunt field is always in circuit, whether there is current used through the meter or not, and it is so arranged that it tends to start the motor. Its purpose is to overcome the friction of the armature so that the meter will register on very small loads. It will be noticed that the connection for the potential circuit is taken off the main at A. This is done so that the meter will register the current used in the potential circuit, and this is one reason why the generator must always be connected on the left side and the load on the right side of the meter. If this form of meter is fed from the wrong side it will run backward. In Figure 107 it will be seen that if the feed were reversed (leaving polarities unchanged) the current through the fields would be in the opposite direction, while that through the armature would remain unchanged, hence the motor would be reversed. Used on direct-current this meter runs as a simple direct current motor and when used on alternating current, at each reversal of the current the polarities of both the fields and armature are changed simultaneously; and the motor will therefore continue to run in the one direction, because changing the direction of current in both the fields and armature of a shunt motor does not change the direction of rotation. There is no iron used in the construction of the motor and therefore no loss from heating.

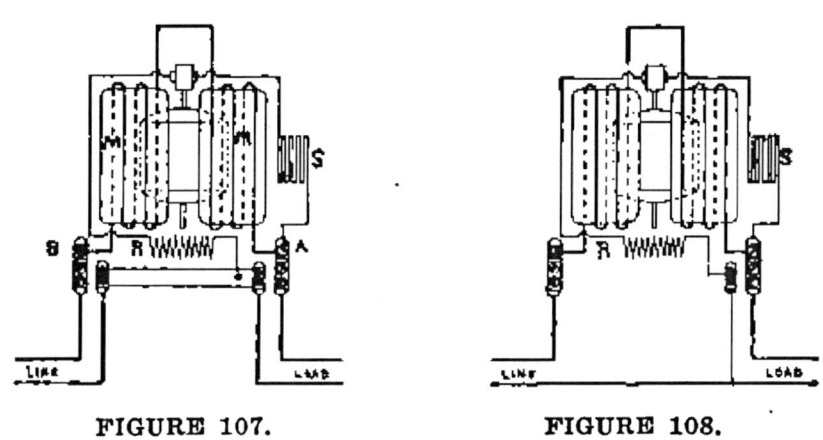

FIGURE 107.   FIGURE 108.

Figure 108 shows the two-wire meter for heavy loads. The circuits in this meter vary from the preceding one only in having but one main carried through the meter with a tap to the other main.

Figure 109 shows the three-wire meter. The two outside wires (positive and negative) are carried through the meter, one through each field, and the armature is connected from one outside to the neutral. In some of the three-wire meters no neutral tap is

RECORDING WATTMETERS

used, the potential circuit being connected directly across the outside mains.

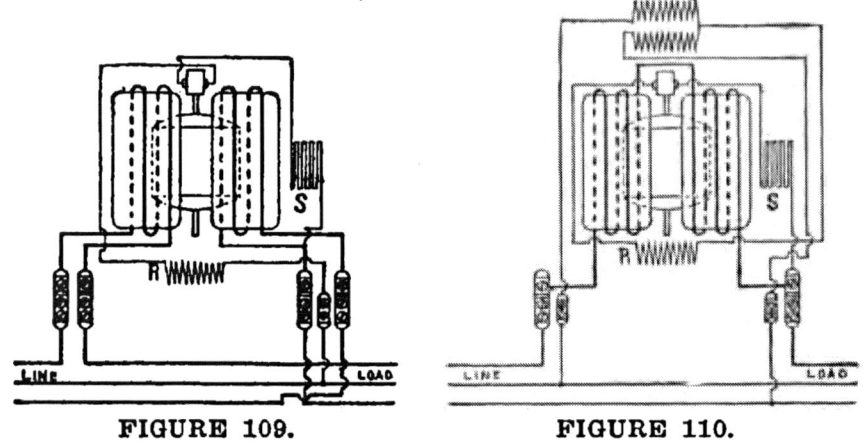

FIGURE 109.   FIGURE 110.

Figure 110 shows a meter for a balanced three phase line.

Figure 111 shows a station meter for use on series arc lines.

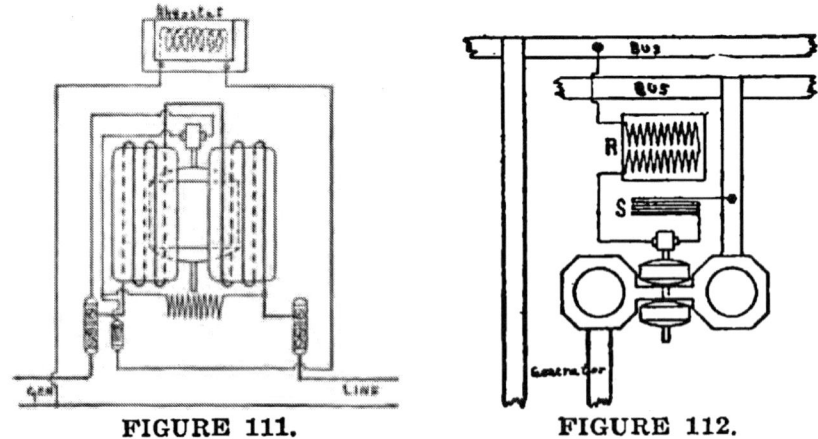

FIGURE 111.   FIGURE 112.

Figure 112 shows a meter used on switchboards to record the entire current passing through the bus bars.

Figure 113 shows the circuits in the Gutmann wattmeter. This meter is used with alternating currents only and depends for its action on an aluminum disk, slotted in spiral lines, operated in joint action with a shunt laminated magnet-coil S' and a pair of series coils S, S. In the two-wire meter the series coils are connected in series with one of the mains and the shunt coil is connected across the mains as shown in diagram. The loss in the shunt coil does not exceed 1½ watts on the 110 volt 60 cycle meter and the drop in the series coil does not exceed ¼ of one volt on full load on the small size meters, and is proportionally less in the larger meters.

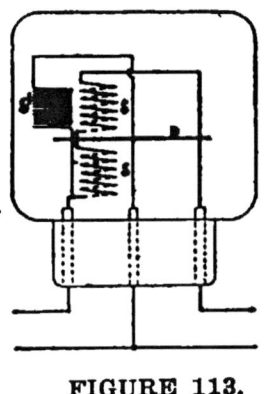

FIGURE 113.

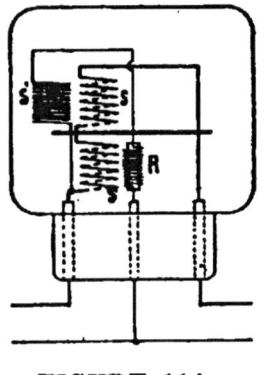

FIGURE 114.

Figure 114 shows the 200-250 volt meter. This meter has in series with the shunt coil a reactance coil R.

Figure 115 shows the three wire meter. In this meter one of the outside mains is carried through one series coil and the other through the other series coil. No tap is taken to the neutral as the pressure circuit is connected across the mains as in the 200-250 volt meter.

Figure 116 shows a meter for use on either 100 or 200 volt systems. The connection shown in the full lines is for 100 volts and the dotted for 200 volts. The reactance coil R is balanced to have exactly the same choke as the shunt coil.

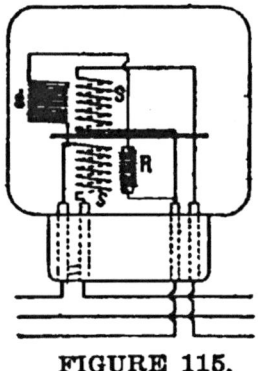 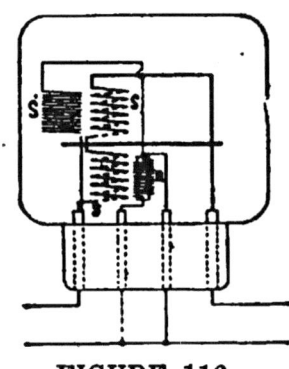

FIGURE 115.   FIGURE 116.

In Figure 117 the connections of an Edison chemical, three-wire meter are shown. The two outsides only are carried through the meter, no neutral connection being used. This type of meter was one of the first used on commercial work, the amount of current having passed through the meter in a given time being determined by the amount of zinc deposited on the negative electrode. These meters are rapidly being replaced by the mechanical meters.

Figure 118 shows a diagram of what is known as the Wright discount or demand meter. This meter is used in connection with recording wattmeters to determine the maximum current which has been used during a given time. It is also used on circuits where it is desired to know the maximum current which has passed through the circuit. In the diagram, B is a glass bulb connected to a tube U which is partly filled with a liquid. Around bulb B is wound a resistance wire which carries the main current. When current is flowing in this wire heat is generated and the air in the bulb is expanded thus forcing the liquid around

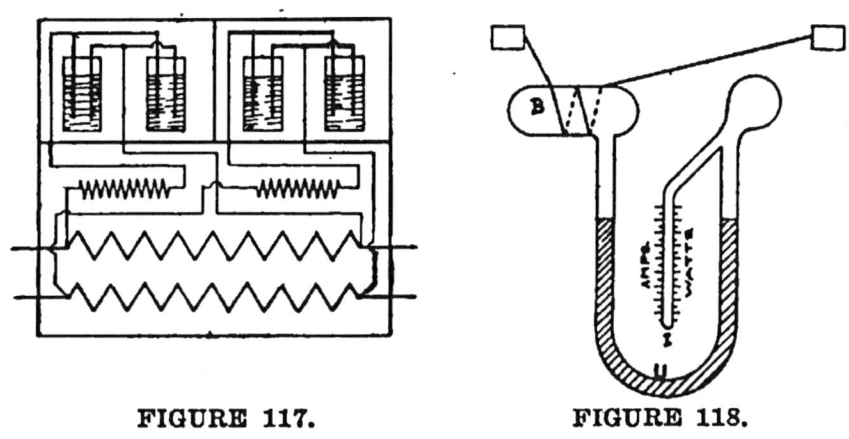

FIGURE 117.   FIGURE 118.

tube U until it reaches the point where the tube U and I join, when it will flow into tube I. The amount of liquid in tube I will depend on the maximum amount of current which has passed through the resistance wire on bulb B. The scale back of tube I is graduated in amperes and watts. The meter is not effected by momentary increases in the current. If the maximum current lasts five minutes 80% will register; ten minutes, 95% will register; thirty minutes, 100% will register.

RECORDING WATTMETERS 130a

The Wright demand indicators described in the previous figure, 118, are influenced only by the current and therefore cannot be used on a. c. circuits having a power factor less than unity. The demand in all a. c. circuits must be measured in watts and therefore several types of demand meters have been de-

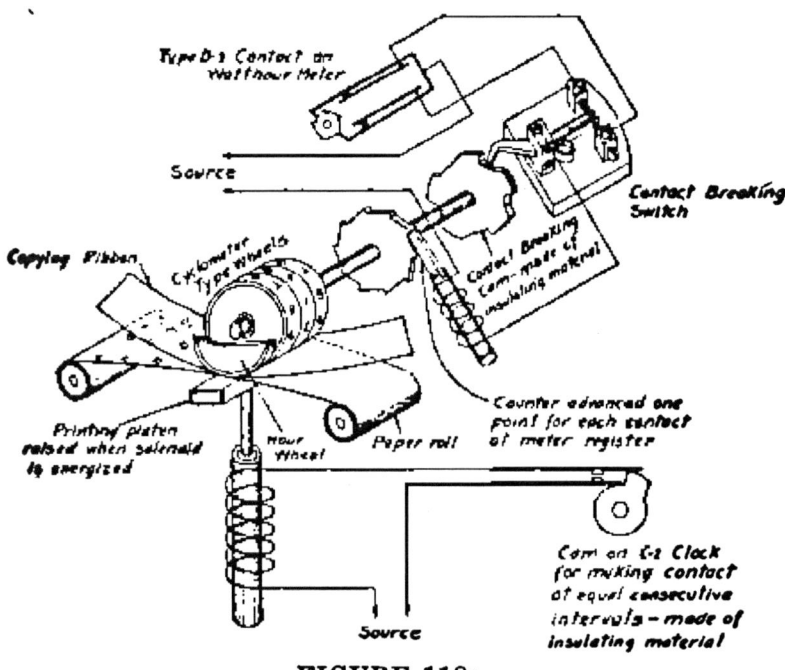

FIGURE 118a.

veloped which are governed directly by the watt meters in circuit. A diagrammatic sketch of one of these is shown in Figure 118 a. This instrument is manufactured by the General Electric Co. and is known as type P or "Printometer." A ratchet wheel made of insulating material is mounted on one of the spindles of the register as indicated in center at top of figure. Two blued steel spring brushes rest diametrically opposite on the ratchet, thus allowing first one and then the other brush to drop off of the ratchet, at equal intervals. A platinum-iridium point is staked in each of these brushes, and as the brush falls off of the ratchet tooth, this point makes contact with another platinum-iridium point which is carried by a second spring-leaf running parallel to the brush. The two brushes resting on the ratchet wheel are charged all of the time with line potential. Thus, when these drop alternately upon the two leaves which connect to the cyclometer coil, we obtain the usual two-way circuit and alternately close the circuit through the cyclometer solenoid. Each time this solenoid is energized it advances the counters one point. A special contact-breaking switch is provided as shown in upper right hand corner and its object is to open the circuit immediately after the solenoid has moved the ratchet shown in center.

This type of demand meter is always accompanied with a clock which is arranged to print the record at certain intervals, usually 30 minutes. This is effected by means of the solenoid and electric circuit shown at bottom of figure. When properly set up and adjusted this instrument will print at predetermined intervals a record of the number of watts consumed in the meter circuits during that interval and the hour of the day at which the energy was used.

Another instrument devised for the same purpose and made by the General Electric Co. is illustrated

RECORDING WATTMETERS 130c

in Figure 118b. This instrument does not print a record but indicates the maximum amount of power used during a predetermined interval by means of a pointer. The registering device consists of a train

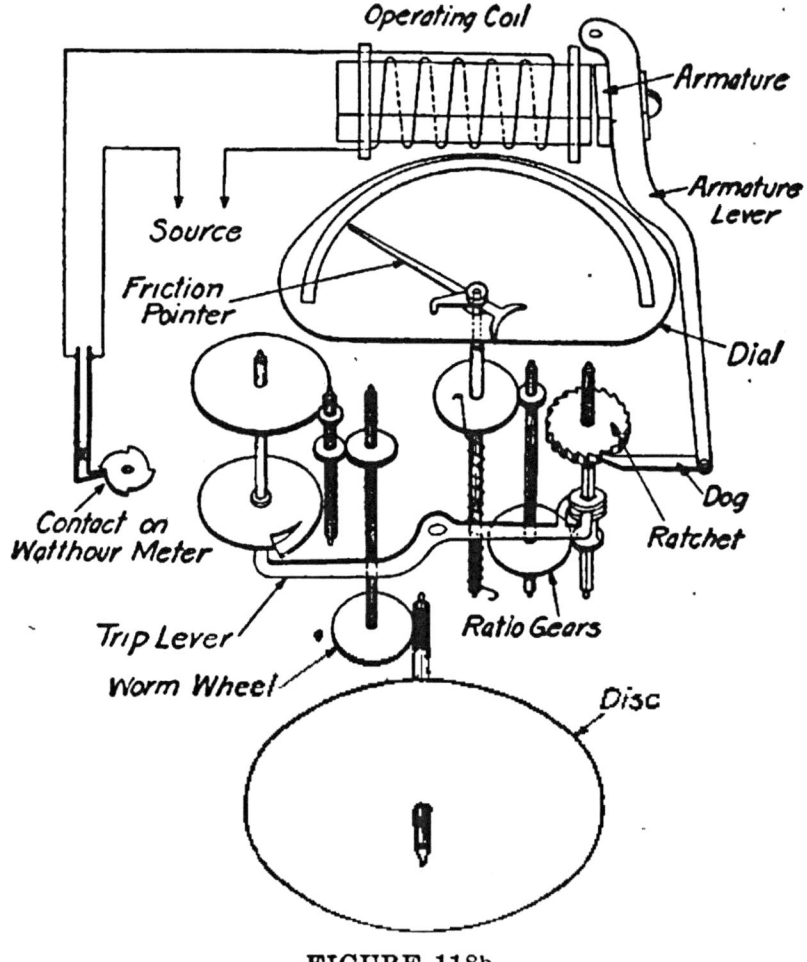

FIGURE 118b.

of gears arranged to drive the pointer forward over a semi-circular dial. The gear wheels are actuated by a ratchet and pawl mechanism which is driven by an electromagnet. This electromagnet is energized once every time a certain number of kilowatt-hours of electrical energy have been registered by the watt-hour meter. It is evident, therefore, that the position of the dial pointer of this demand meter is directly dependent upon energy consumption as registered by the watthour meter.

Since the demand meter gives the demand for a definite time interval, it is necessary that the mechanism which drives the dial pointer forward over the scale shall be reset to zero position at the end of the time interval, but shall leave the dial pointer at the most advanced point on the dial scale to which it has been carried. This resetting of the register mechanism to zero is accomplished by a mechanism governed by a constant speed device so that the resettings are accurately timed. When used in connection with a.c. circuits the device is operated by a small constant speed motor. For d.c., clock work is used.

The above instruments are usually set to make complete records of loads that last for some time. If the load during that time is fairly constant, they may be considered as giving the true instantaneous maximum load. If the actual instantaneous value of current or wattage is wanted, some form of chart-drawing instrument is usually inserted in the circuit. If none such is at hand a curve representing with pretty fair accuracy the fluctuations in the circuit may be obtained in the following manner, which has been successfully employed by the authors: Take an ordinary sheet of paper and write upon it in straight lines the numbers, 1, 2, 3, etc. Let each of these numbers stand for seconds and let there be as many as will cover the time during which observations are to be taken. Let one man observe the disk of wattmeter and be prepared to give some signal each time the disk completes one revolution. Let another man hold a watch and count off the seconds as the watch ticks them off. A third man must now be prepared to follow with a pencil the numbers on the paper in the order as the watch holder reads off the seconds. With a little practice the man in charge of the paper will soon learn to follow along in synchronism with the time indicated by the watch, and at every signal from the disk reader, make a mark upon the paper. With a few minutes' practice three men will learn to co-operate very nicely in this way. The rate at which energy is consumed in the circuit will be inversely proportional to the time required for the disk to make one revolution. If the load carries with it some sudden high peaks, the disk reader may let two revolutions of the disk occur before giving the signal, but he should then have some distinctive signal for the marker so that he will understand and mark accordingly.

CHAPTER XII.

DIRECT CURRENT MOTORS.

Figure 119 shows the winding of a series motor for use on constant-potential circuits. In this motor the fields and armature are in series across the main circuit. The purpose of the starting box SB is to insert a resistance in series with the armature when

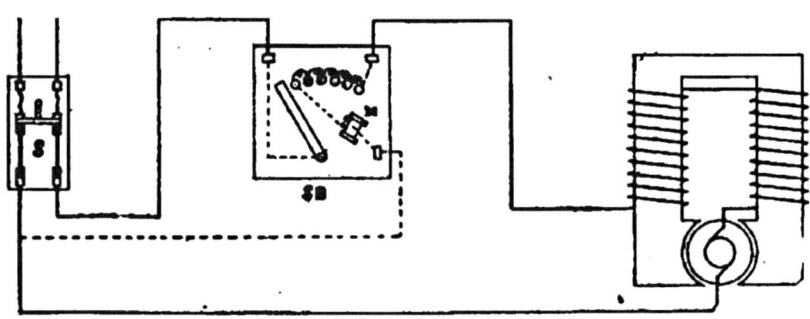

FIGURE 119.

starting, to prevent an excessive flow of current which would result were the main current thrown on fully with the armature at rest. To start the motor the main switch S is closed, and the arm of the starting box is moved gradually from one contact to another until it has reached the position where no resistance is left in circuit. It is then held by means of the small magnet M in this position until the current is cut off, or for some reason ceases to flow, when, by means of a spring attached to it, the arm will fly back to its original position. This makes it impossible to throw the current on while all the resistance is out of the armature circuit. The small magnet M is connected directly across the mains, generally having a resistance in series with it to reduce the voltage on the winding. This resistance is placed in the starting box, and is not shown in the drawing. In some motors the automatic coil M is connected in series with the main current, but in this case the variations in the current from no load to full load make its use unsatisfactory.

The speed of a series motor varies with the load, decreasing as the load increases and vice versa. If the load is entirely removed the motor will run away, unless, as in the case of very small motors, the ohmic resistance of the field and armature is sufficient to control it. This type of motor is also used on street car work, although in this case the starting box is replaced with a controller which, by varying the resistance or connecting the motors in series or multiple (where two motors are used), varies the speed. [See Figure 127.] Reversing either the field or armature connections will reverse the direction of rotation. If the field and armature are both reversed the motor will run in the same direction.

This motor is always protected from overload by a fuse or circuit-breaker placed in the main circuit. Fuses are shown in the drawing on the motor switch.

DIRECT CURRENT MOTORS 133

Figure 120 shows the winding of a shunt motor. The field and armature of this motor are placed in shunt across the main circuit. The starting box SB is placed in the armature circuit and performs the same service as in the constant-potential, series motor. The automatic coil of the starting box is connected in series with the field circuit. The speed of a shunt motor is practically constant, and for this reason this type of motor is extensively used. The motor is

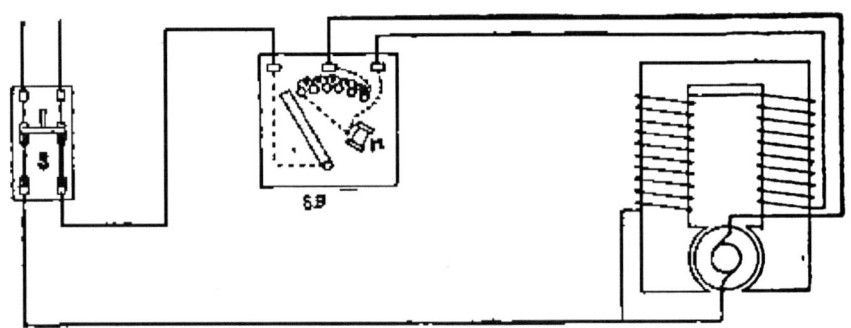

FIGURE 120.

started in the same way as the series motor, and is protected from overload in the same way. If either the field or armature connections are reversed the motor will run in the opposite direction. The speed of a shunt motor may be varied by inserting resistance in either the armature or field circuit [See Figure 124], or by shifting the brushes.

It must also be remembered that the loss in the line in long runs feeding a motor will cut down the P. D. at the armature, and this will decrease the speed as the load increases. To obviate this the size of wire should be chosen so that the drop in potential shall be as small as possible.

Figure 121 shows the winding of a compound motor. In addition to the shunt winding on the fields an extra winding is added, which is in series with the armature. The starting box is connected in series with the armature, and the automatic coil M is connected in series with the shunt field as in the shunt

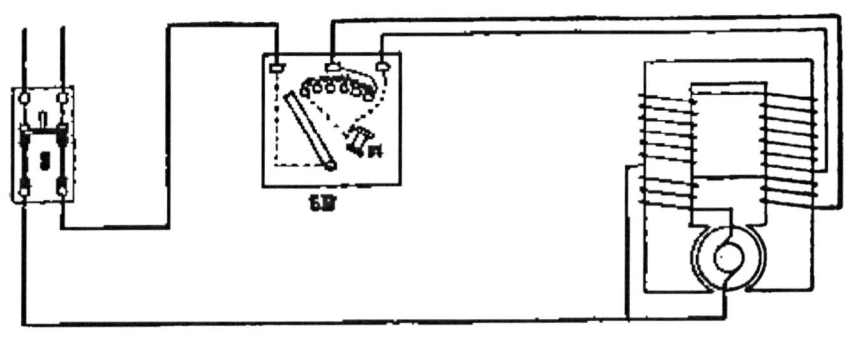

FIGURE 121.

motor. The series winding of these motors is connected in either of two ways, known as the "cumulative" or "differential." The winding shown in the diagram is cumulative, the current in the shunt and series winding being in the same direction. In the differential winding the current in the series coil travels in an opposite direction from that in the shunt coil.

Motors having the differential winding will maintain a more constant speed; for, as the load increases,

DIRECT CURRENT MOTORS

the increased current in the series winding will partly neutralize the effect of the shunt winding and decrease the magnetism of the field, thus tending to increase the speed of the motor. On loads which have a constant variation, such as the planer, for instance, when, at the end of each stroke a great increase of load comes on, the differential motor is apt to spark badly. The cumulative motor will in the same case slightly decrease in speed at each stroke. The differential motor is not as efficient as the cumulative form from the fact that there is a waste of current due to the two fields opposing each other.

Where motors are used in isolated plants the motor switches should be opened before the plant is shut down.

A number of different connections by which the speed of a motor may be varied or the direction of rotation reversed, are shown in Figure 122. Where the three-wire system is in use the speed of a motor may be varied by using the three-wire, double-throw switch shown at the left of the diagram. With the switch thrown to the upper position the armature will obtain the full line voltage, and with the switch on the lower position the armature will receive the voltage between the outside and the neutral; while the field will receive in both cases the full voltage of the line. In the 110-220 volt system the upper connection gives 220 volts and the lower connection 110 volts on the armature, the field receiving 220 volts. It is customary to use a three-wire, single-throw switch to connect the service to the motor, this switch being

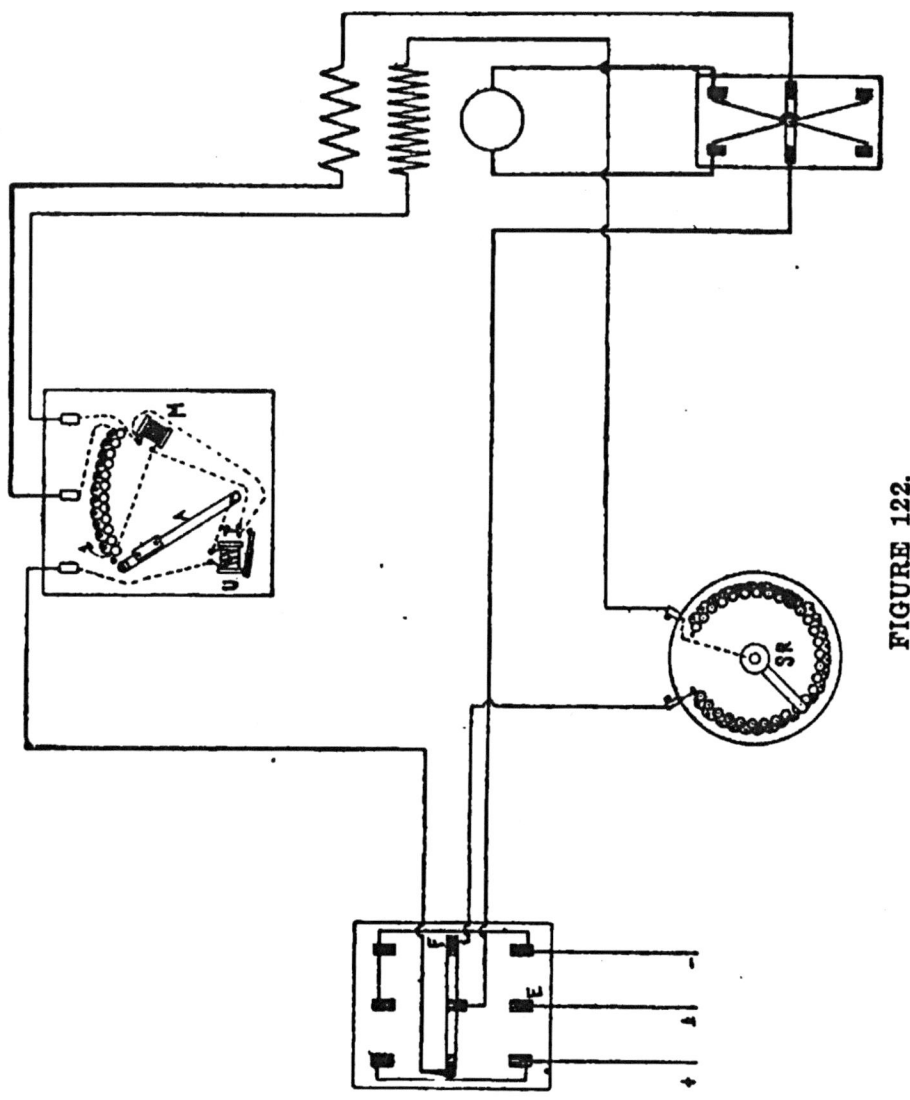

FIGURE 122.

placed in the line before the double-throw switch and being used whenever it is desired to shut down the motor. The double-throw switch is only operated when the motor is at rest.

In the upper part of the diagram are shown the connections of the Cutler-Hammer underload and overload starting box. With the movable arm A on contact shown in drawing no current will flow. If the arm is moved to contact 1 current will flow from the main through magnet U to the arm A, through all the resistance to the series field and armature and to the other side of the line. As soon as the movable arm has made contact with 1, current will also flow through the winding of magnet M and out to the shunt field and opposite side of line. The arm A is gradually moved to the right until it reaches the last contact, where all the resistance is cut out of the armature circuit. When it reaches this point the magnet M, which is energized, attracts the armature on the arm A and holds it in this position as long as current is flowing through the magnet.

If the main supply were for any reason shut off, the magnet M would be de-energized, and the arm A (which is equipped with a spring) would fly back to the "off" position. This makes it impossible for the supply current to be momentarily cut off and then thrown on again while all the resistance is cut out of the armature circuit. In case the field circuit should open, by the breaking of a wire, for instance, the magnet M would be de-energized and the current cut off. When the motor is shut down by opening the motor switch, the arm A will not fly back until the speed of the motor has considerably decreased, owing to the fact that the motor is acting as a generator and sending current around the shunt field and coil M.

The purpose of the magnet U is to protect the motor from any excessive rise in current, due either to a short circuit in the motor or to the throwing on of too heavy a load. With the normal current flowing through the winding of U, the armature below it will not be attracted; but if the current exceeds a certain amount the armature is attracted, and the winding of the automatic magnet M short-circuited at the point P, thus demagnetizing M and allowing the arm A to fly back and shut off the current from the motor. The armature below magnet U is adjustable, so that it may be set to operate at whatever current is desired.

Similar apparatus to the above may be used to regulate the speed of the motor by applying resistance in series with the armature, and thus cutting down the current; but in such case the apparatus is designed to carry the full current for an indefinite time. The automatic coil M is arranged to attract an armature which is connected to a pivoted lever, having a point at the other end which fits into a series of indentations on the lower part of arm A, and holds the arm squarely over the contacts in whatever position it may be placed for the required speed.

Strengthening the field of a motor tends to decrease

the speed, and weakening the field to increase the speed. SR is a rheostat connected in series with the shunt field by means of which more or less resistance may be cut in series with the fields. Cutting in more resistance will reduce the current in the fields, and thus weaken them and increase the speed, and cutting out resistance will act in the opposite way.

The two-pole, double throw switch shown in lower right-hand corner may be used to reverse the direction of rotation of the armature. With the switch thrown to the upper contacts the current will enter the armature from the right-hand side, and with the switch thrown to the lower contacts current will enter on the left-hand side of the armature, thus reversing the direction of rotation. This switch should never be thrown while the motor is running, but should be thrown over while the armature is at rest.

Figure 123 shows connections for the Cutler-Hammer printing-press controller, as used with a shunt motor. R is a resistance box generally in the larger size motors installed separately from the controller, and connected to it by wire leads. The automatic coil M is connected in series with the field circuit, and when current is on attracts an armature (not shown in drawing) which is connected to a pivoted lever, the other end of which fits into a series of indentations on the lower end of the arm A and holds the arm in whatever position it may be placed. The arm A is made in two pieces, separated by an insulator so that the upper and lower parts are not in electrical connection. As the arm is moved to point 1, current from the mains enters the lower part of the arm and goes to the copper segment S. From there it is carried to the armature and back to the segment T. It

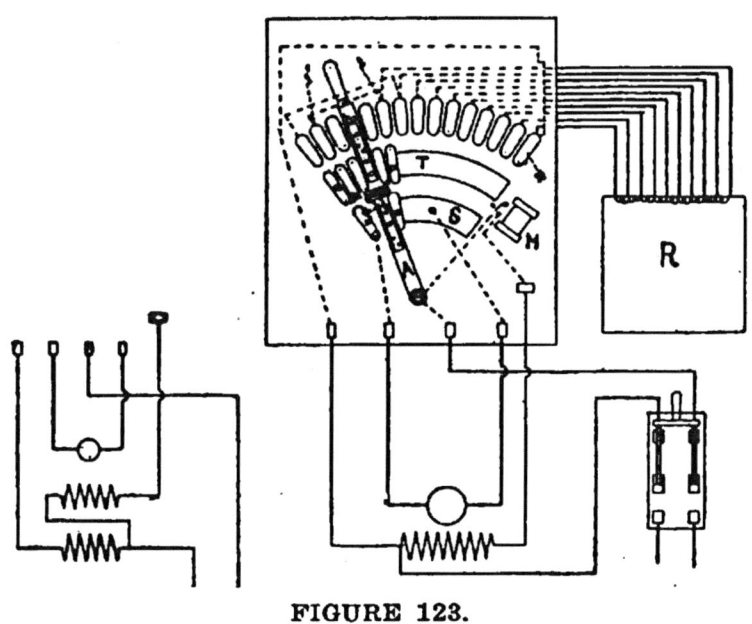

FIGURE 123.

then crosses the upper part of the arm to the contact 1 and through all the resistance in R and back to point 10 to the other side of the line. The field is simply connected across the mains through coil M. If the arm A is moved to point 1, the current will then flow through the armature in the opposite direction, thus reversing the direction of rotation. With the arm on contact 10 all the resistance is cut out of the armature circuit. This controller has ten variations in speed forward, and two backward. At the

DIRECT CURRENT MOTORS 141

left is shown a diagram of the connections of this starting box when used with a compound motor.

In Figure 124 are shown connections for the Cutler-Hammer self-starter used with a motor driven pump. The connections shown are for a compound motor.

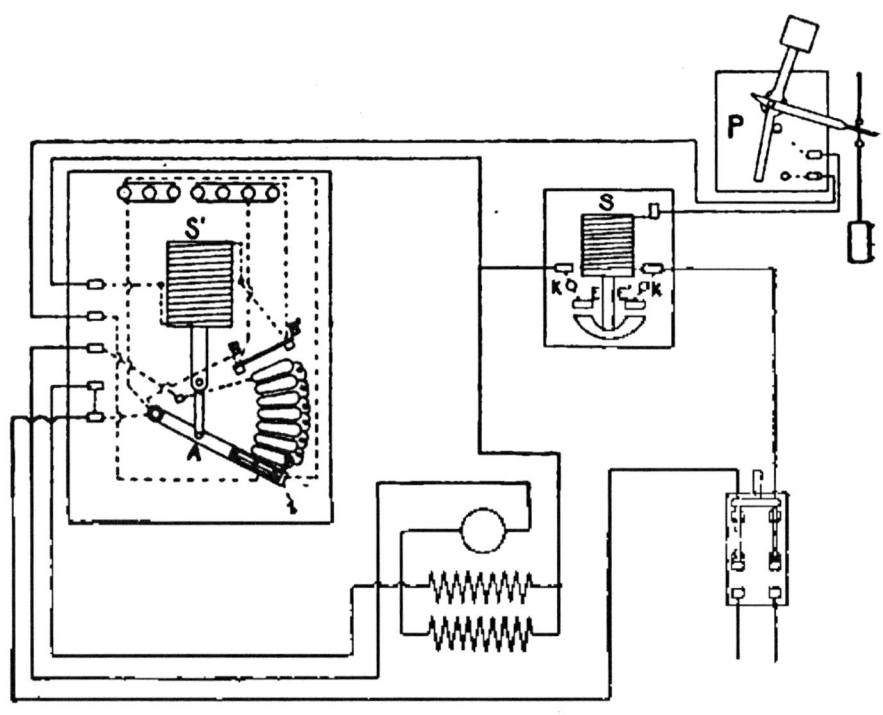

FIGURE 124.

S is a solenoid connected across the mains through the switch P and the arm A of the self-starter. The current in this circuit varies from $\frac{1}{4}$ to 1 ampere, according to the size motor used. The switch P is controlled by a float in the tank, and is so arranged that it will close as the level of the water lowers and open again when the tank has become filled. This switch may be placed any distance from the motor. When the switch P closes, the solenoid S is energized, and the core, at the lower end of which is attached a copper contact piece, closes the contacts E, E', thus allowing current to flow through the series field and armature of the motor and through all the resistance in the starter. At the same time, when E, E' is closed current passes through the solenoid S' and through the small spring connecting contacts B B'. This energizes the solenoid S' and draws up the core and arm A, thus gradually cutting resistance out of the armature circuit. When the arm reaches the upper contact, the circuit through the solenoid S' is opened at B and the lamps thrown in series with it. This is done to cut down the current flowing through the solenoid, as less current is required to keep the arm in place than to move it over the contacts. The circuit from the small solenoid S is connected to the contact 1 so that when the arm A moves upward lamps are thrown in series with this circuit, to cut down the current in the solenoid S to that required to just hold it; so that, if for any reason the supply current is cut off, the contact E E' cannot be closed until the arm A has moved to the lower point, where all the resistance is in the armature circuit. The number of lamps used varies with the size of motor. This same apparatus can be used with any air pump, or elevator in which the motor does not reverse, the switch P being replaced with the necessary switch.

On the solenoid S the small magnets K are used to extinguish the arc at the break.

Figure 125 shows a diagram of the connections of a shunt motor used for blowing a pipe organ. The arm of the resistance box R is mechanically connected to the bellows of the pipe organ so that its position is determined by the amount of air in the bellows. When all of the air is out of the bellows the arm of

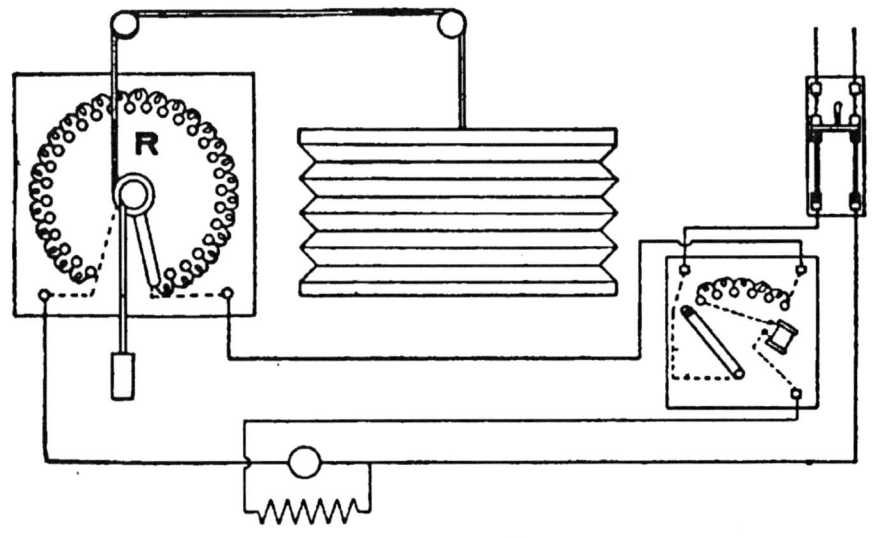

FIGURE 125.

the rheostat is in the position where no resistance is in circuit, or as shown in the diagram. As the motor speeds up and air is forced into the bellows the rheostat arm slowly moves over the series of contacts cutting resistance into the circuit at each step. When the bellows are completely filled the arm is on the last contact where all of the resistance of the box R is in series with the motor, this resistance being great enough to completely stop it. From the above description it will be seen that the action is automatic, the speed of the motor being governed by the amount of air taken by the organ. After the organ has been at rest for some time the air gradually leaks out of the bellows and the rheostat arm moves to the point where no resistance is in circuit. For this reason a starting box is always provided.

Figure 126 shows the connections of the Cutler-Hammer compound drum controller, this type of controller being used on printing presses, cranes and other work requiring a frequent change in speed and direction of rotation. In the upper part of the diagram is shown the drum laid out, the contact rings X, Y, Z, Y', Z' and W, and the segments below being mounted on a revolving drum, while the contacts 1 to 7 and B, A, SF, B' A', SF' and L are stationary, being supplied with fingers which make contact with the segments opposite as the drum is revolved.

With the drum moved to the first point on the forward motion the rings X, Y, Z will come in contact with A, SF and 1 respectively, and the rings W, Y' Z' with B', SF' and L. Current will then flow from the + main through the series field to the resistance box R and through all the resistance to the point 1 of the controller. From 1 it passes to contact ring Z, and then through ring X and contact A to the armature and back to B' and ring W to ring Z' and contact L to the negative side of the line. As the drum is moved

DIRECT CURRENT MOTORS

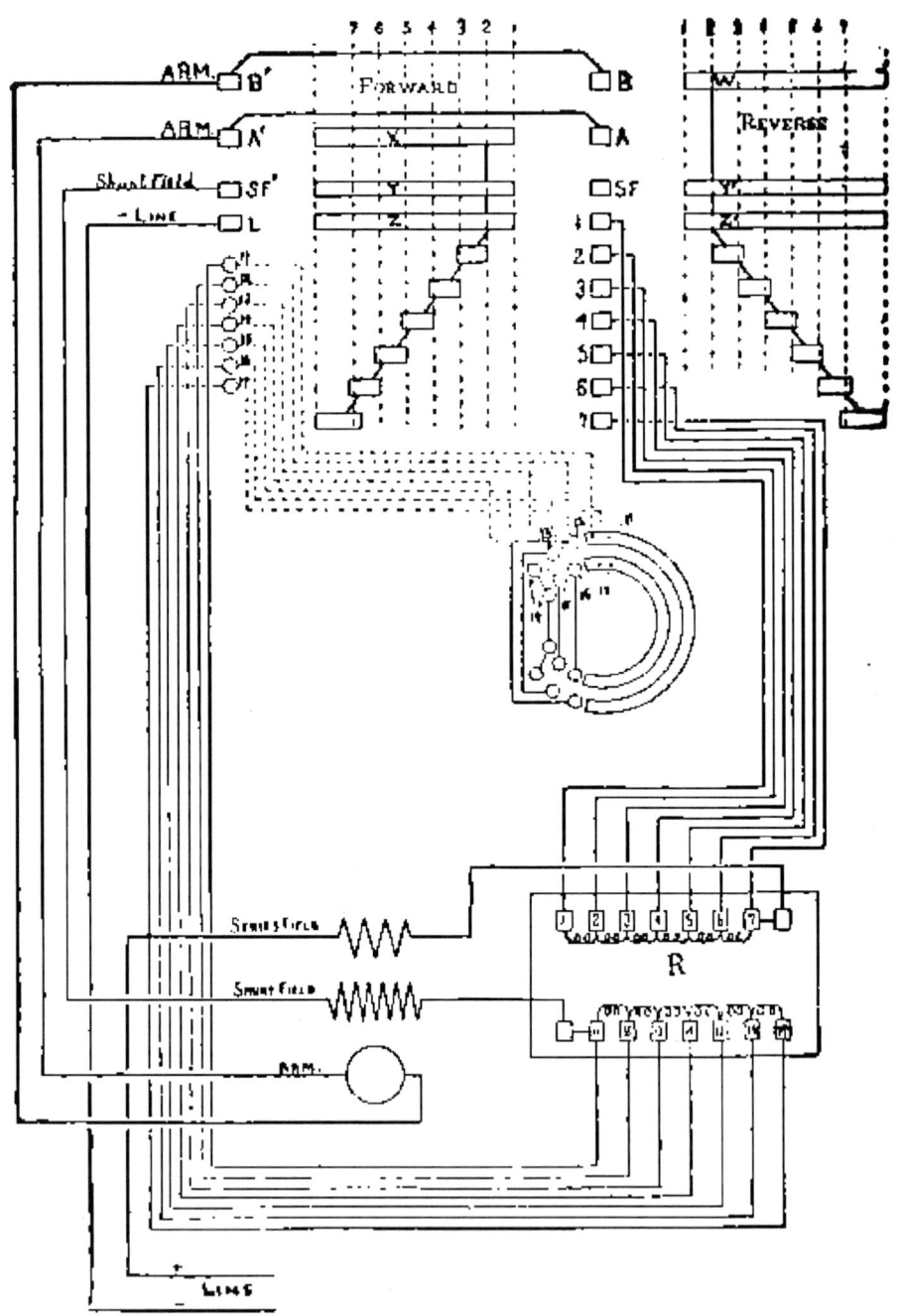

FIGURE 126.

toward point 7 at each step, part of the resistance in series with the armature is cut out, until at 7 the armature and series field are connected directly across the mains.

In the bottom of the controller are located two copper rings and a number of contacts, which are connected to their respective points in resistance box R. A small, movable contact shoe short-circuits rings 11 and 17, while the controller is moved from points 1 to 7, thus allowing current to pass from the positive side of the line to 17, on to 11, and then through the shunt field and out to bar Y' on controller and to negative side of line. As the drum passes point 7 the contact shoe connecting 17 and 11 will then connect 17 and 12, thus cutting the resistance between points 11 and 12 in the resistance box R in series with the field and increasing the speed of the motor. As the controller is moved still further, more resistance is cut in series with the field, until at point 14 all the resistance is cut in and the motor has reached its highest speed.

If the drum is moved to 1 on the reverse motion the same connections are made with the exception of the armature. In this case current from contact 1 passes to ring Z' and then to B and armature, this causing current to flow in the opposite direction in armature and reversing the direction of rotation. In printing press work a stop is used which allows the

DIRECT CURRENT MOTORS 147

reverse motion to take in two contacts only, thus limiting the reverse to two speeds.

Figure 127 shows the connections of the General Electric K2 street car controller. This controller is of the series parallel type, and varies the speed of the

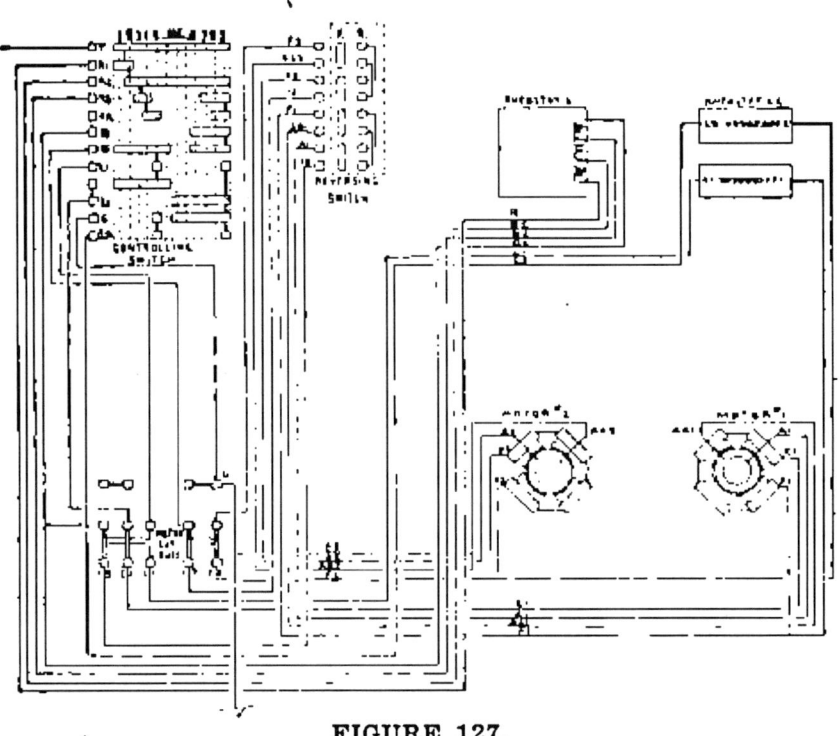

FIGURE 127.

car by connecting the motors first in series and then in parallel, suitable resistance being used to give a gradual starting current. In Figure 128 are shown the various connections between the rheostat and motors obtained at the different points of the controller. In the upper left-hand corner the drum of the controller is laid out. T, R1, R2, etc., are stationary contacts with fingers which make contact with the various segments on the drum as it is revolved.

At the right of the controller is the reversing switch, by means of which the car can be made to go in either direction. The reverse switch is also a drum on which are placed two sets of contacts, these making connection with the stationary points F2, AA2, etc., as the drum is revolved. If the controller drum is moved to point 1, the current from the trolley wire enters at T, then to segment on drum opposite T. From there it passes to contact R1, then to rheostat K, through all the resistance to the point 19 on the reverse switch. With the reversing switch on F it will then pass to A1, through the armature of motor No. 1 back to AA1, on the reverse switch and through field of motor No. 1 to the point E1 on the controller. From E1 it passes to the point 15 by means of segments on the drum, and to 15 on the reversing switch and to armature of motor No. 2 back to AA2 on the reversing switch, and to the field of motor No. 2 and back by means of E2 to the ground. The two motors are now connected in series with all the resistance in rheostat K in series with them. This is shown in 1 of Figure 128.

As the controller is moved to points 2 and 3, part of the resistance in rheostat K is cut out, until at 4 the two motors are running in series with no resistance. At point 5 the fields of both motors are weakened by shunting them around the resistance in rheostat K2, thus further increasing the speed. The points between 5 and 6 are used to change the connections from series to multiple. At point 6 the motors are in multiple, in series with part of the resistance in K. At points 7 and 8 part of this resistance is cut out, while at 9 the motors are connected in multiple with the fields weakened.

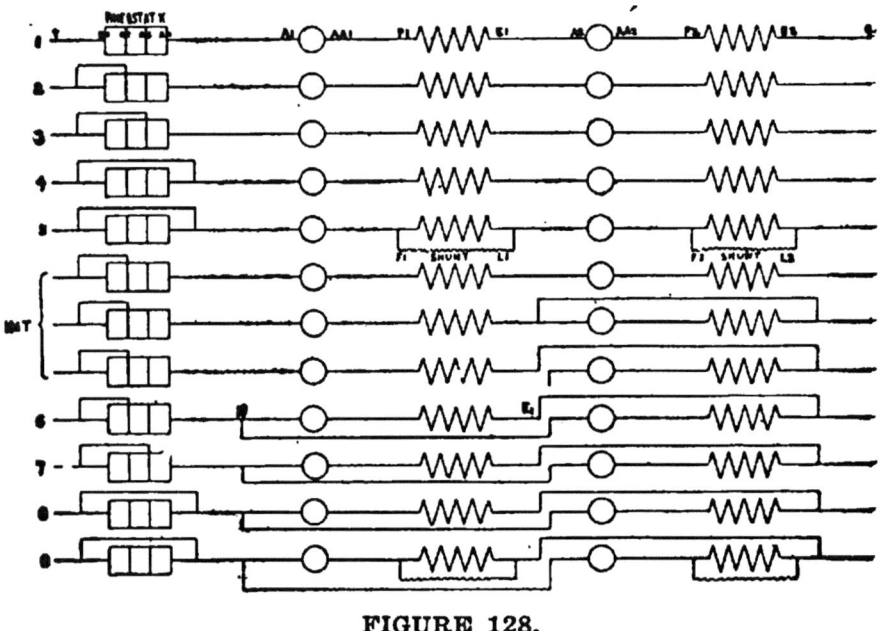

FIGURE 128.

In case it is necessary to cut out one of the motors, this may be done by means of the switches shown below the controller. If the switch at the left-hand is thrown to the upper contacts, motor No. 1 will be short-circuited. Throwing the other switch up short circuits motor No. 2. When one of the motors is cut out, a stop comes into play which allows the controller to move over the first five points only. If this were not done and the controller moved to point 6, the trolley would be directly connected to ground through the rheostat K. This can be seen by reference to 6 in Figure 128, where cutting out motor No. 1 short-circuits 19 and E1. The car should never be run with the resistance in rheostat K in circuit, therefore points 4, 5, 8 and 9 only should be used for any great length of time. The diagram shows one set of controlling apparatus only, this set being duplicated at the other end of the car.

The speed of a constant current series motor varies with the load, decreasing as the load becomes greater and increasing in speed as the load becomes lighter. If the load is entirely removed the motor will "run away." No satisfactory method of winding has been devised which would make these motors self-regulating, so that if the motor is to be used on a varying load some mechanical device must be employed to regulate the speed.

In Figure 129 the arm A moves over a series of contacts which are connected to different points of the field winding. This arm may either be moved by hand, or, as is more common, connected to a centrifugal governor. As the load on the motor increases, its speed will slightly decrease, thus decreasing the speed of the governor and moving the arm upward. This cuts out part of the field winding and speeds up the motor.

DIRECT CURRENT MOTORS 151

In Figure 130 the arm A moves over a number of contacts which are in connection with the resistance

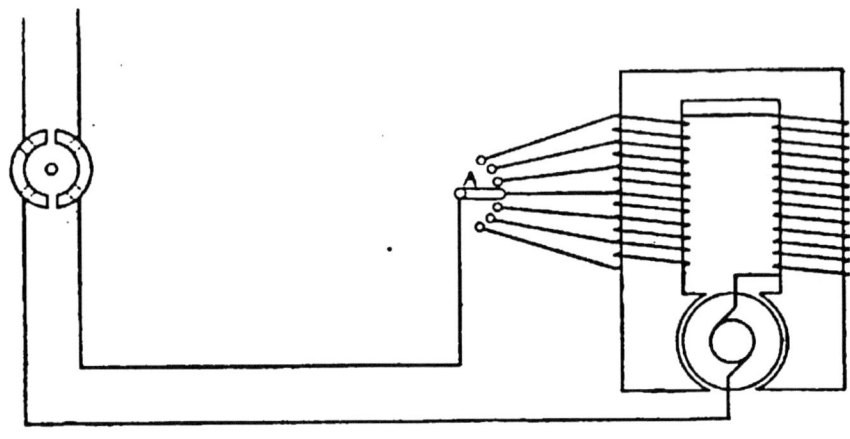

FIGURE 129.

wire R. Current coming from the left-hand main passes through the lower part of the resistance R and is shunted at the arm A, part of it passing

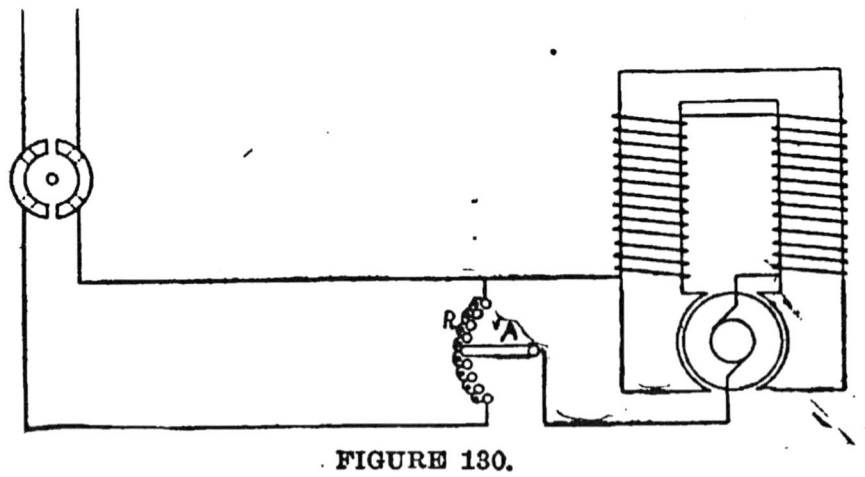

FIGURE 130.

through the remaining resistance and part of it going to the motor. By changing the position of the arm, more or less current can be sent through the motor, the greatest amount passing through it when the arm is at the lowest contact. The arm may either be moved by hand or used with a centrifugal governor, as described in the preceding paragraph. It will be seen that this method is not very efficient, as a great deal of energy is consumed in the resistance wire. There are a number of other methods used for constant current series motor regulation, but they are mostly variations of those shown.

This type of motor is fast being replaced by the constant potential motor. Fuses are never used on these motors, as the current is always the same, and the switch used to start and stop the motor closes the main line when it opens the motor circuit. The ordinary snap switch cannot be used.

Figure 130a shows diagram of a printing press controller generally known as of the Kohler system and built by the Cutler Hammer Co. This system is widely used and there are many variations; modifications being made in some cases to fit different voltages and also to obtain different results as not all presses are run in the same way.

In the diagram M is the main magnet which when energized closes the armature circuit at A. The two circles below A represent blow out magnets which are not always used. The circuit can readily be traced along the heavy lines and through the rheostat R. N is another magnet or solenoid which when energized

DIRECT CURRENT MOTORS 153

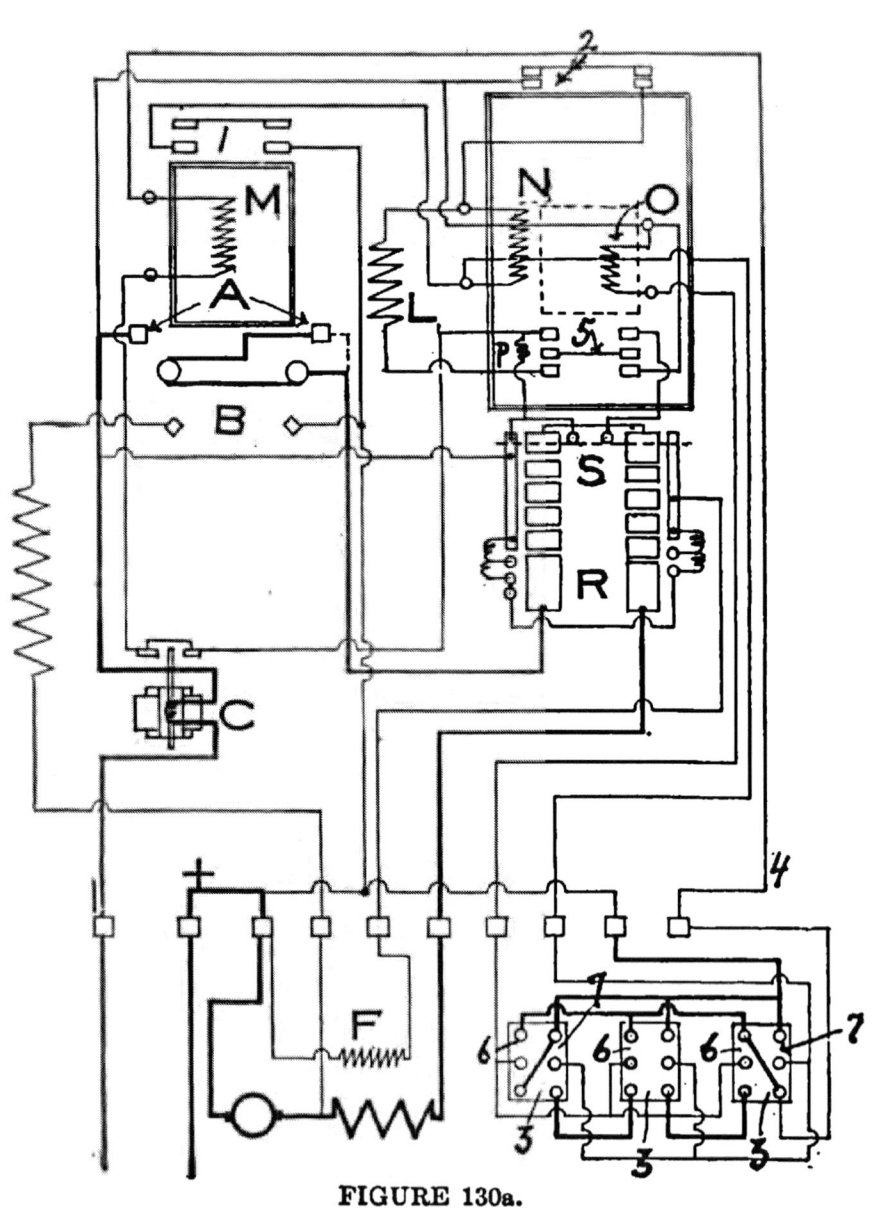

FIGURE 130a.

pulls up the contact bar of the rheostat R until it rests as indicated by dotted lines, thus cutting all of the resistance of R into the armature circuit.

When at rest in any position the solenoid is held in place by a ratchet device (not shown) and also by current which passes through N and the auxiliary resistance L at the left. The ratchet and also the circuit through N are controlled by another magnet O. This magnet when energized withdraws the ratchet and allows the bar to slip down and also opens the circuit through N. at 5. When the circuit of O is closed the solenoid N begins to move downward cutting out resistance until the circuit of O is opened when it comes to rest wherever it happens to be. Thus more or less of the resistance R may be left in the armature circuit.

The field circuit F can readily be traced and it can be seen that as the solenoid moves down to its lowest notch resistances are cut into the field circuit which weaken the field and cause the motor to attain its highest speed.

B is the brake circuit and when M descends after being deenergized it closes the armature circuit at B, thus short circuiting the armature and quickly bringing the motor to rest.

C is a circuit breaker and the plunger shown opens the circuit through M when the armature current exceeds its allowable value.

The various buttons by which the motor is controlled are shown in the lower right hand corner. There may be any number of these buttons and they may be located at different convenient places about the machinery. From any one of these buttons the motor may be started or stopped. The operation is as follows: The motor cannot be started unless the solenoid N has drawn up the contact bar of the rheostat to its highest point closing the safety circuit at S. This is accomplished as soon as the main switch (not shown) is closed. Current passes from the positive pole of the circuit to point 1 which is closed until M is energized, thence through N to point 2 which is closed until N has acted, and from there to the negative pole of the line.

The middle bar at 5 rests upon the lower contacts there shown except when O is energized. When O is active this bar is drawn up against the upper contacts. Before current can be gotten into the armature circuit all of the points 3 on the buttons must be closed. When this is done circuit is established through wire 4, magnet M, resistance P and the negative pole of the line. Owing to resistance P this current is not of sufficient strength to close the armature circuit at A. When now one of the buttons is closed at 6 current is established through O to the negative pole of the line. This releases the ratchet before mentioned and also draws up 5, establishes a shunt circuit around P through S and strengthens the current in M sufficiently to draw up the core and close the armature circuit at A. This starts the motor at its slowest speed and allows the contact bar of R to descend, thus cutting resistance out of the armature circuit and speeding up the motor. When the button 6 is released 5 again closes the circuit through L and holds N wherever it may be, thus keeping the motor running at that speed.

If the speed of the motor is to be reduced pressing one of the buttons 7 will cause the contact bar of N to rise and cut in more resistance into the armature circuit. The motor can be stopped by opening any one of the buttons 3, but all of them must be closed before it can be started. This is a safety arrangement of great value.

Another diagram of Kohler system printing press controller is given in Figure 130b. In this case the motor is reversible but can be used in the reverse direction at the slowest speed only. There is also a lock mechanism shown at P which can be set so that the motor can be operated at a fixed speed only. In this case it is intended that the pressman shall have no control over the speed but have full control over starting and stopping of motor.

The field and armature circuits can easily be traced and will need no explanation. There is also the brake circuit as in the preceding Figure 130a.

With the reversing switch indicated in the lower right hand corner thrown to the right, circuit is at once established through wire 1 solenoid N points 2 and 3, and the negative pole of the line. When N acts the circuit at 2 is opened and current is now forced through

DIRECT CURRENT MOTORS

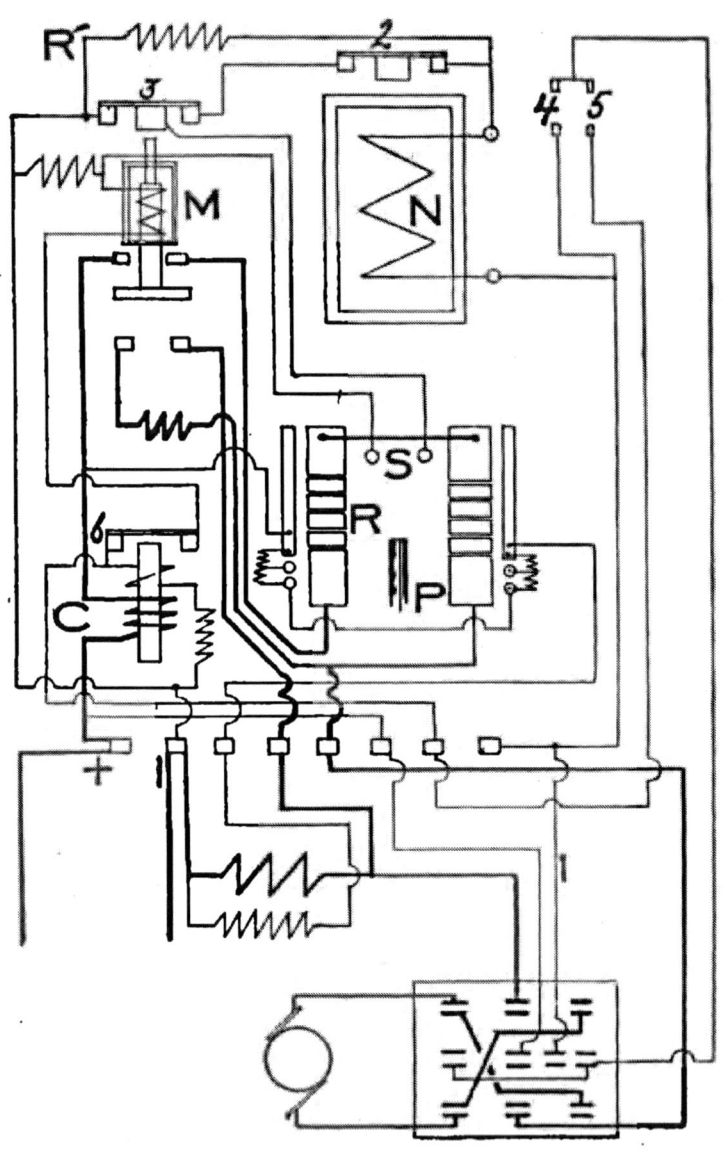

FIGURE 130b.

R' which reduces it so as to be only sufficient to maintain N in its position. With the reversing switch thrown to the left there is current in N only while button 4 is closed and when this is opened the contact bar descends until it strikes the locked plug P the position of which determines the speed at which the motor shall run.

To close the armature circuit it is necessary to close button 5. This sends current through point 6, solenoid M, safety S, point 3 and negative pole of line. There is also a parallel circuit around the circuit breaker C which keeps the circuit open after an overload in the armature circuit has caused the breaker to act. For normal operation in the forward direction button 4 must be closed and remain closed until 5 is closed. When 5 is closed the armature circuit is closed and the motor starts at its slowest speed. To speed it up 4 must be opened; this allows N to descend and cut out resistance and speed up the motor.

CHAPTER XIII.

AUTOMOBILES.

ELECTRIC AND GASOLINE, CHARGING STATIONS, GAS ENGINES.

The following diagrams illustrate some of the methods of electric automobile wiring employed by the Woods Motor Vehicle Co., and much of the information herein given is taken from Mr. C. E. Wood's work, "The Electric Automobile."

Figure 131 shows one of the earlier methods and gives three speeds. The first speed is obtained by grouping the batteries four in parallel and ten in series. This connection is made when the controller connects all of the points along line a with the opposite points along line b. The circuit can readily be traced, the current passing from the + poles of the cells to bar 1, thence to Y, through both fields, F, to the reversing switch R; back to both armatures; through other side of reversing switch and to X, bar 2 and the — side of the batteries.

The second speed is obtained when the controller connects the points along line a with those along c. This places the battery in groups of two in parallel and twenty in series. The third step, by connecting *a* and *d*, places all forty cells in series with the fields and armatures.

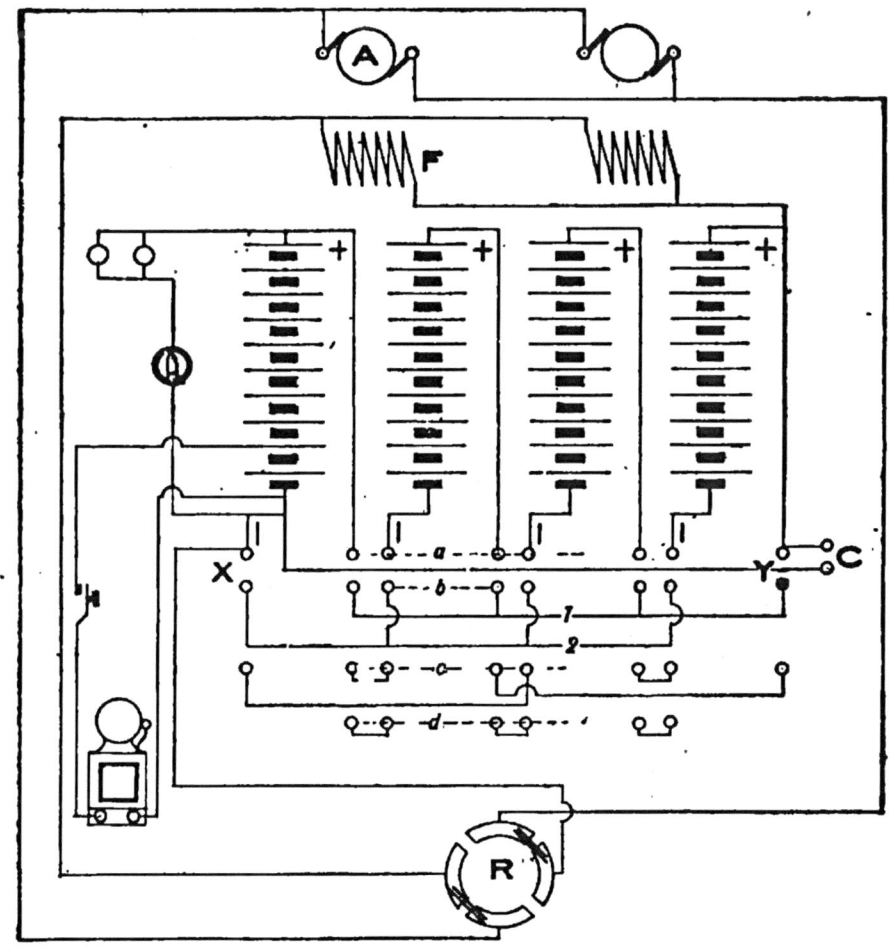

FIGURE 131.

Figure 132 shows an arrangement giving four speeds and in which not so many changes are made in battery connections, but more in those of the fields. As in the previous diagram both armatures always remain in parallel.

AUTOMOBILES

The first speed is obtained when the controller connects the points along *a* with those along *b*. The two halves of battery are now in parallel and work through both fields in series, the current passing from

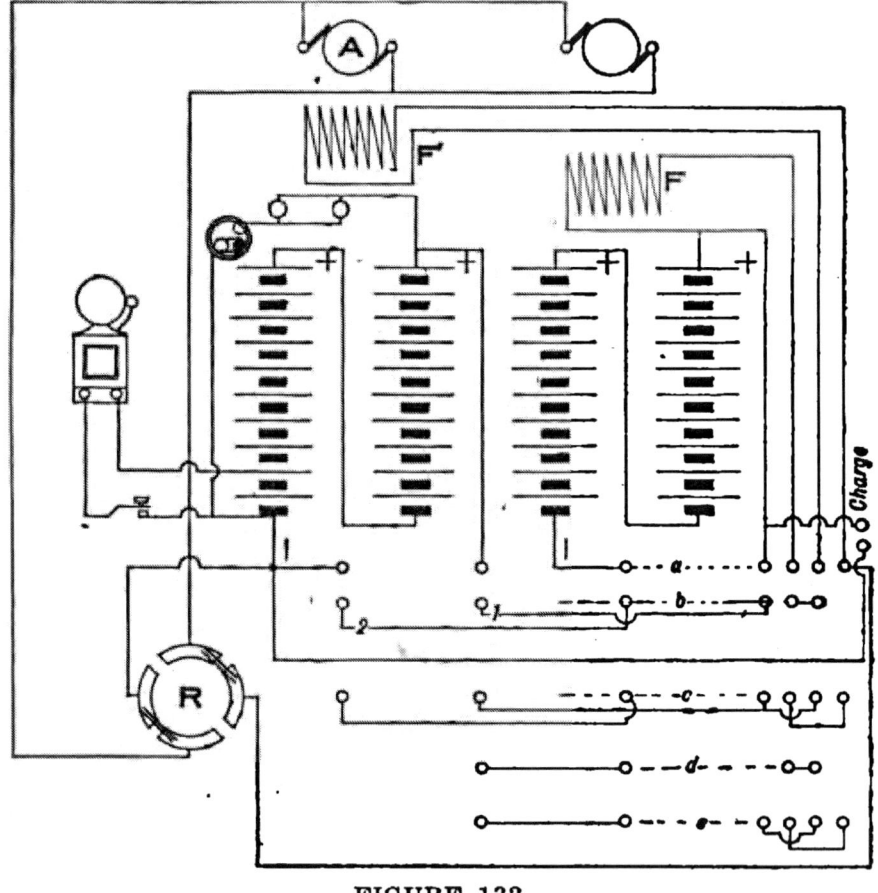

FIGURE 132.

the positive pole of battery to bar 1, thence to field F, back to controller and through F′, thence back to reversing switch R, through both armatures and again through reversing switch and back to negative pole of battery and bar 2.

The next step on the controller combines *a* and *c* and leaves batteries still in parallel and at the same time throws the fields in parallel thus weakening the fields and speeding up the motor.

The third step, combining *a* and *d*, throws the batteries all in series and the fields also, increasing speed through increased E. M. F.

In the fourth speed, connecting *a* and *e*, the batteries remain in series and the fields are again placed in parallel. The charging plug is shown at the right and to charge, the batteries are thrown in series. Connections for electric gong and lamps are also shown.

It will be noticed that with these motors fuses or circuit breakers are not used. It would indeed be quite dangerous to have a fuse blow out when climbing a steep hill. The whole wiring is therefore so designed that it can safely carry for a short time all that the battery can deliver. These diagrams show no resistances used as with other motors; the reduction of E. M. F. at starting by placing cells in parallel is far more economical and satisfactory. Vehicles, have, however, been built which combine resistance control with the methods just described.

Figure 133 shows the arrangement of an automobile charging station. By means of the rheostat R the current is regulated to the needs of the battery. The charging plug P is usually so made that it can be inserted only one way so that the polarities of the charging dynamo and the batteries will always be correct. The voltmeter may be used to test the condition of the battery and also to indicate polarity of dynamo or battery if these are not known. The double-throw switch shown is needed only in case it is desired to test or "form" batteries. It provides an easy connection for discharging batteries.

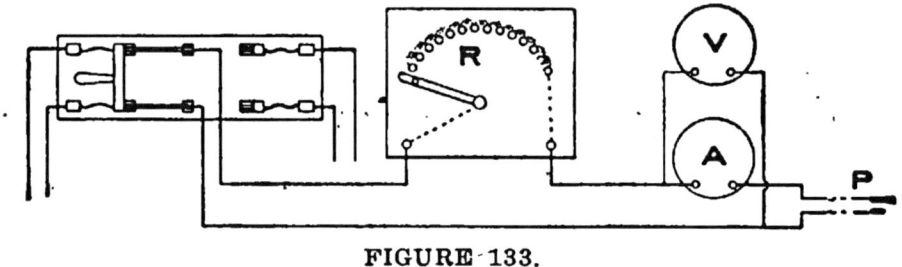

FIGURE 133.

In Figure 134 is shown the general principle of ignition used in gasoline automobiles. A jump spark is almost invariably used and this is produced by means of an induction coil capable of giving a very

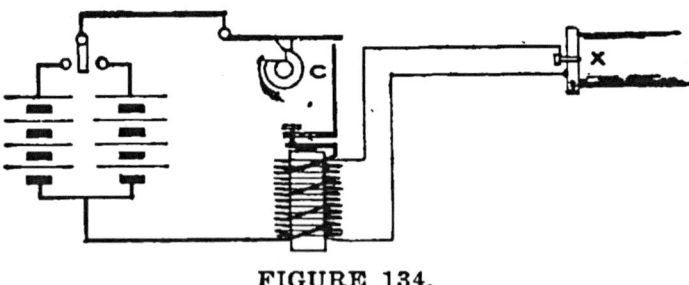

FIGURE 134.

high voltage. The figure shows an induction coil equipped with a vibrator, but this is not always used and many equipments dispense with it entirely. The cam C is connected with the gearing and adjusted so that it makes and breaks the circuit at just the proper time for ignition. Whenever the current at C is broken a spark occurs at X. At this point a "spark plug" equipped with proper terminals across which the spark is to jump is fitted into the end of the cylinder.

Figure 135 shows a four-cylinder engine equipped with four sets of batteries and independent coils.

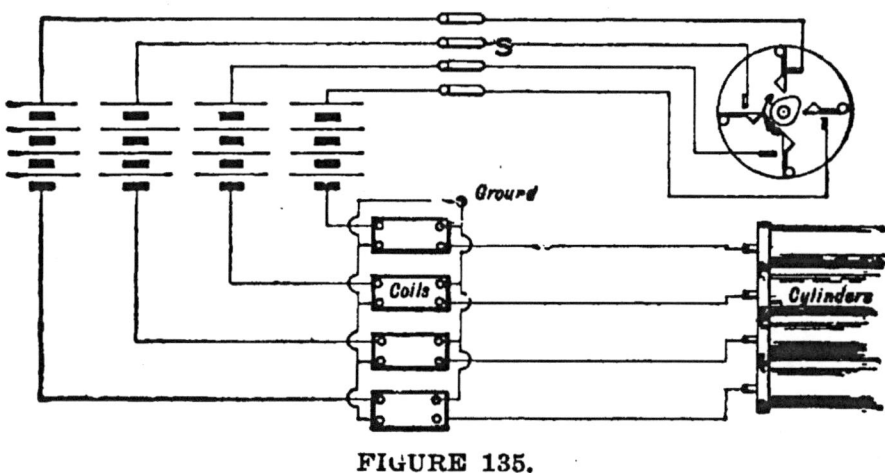

FIGURE 135.

An arrangement using either battery or generator is shown in Figure 136. Generators used in this connection are usually fitted out with some form of governor which keeps them running at a sufficiently uniform speed to allow of practical operation whether the car be running fast or slow. This figure also shows wiring arranged for a "double spark gap." A spark plug is very apt to "foul"; that is, to become covered with soot from the combustion of gas in the cylinder. When it is thus "fouled" the current leaks through the carbon from one terminal to the other and, of course, there is no spark. The proper remedy is to either provide a new plug or clean the old one. It is, however, claimed by some automobile users that if another spark gap be introduced in series with the one which is "fouled" that both will then spark. Whether

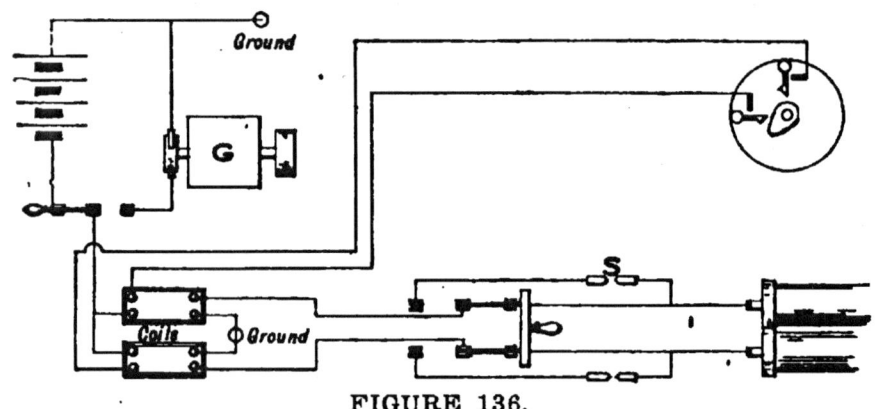

FIGURE 136.

this be true or not it can at best be only a temporary relief, for in time the plug in the cylinder will become so completely covered that it cannot possibly spark. The throw-over switch in Figure 136 admits using a single or double spark gap.

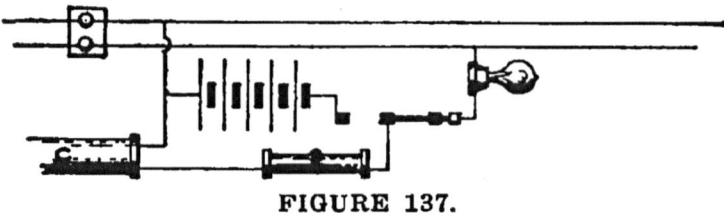

FIGURE 137.

In Figure 137 are shown the connections of a gas engine igniter where the gas engine is used to drive a dynamo supplying electric lights. The current is taken from an electric light circuit while the dynamo is running, a 50 c. p. lamp being placed in series with the spark coil. While the engine is starting the battery is used to supply current for igniting the gas. The single-pole throw-over switch is arranged to make connections either way. This arrangement has the disadvantage that it usually "grounds" the electric light system and is therefore not approved by most insurance companies and inspection bureaus.

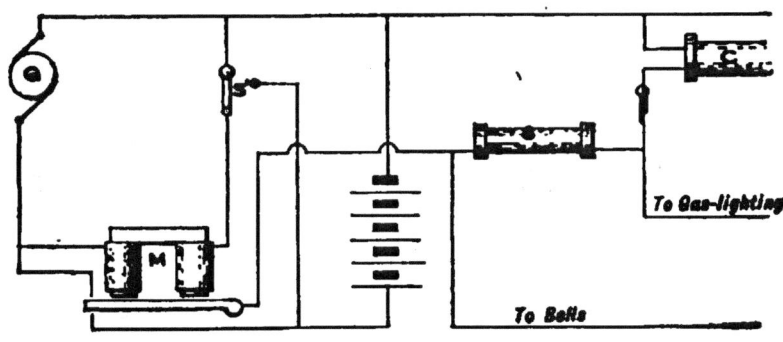

FIGURE 138.

Figure 138 shows another arrangement of gas engine ignition. The small generator G is coupled to the gas engine and driven by it. While the engine is at rest the armature of the magnet M closes the battery circuit on the spark coil and cylinder C of the engine. As the engine gains speed the generator G sends current through the magnet M and raises the armature, thus disconnecting the battery and closing its own circuit on the spark coil. If a storage battery is used it may be charged from time to time by throwing the switch S' over. The switch near C may be opened to prevent accidental short circuits while the engine is at rest.

Figure 138a shows a typical wiring diagram of an automobile ignition circuit. The electrical system consists of a magneto geared to the engine drive shaft. There are two windings on the armature, a primary or low-voltage winding and a secondary or high-voltage winding. A circuit-breaking device, which is operated mechanically at each revolution of the arma-

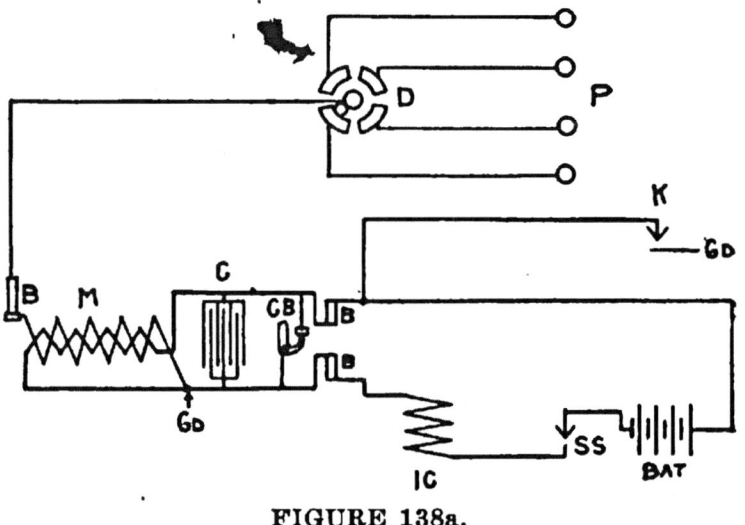

FIGURE 138a.

ture, is attached to the armature shaft. A condenser, also on the armature, is connected directly across the circuit-breaker terminals. When the automobile is started the starting switch SS is closed and the circuit is completed through the dry batteries, intensifying coil and primary winding of the armature. When operated at the low speed of starting, the current generated by the magneto is not sufficient to produce a suitable spark and the generator current is therefore intensified by the dry batteries. The circuits in starting are as follows: Through the primary winding of the armature and through the circuit breaker which is closed. Paralleled with this is the battery circuit, through the intensifying coil IC, and then by means of the brushes BB through the circuit breaker CB. At the proper time for ignition the circuit breaker opens and the combined currents of the magneto and dry batteries induce a current in the secondary winding

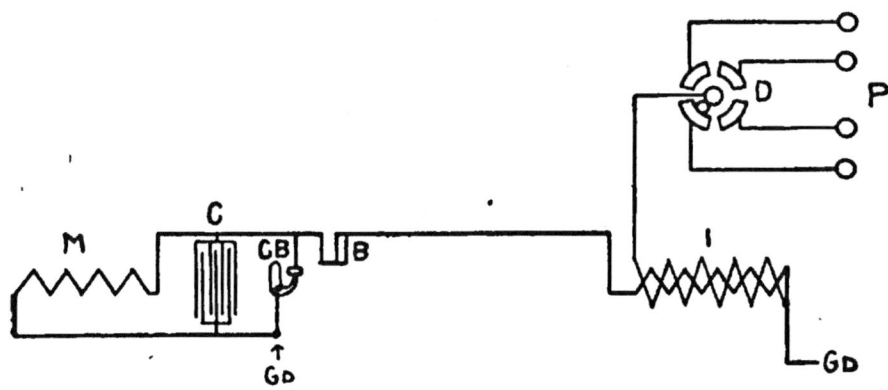

FIGURE 138b.

of the magneto, this winding acting as the secondary of a transformer. The induced, high-voltage current passes out through the brush B and by means of the distributor D to the proper cylinder. The secondary winding also generates a current which is added to that induced by the current in the primary winding. It is necessary to connect the battery so that the current flows in a certain definite direction through the circuit breaker, otherwise it will tend to neutralize the effect of the current generated by the magneto. The switch shown at K is operated by the insertion and extraction of a key. When the key is withdrawn the switch is closed to ground and the circuit breaker is therefore shunted directly across and made inoperative. The insertion of the key opens this switch and permits the circuit breaker to perform its proper function.

Figure 138b shows the wiring diagram of an ignition system using, in place of the secondary winding on the armature of the magneto, an induction coil. The electrical action is similar to that described in Figure 138a except that the breaking of the magneto circuit induces a high-voltage current in the secondary of the induction coil. The condenser shown in both of these diagrams is provided to reduce the destructiveness of the arc which occurs when the circuit is opened at the circuit breaker. There are many variations of the circuits shown, but the principle is the same in most of them.

CHAPTER XIV.

DIRECT CURRENT GENERATORS, COMPENSATORS, ALTERNATORS.

A diagram of the circuits in the Western Electric Co.'s series arc dynamo is shown in Figure 139. Constant-current, series dynamos, like the constant-current, series motors, are not self-regulating, so that some mechanical means must be employed to keep the

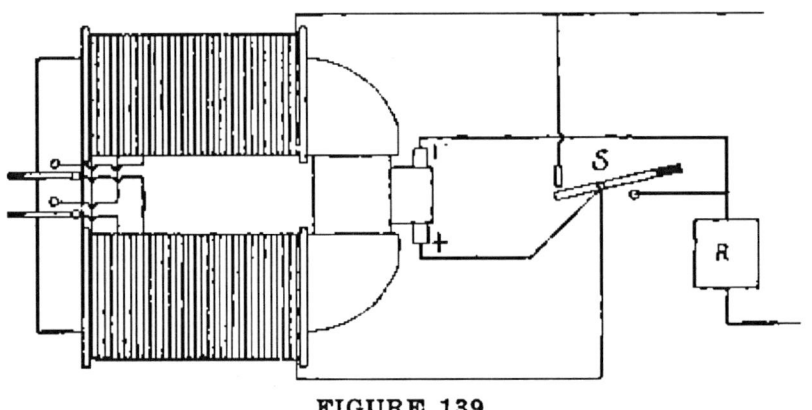

FIGURE 139.

current constant. This is accomplished by shifting the location of the brushes, or varying the number of exciting turns on the fields, or in some cases by both these methods combined. In the machine shown the voltage is regulated by shifting the brushes. In the diagram, current flows from the lower or positive brush to the center connection of switch S, and then around the fields and out to the positive side of the line, returning through the regulator R to the upper brush. The switch S is used in starting and shutting down; in the position shown switch is set for running.

When it is desired to shut down, the switch S is closed. This first short-circuits the fields and then the armature. The switches shown at the left are used to cut down the current by short-circuiting part of the field windings. They are used where it is desired to operate either the 1200 c. p. arc lamp taking 6.8 amperes, or the enclosed arc lamp taking 6 amperes. With the switches in the position shown the machine will generate 9.6 amperes, the current generally used on the 2000 c. p. arcs. To reverse the direction of current the armature leads are reversed. In connecting two arc machines in series the + of one machine is connected to the — of the other. The positive side of the machine must always be connected to the positive side of the line.

Figure 140 shows the connections on a shunt-wound dynamo. The winding varies from that of the series dynamo in having the field magnets, which are wound with a great length of fine wire, connected in shunt across the dynamo brushes. The current in this field is then in shunt with the main circuit, and is generally about 2 or 3 per cent. of the whole current generated by the machine. Shunt-wound dynamos are used where a current of constant potential is desired, such as the lighting of incandescent lamps in parallel, furnishing power for motors and in storage battery charging and electro-plating. Although the voltage of a shunt dynamo is practically constant, still, as the load is increased, the voltage will gradually fall, and this must be regulated by means of the rheostat R which is connected in series with the field. If resistance is cut out of the rheostat the current in the fields is increased, and the voltage of the machine rises, and *vice versa*. This dynamo is always protected from overload by a fuse or circuit-breaker placed in the main circuit.

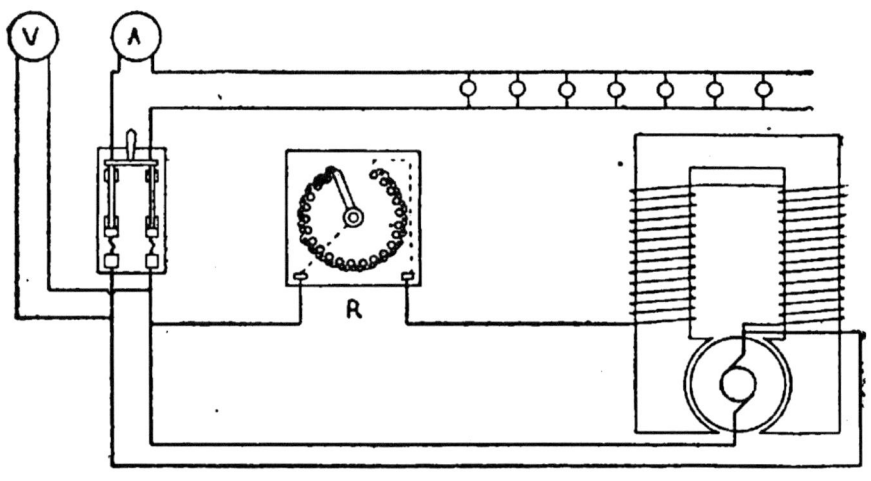

FIGURE 140.

To start the dynamo it is first brought up to speed and the voltage regulated by means of the rheostat R and the voltmeter V, and the main switch is then thrown in. The connection for the field is taken off the dynamo leads so that the opening of the main switch will not open the field circuit, and for this reason the field will begin to build up as soon as the machine is started. Pilot lamps are sometimes used in place of voltmeter V, the voltage being determined by the brightness of the lamp. This is a very unsatisfactory method and is very little used at the present time. If either the armature or field connections are reversed current will flow in the opposite direction.

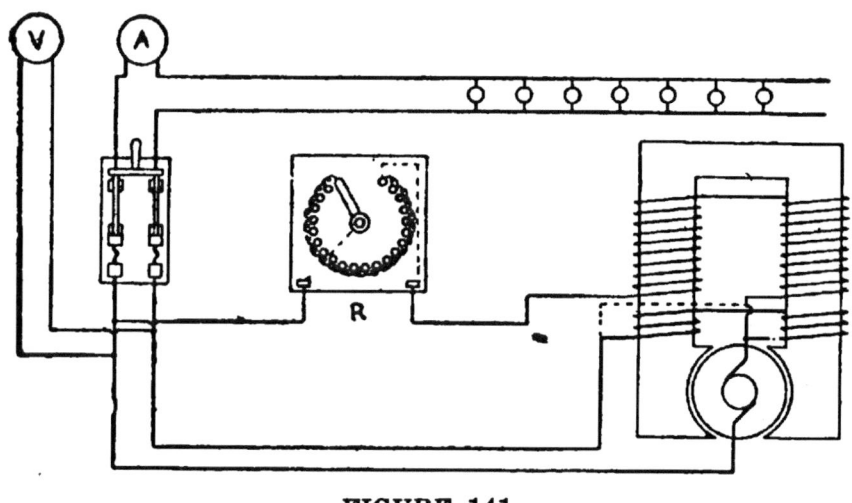

FIGURE 141.

Figure 141 shows the connections of a compound-wound dynamo. This machine, like the shunt-wound machine, is used where a current of constant potential is desired, but it has the advantage over the shunt machine in that it maintains the voltage more constant over a greater variation in load. The winding varies from that of the shunt dynamo in having, in addition to the shunt field, an auxiliary field which is in series with the armature. It is in reality the winding of both the shunt and series machine on one machine. As the current supplied by the dynamo increases, the current in the series field winding increases, thus increasing the field magnetism and the voltage. In this way the voltage is kept practically constant.

When a dynamo of this kind is used to supply a large load located at some distance from the generator, it is sometimes desirable to have the voltage at the dynamo terminals increase as the load increases, to overcome the increased drop in the line due to the losses from increased current. To accomplish this a method known as over-compounding is used, the series windings being so calculated that, as the current increases, the voltage will rise accordingly.

In some cases the shunt field is connected between one brush and the end of the series winding, as shown in the dotted lines. This is known as the long shunt, the method of connecting directly across the brushes being known as the short shunt. A rheostat R is connected in the shunt field and serves the same purpose as in the shunt machine.

Figure 142 shows the connections when two shunt-wound machines are to be run in parallel. The winding of these machines is the same as shown in Figure 140. The positive lead of each machine is connected to the same bus bar. In starting, if it is desired to use but one machine, the method described in Figure 140 is followed. When one of the machines is running and the other is to be thrown in, the idle machine is brought up to speed with the main switch open and the voltage regulated by means of the rheostat and voltmeter until the voltages of the two machines correspond. The main switch is then thrown in and the load on the two machines, which is ascertained by the ammeters, is equalized by means of the rheostats. If there is any great difference in voltage between the

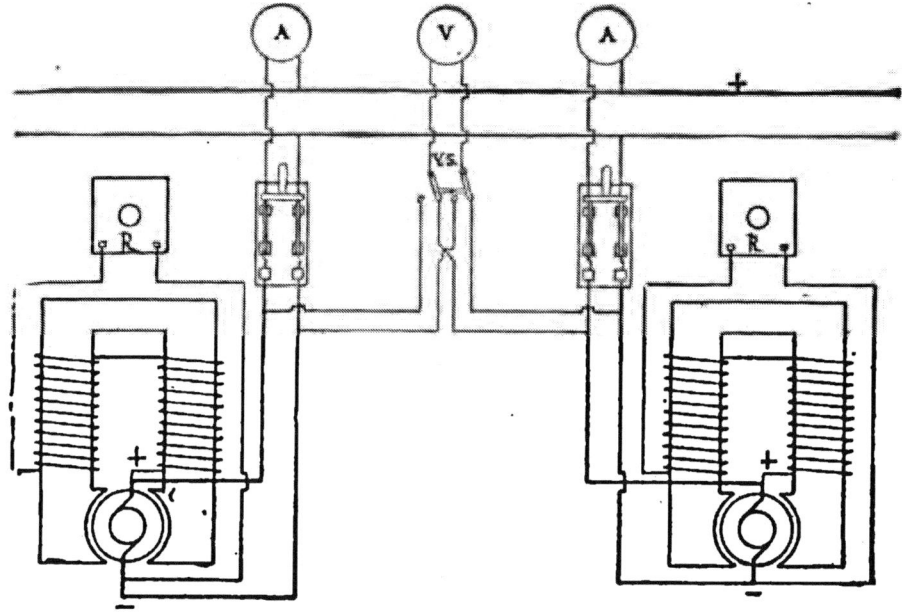

FIGURE 142.

machines, the higher one will run the other as a motor without changing the direction of rotation. The field current will remain unchanged and the armature current of the low dynamo will be reversed, which will cause it to run in the same direction as a motor as it ran as a dynamo.

DIRECT CURRENT GENERATORS

When a plant feeding motors is shut down the switches on motors should first be opened, or very likely motor fuses will blow. As the voltage goes down the motors will draw more current to do the work. If a plant is shut down with the motor switches "on" it will generally be found impossible to start up a shunt dynamo, the low resistance in the mains not allowing enough current to flow around the shunt fields to energize them.

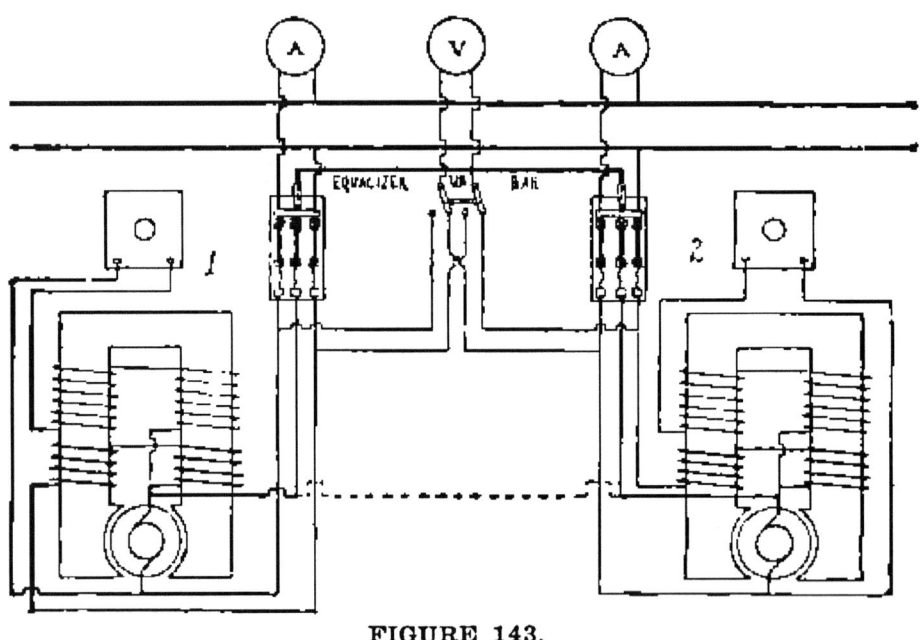

FIGURE 143.

Figure 143 shows connections for two compound-wound dynamos run in parallel, the winding of each machine being the same as in Figure 141. When two or more compound-wound dynamos are to be run together, the series fields of all the machines are connected together in parallel by means of wire leads or bus bars, which connect together the brushes from which the series fields are taken. This is known as the equalizer, and is shown by the line running to the middle pole of the dynamo switch. By tracing out the series circuits it will be seen that the current from the upper brush of either dynamo has two paths to its bus bar. One of these leads through its own fields, and the other, by means of the equalizer bar, through the fields of the other dynamo. So long as both machines are generating equally there is no difference of potential between the brushes of Nos. 1 and 2. Should, from any cause, the voltage of one machine be lowered, current from the other machine would begin to flow through its fields and thereby raise the voltage, at the same time reducing its own until both are again equal.

The equalizer may never be called upon to carry much current, but to have the machines regulate closely it should be of very low resistance. It may also be run as shown by the dotted lines, but this will leave all the machines alive when any one is generating. The ammeters should be connected as shown. If they were on the other side they would come under the influence of the equalizing current and would indicate wrong, either too high or too low. The equalizer should be closed at the same time, or preferably a little before, the mains are closed. In some cases the middle, or equalizer, blade of the dynamo switch is made longer than the outsides to accomplish this. The series fields are often regulated by a shunt of variable resistance. To insure the best results, compound-wound machines should be run at just the proper speed, otherwise the proportions between the shunt and series coils are disturbed.

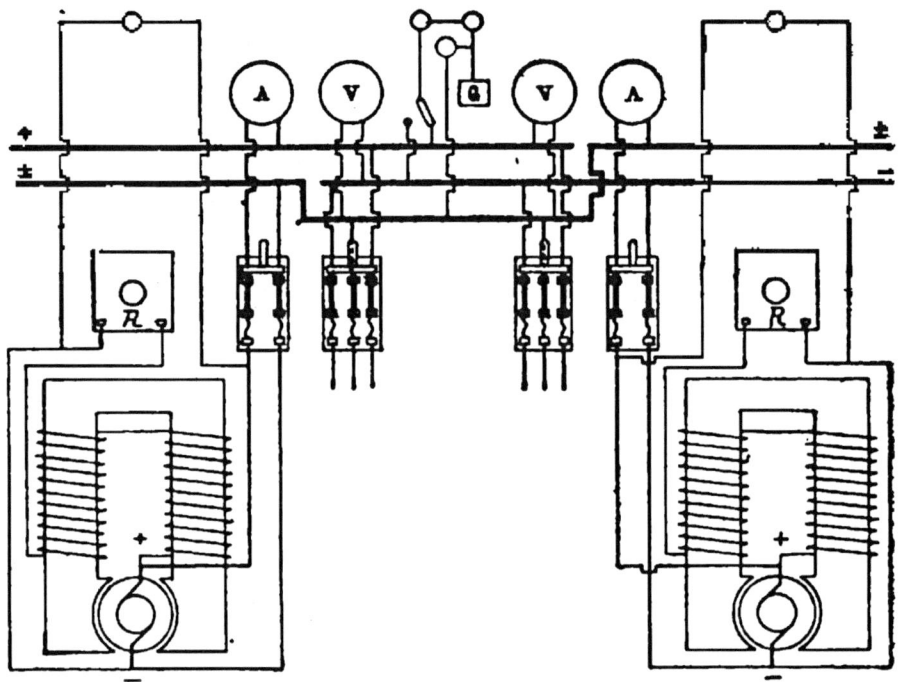

FIGURE 144.

Figure 144 shows connections where two shunt-wound machines are connected to operate on what is known as the three-wire system. The two dynamos are connected in series, three wires being carried from them; one from the outside pole of each machine and one from the junction of the two machines. The voltage between these outside wires is equal to the combined voltage of the two machines, and the voltage between the outside and the central or neutral wire is equal to the voltage of the corresponding machine. If the load on both sides of the system is equal there will be no current flowing in the neutral wire, while if the loads are unequal the neutral wire will have to carry only the difference in currents between the two outsides.

The advantage derived from the use of the three-wire system lies in the fact that one wire (which would have to be used were the two machines operated on two separate circuits) can be done away with, and on account of the voltage being doubled the wires can be of much smaller capacity. For the same per cent of loss the amount of wire required to operate the three-wire system, when the neutral wire is of the same size as the outsides, is but three-eighths of that required with a two-wire system. This system is used to a great extent in the large cities for central station, direct current distribution, and it is also used on the secondary mains in alternating current work.

In the feeder lines of the direct current system the neutral wire is generally made one-third the size of the outsides, while in the secondary mains in both direct and alternating current work all three wires are made of the same size; for, if one of the outside fuses should blow, the neutral would have to carry the full current.

Figure 145 shows a diagram of the winding and connections of a Western Electric compound-wound compensator set. This apparatus is used in connection with 220 volt generators and by means of it a three-wire 110-220 volt system is obtained. This set consists of two motors, the armatures of which are mounted on the same shaft so that both run at the same speed. When the machines are started the switch P and the circuit-breaker are left open and the switch shown at the left closed. The machines are then started by means of the starting box. Tracing out the circuits it will be seen that the main current from the positive pole of the switch passes through the starting box, through the armature and series fields of machine B then through the armature and series fields of machine A and back to the negative side of the line. The circuit for the shunt fields is connected to the starting box, current flowing through the resistance box, R, and then through the shunt fields of machine A and machine B, these fields being connected in series, to the negative side of the line. It will be noticed by the direction of the arrows that the current in the series fields and the shunt fields are in opposition. This remains so in both motors only while the load on both sides of the neutral is even and under this condition the amount of current in the series fields is very small. If an additional load is thrown on one side, say ten lamps at X, part of the excess current flows along the neutral wire to the

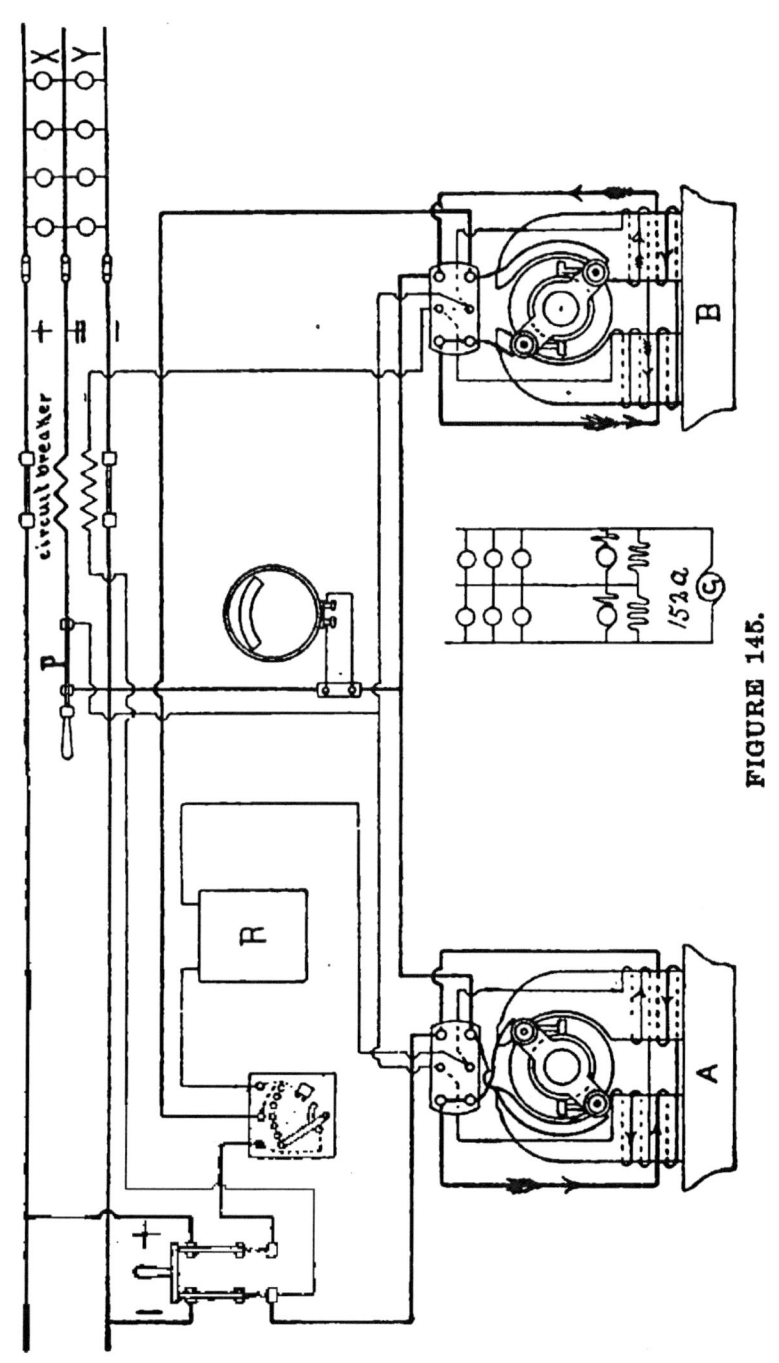

FIGURE 145.

armature and series fields of machine A. This current being in opposition to the current in the shunt fields weakens them and tends to speed up this motor. This speeding up increases the counter E. M. F. of machine B, the fields of which have not been weakened, and current flows out of the armature and through the series fields in a direction opposite to that shown by the arrows. The current in both field coils in this machine will now be in the same direction and the machine will act as a compound-wound generator. It cannot as a generator give out more power than it receives from A as a motor and will generate a little less than one-half of the excess current used at X. This is shown a little plainer by the diagrams in Figure 146. With no load, or with the load evenly distributed on both sides of the neutral, the conditions will be as shown in the upper diagram, both machines acting as motors. With excess of load between the positive and neutral approximately one-half of the excess current will pass along the neutral wire through the lower machine causing it to act as a motor while the balance of the excess current is supplied by the upper machine acting as a generator. The lower diagram shows the conditions with excess load between the neutral and the negative. In the operation of these machines, when they have attained full speed after starting, their voltages are equalized by means of the resistance box R, this box being placed in the strongest field. When automatic starting boxes are used, as in this case, it is almost always necessary to place the resistance box in the opposite field to balance the resistance of the magnet on the starting box. For equalizing the voltages connections are made to the voltmeter as shown in Figure

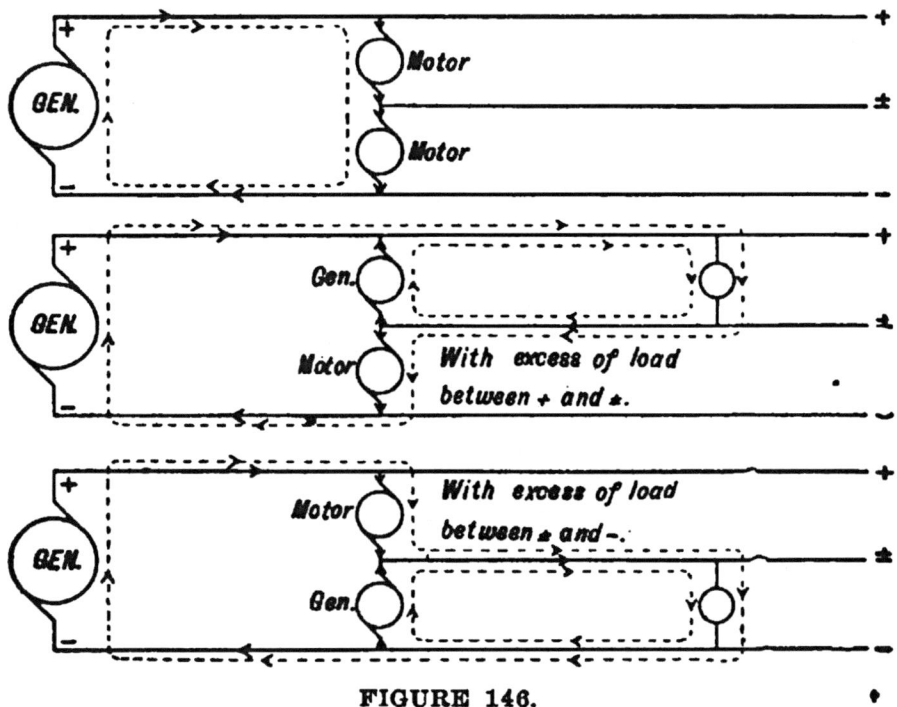

FIGURE 146.

143, so that reading for both machines can be taken. When the machines are at even voltage the circuit breakers are thrown in.

Figure 147 shows the switchboard and machine connections for two Compensator sets in parallel. The two panels at the left are for the 220 volt generators, the two at the right are for the feeders while

COMPENSATORS 181

the two center panels are for the operation of the compensators. By following out the circuits for the

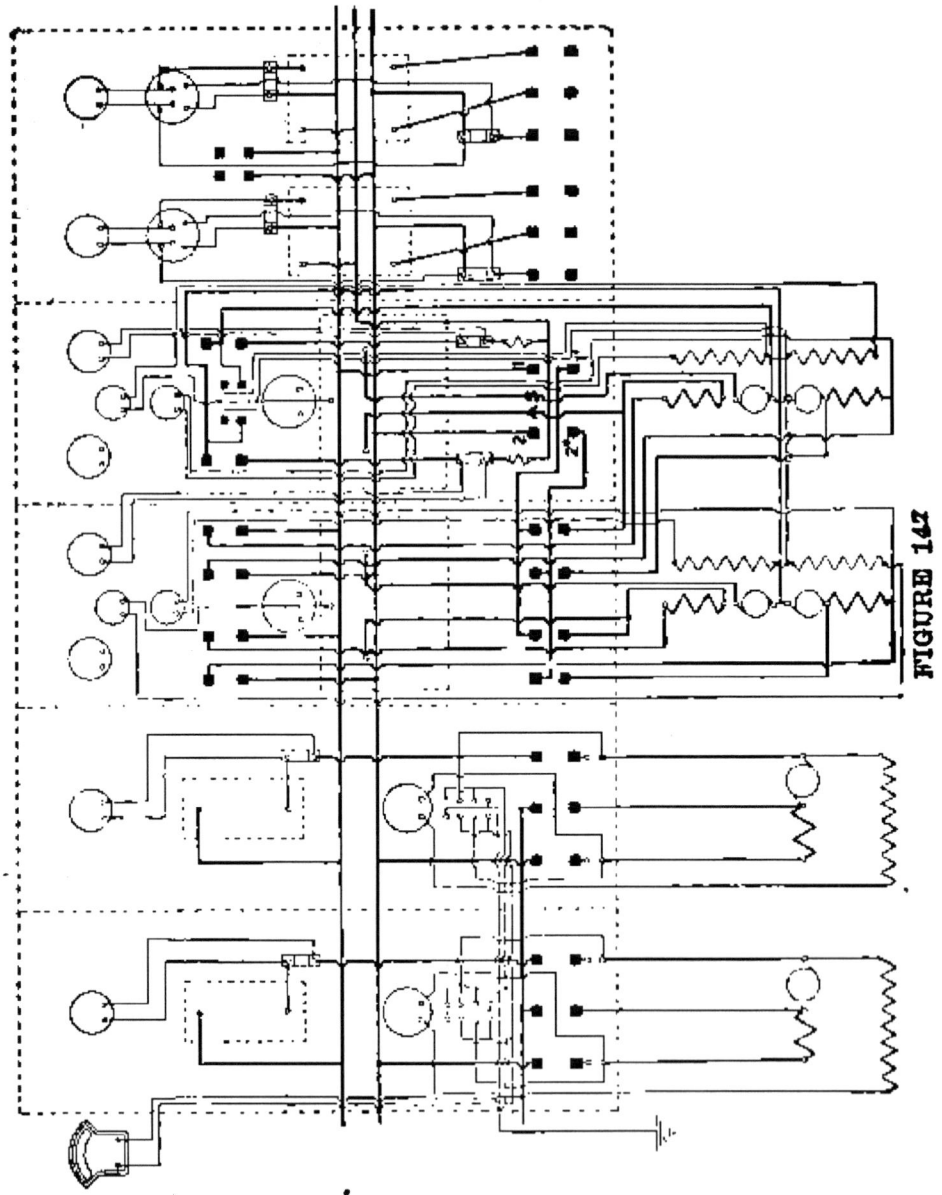

FIGURE 142

individual compensators it will be seen that, with few exceptions, they correspond to the circuits shown in

Figure 145. A resistance box is installed in each shunt field circuit while in Figure 145 there is only one resistance box.

The principle of the Westinghouse Three Wire Generator is illustrated in Figures 147a, 147b, and

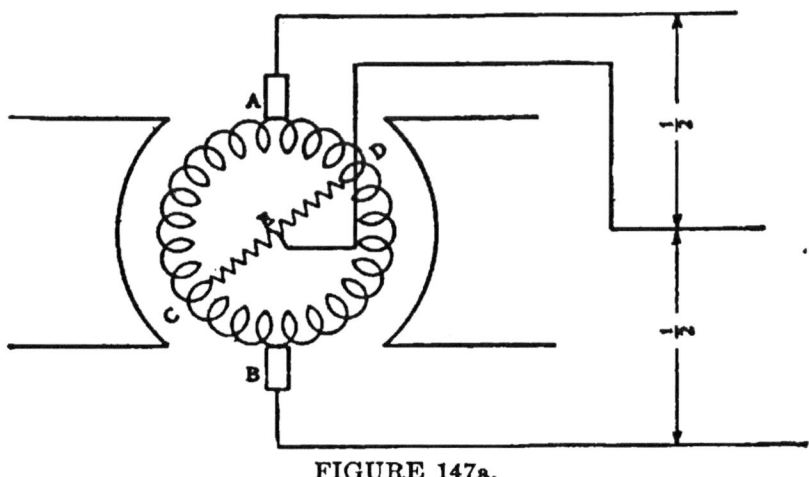

FIGURE 147a.

147c. Figure 147a shows the connections of the dynamo armature. The outer circle represents the ordinary armature winding connected by means of the commutator to the brushes A and B. The fine coils shown running through the center from C to D represent taps taken from diametrically opposite points of the direct current winding. If these taps are joined through resistances as indicated alternating currents will circulate in them and at E there will be a point at which just half of the voltage of the direct current system exists. The wire connected to this point can therefore be used to fulfill the same requirements as the neutral wire in the ordinary two generator three wire system.

ALTERNATING CURRENT GENERATOR 133

The connections of a single machine are shown in Figure 147b. In actual practice the alternating current connections of the armature are connected to two auto transformers as shown. These auto transformers are known also as balancing coils.

Figure 147c shows the switchboard connections for two such generators operating in multiple. On

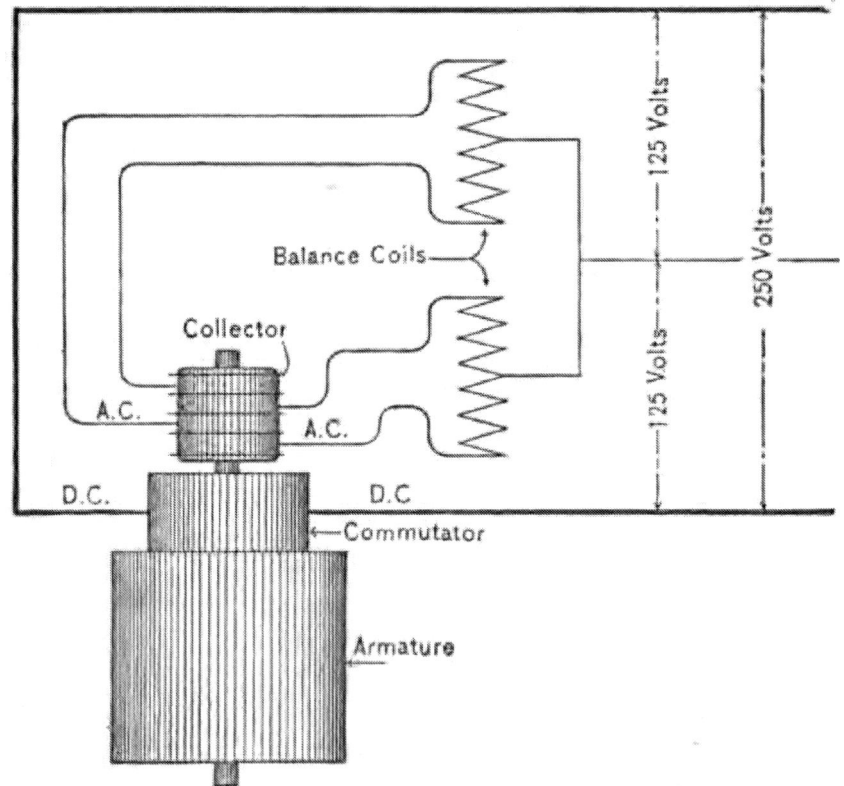

FIGURE 147b.

account of the fact that the load is often unbalanced an ammeter is provided in each leg leading from a machine to the switchboard. The series fields of each machine are also divided so that current from each leg may pass through half of each field. Since the series fields are divided it is necessary to run an equalizer for each division and two are therefore shown.

The balancing coils should be mounted as near to the dynamos or switchboard as practicable. Any great resistance introduced into their circuit will affect the voltage existing between the neutral point and the outside wires. It should be noted that both the positive and negative equalizer connections as well as both the positive and negative leads are run to the cir-

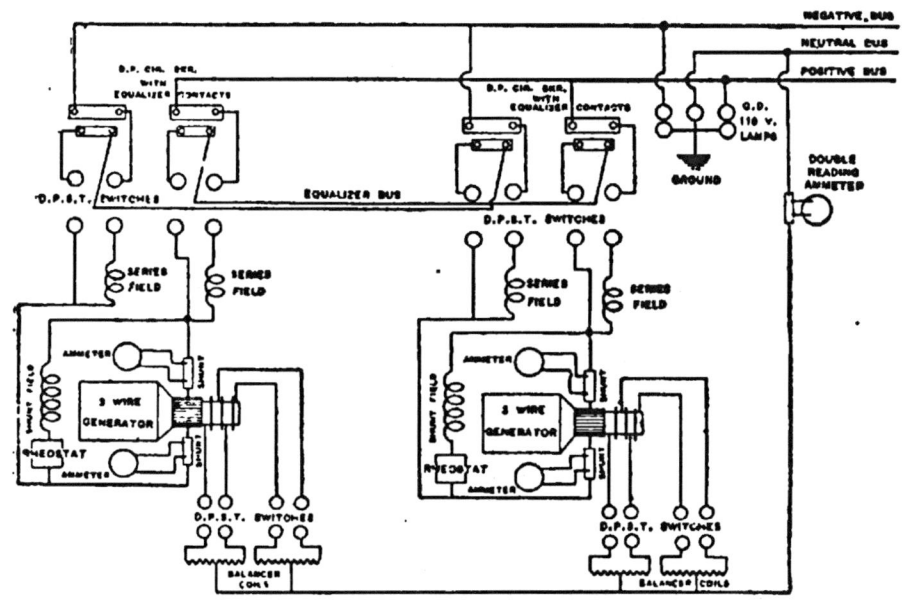

FIGURE 147c.

cuit breakers in addition to the main switches on the board. This is necessary in all cases. Otherwise, when two or more machines are running in parallel and the breaker comes out opening the circuit to one of them but not breaking its equalizer leads, its ammeter is left connected to the equalizer bus bars and current is fed into it from the other machines through the equalizer bars either driving it as a motor or burning out the armature.

Once properly installed, the balancing coils require no further attention and give no trouble. Provision should however be made so that their circuit cannot be opened accidentally while in operation.

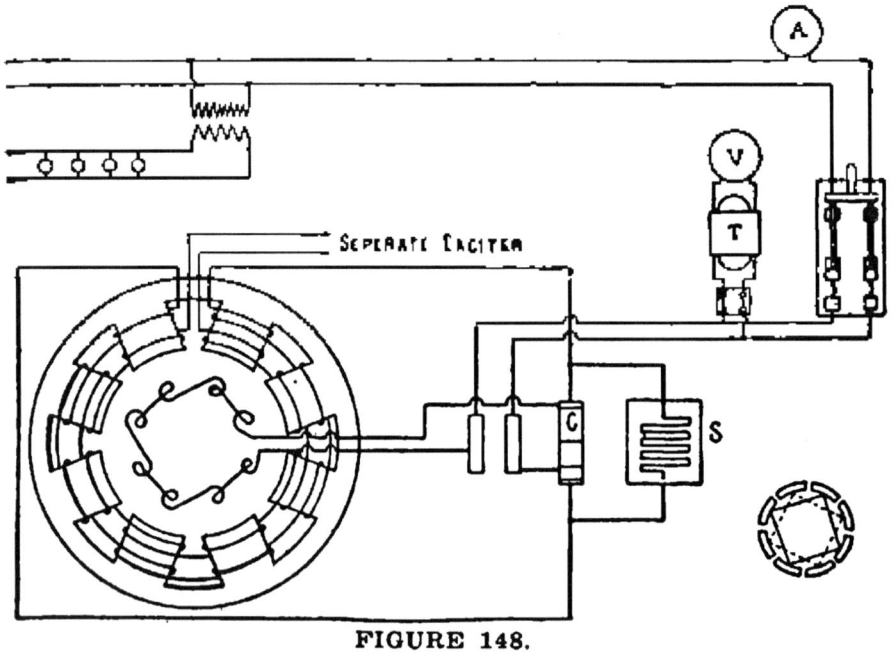

FIGURE 148.

Figure 148 shows the connections of a single-phase, alternating current generator. The field of this machine is excited by a direct current, part of which is taken from some outside source (generally a small dynamo belted to the shaft of the alternator) and part of which is taken from the windings of the alternator, the current being rectified by means of the commutator C. This commutator has as many segments as there are poles to the dynamo, and the alternate segments are connected together as shown in the small diagram. S is a German silver resistance which is connected in shunt across this rectifying commutator. The main current coming from the armature is shunted, part going through the shunts, the remainder around the field winding.

It will be seen that this method of field excitation is very similar to that used on the compound-wound direct-current dynamo. In the diagram shown both

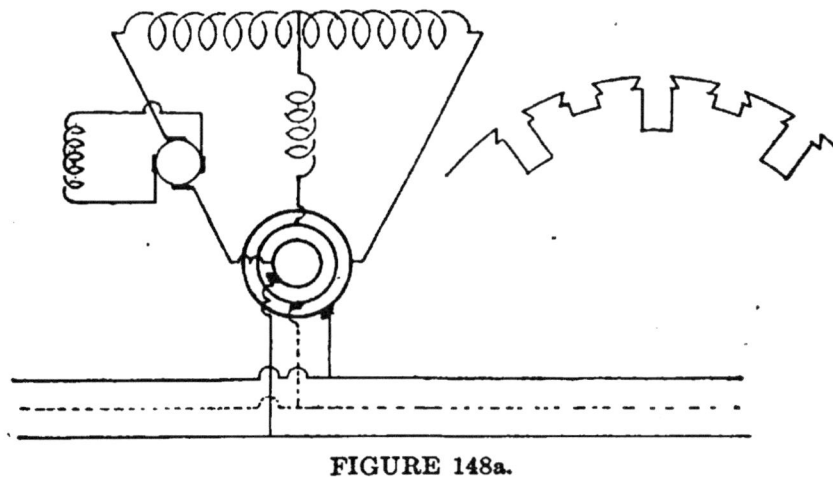

FIGURE 148a.

of the field windings encircle every pole, but in some machines the rectified current will traverse a few poles only, the current from separate exciter traversing the remainder. Current on these machines is usually generated at high voltage, and transformers are used at the point of supply to cut the voltage down to that required. The transformer T is used

ALTERNATING CURRENT GENERATOR 187

in connection with voltmeter V to reduce the voltage on that instrument.

Figure 148a shows a theoretical diagram of a monocyclic generator of the General Electric Co. Such generators are sometimes used on systems where the lighting load is the main factor and only a few self starting motors are to be operated. It is essentially a single phase alternator with an extra winding of smaller capacity placed so as to produce a phase difference of 90 degrees between the currents in the main coil and those in the smaller. The smaller winding is known as a "teazer" coil, and the middle wire to which this coil attaches is spoken of as the "teazer" wire. The machine carries three collector rings. The arrangement of the wires placed upon the armature can be seen from the figure at the right. The main coils are placed in the deep slots and the teazer coils into the shallow ones.

In the General Electric generator, if the voltage between the two main wires is 2080 there will be difference of potential between either of the outsides and the teazer of 1160.

The field connections of a monocyclic generator are shown in Figure 148b, and the diagram is self explanatory.

The armature connections are given in Figure 148c, and the following instructions are quoted from the General Electric Co. "The armature of a standard monocyclic generator rotates in the counter-clockwise

WIRING DIAGRAMS

CONNECTIONS OF MONOCYCLIC GENERATOR

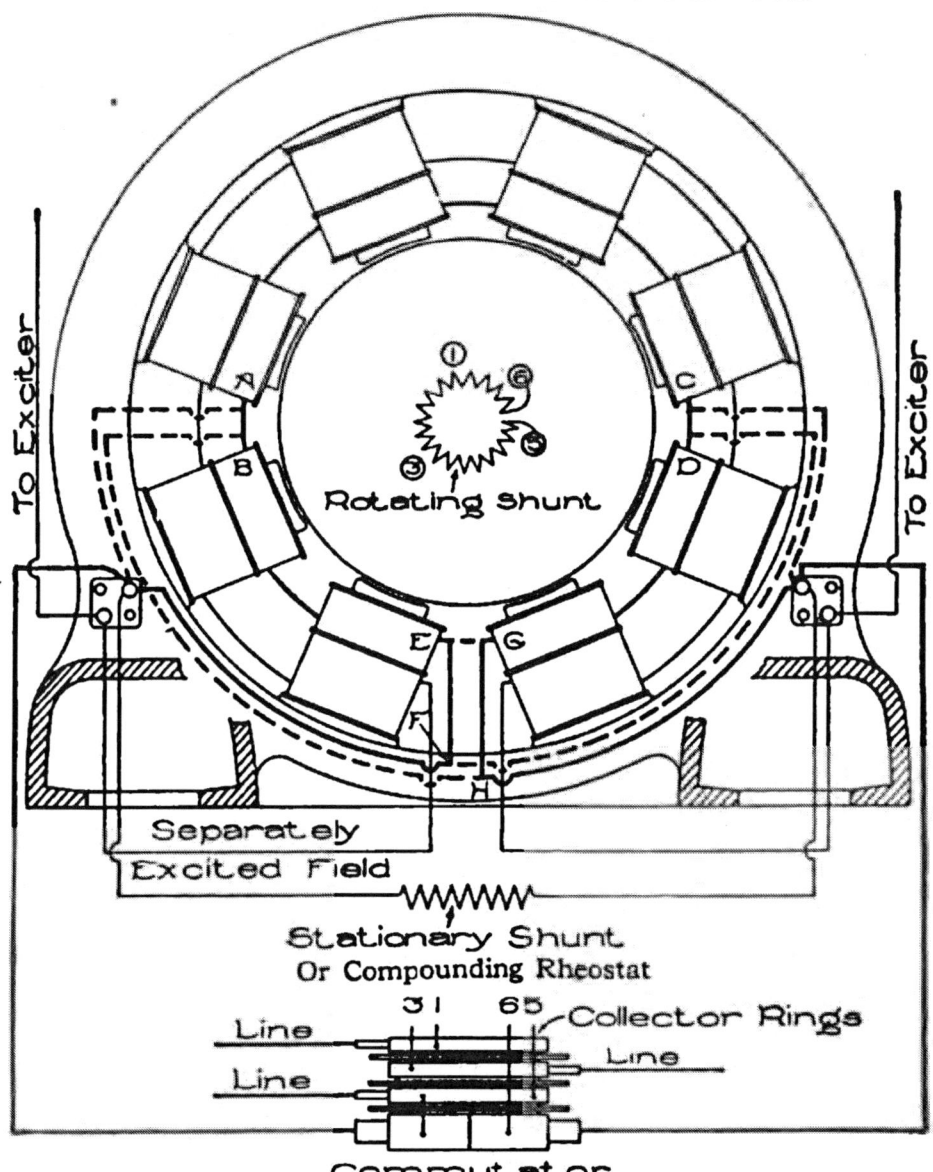

For 2300 Volt Generators, connect as shown by solid lines.
For 1150 Volt Generators, omit connections A to B, C to D, E to F, and G to H, and connect as shown by dotted lines.

FIGURE 148b.

ALTERNATING CURRENT GENERATOR

direction as one faces the commutator. When the generator is loaded, the voltage between the teazer coil and the two terminals of the main coil may be different; therefore, it is necessary to have the commutator connected in corresponding ends of the main coil.

"If the machine has not been arranged for clockwise rotation the following change in the connections on the commutator-collector must be made if the machine is

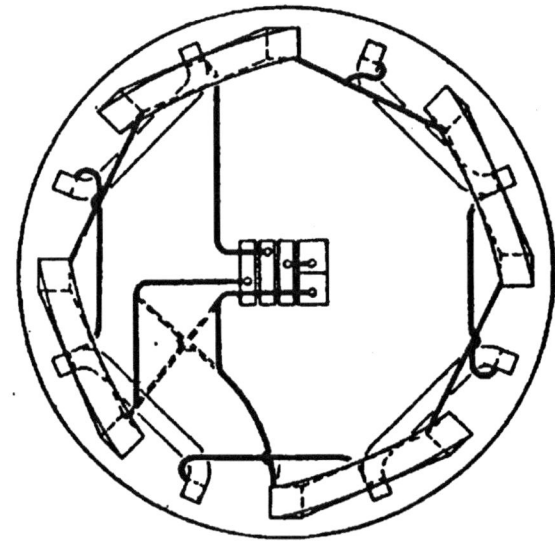

FIGURE 148c.

to be run in parallel with another. The diagram Figure 148b shows the connections of monocylic generators. In this diagram the studs on the commutator-collector marked 1 and 6 are the terminals of the main coil. These should be reversed.' The numbers are stamped on the end of the stud and may be seen with the aid of a mirror. By referring to the diagram it is

WIRING DIAGRAMS

CONNECTIONS OF THREE-PHASE GENERATOR

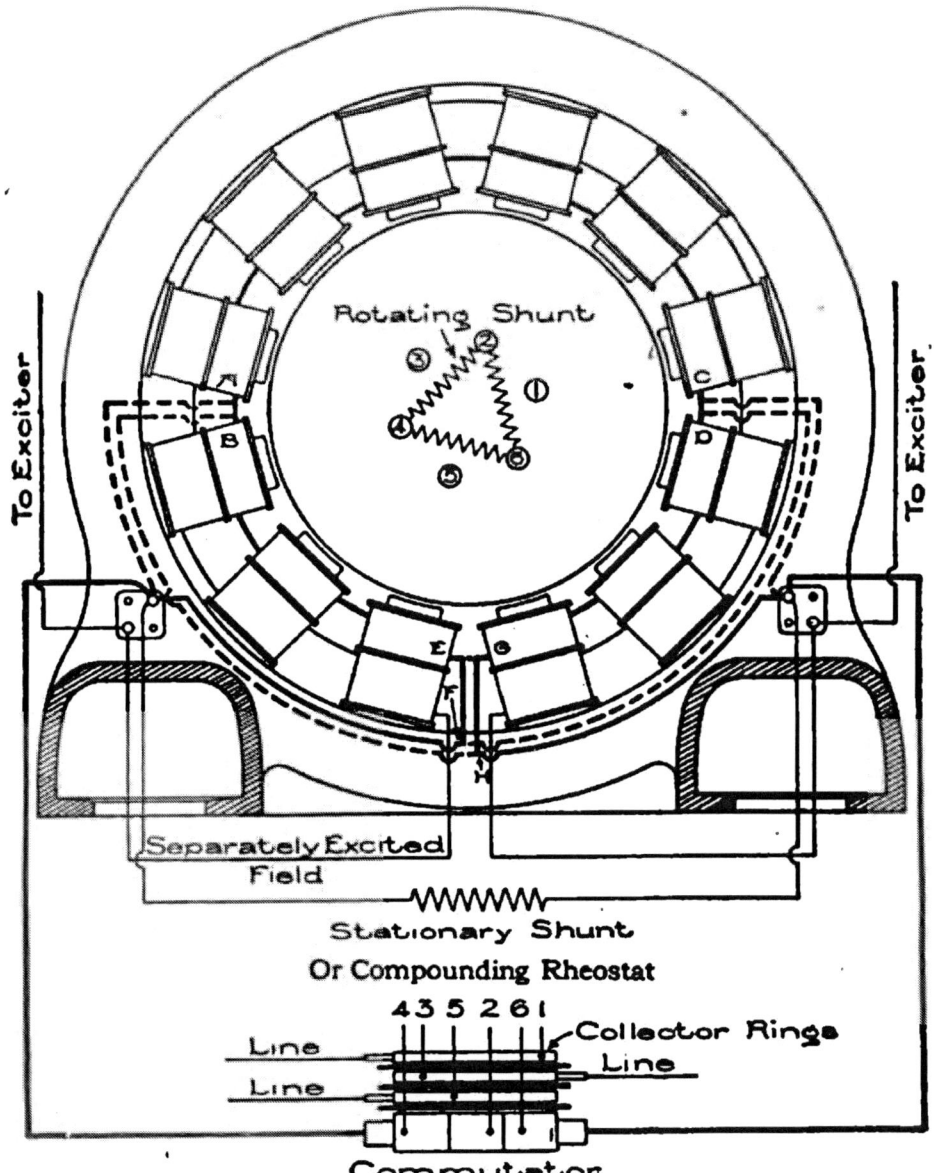

For 2300 Volt Generators, connect as shown by solid lines.
For 1150 Volt Generators, omit connections A to B, C to D,
E to F, and G to H, and connect as shown by dotted lines.

FIGURE 148d.

a simple matter to trace out the connections with the aid of a magneto, after the armature leads have been disconnected and the brushes raised."

Figure 148d shows the connections of a General Electric three phase generator. This machine, as well as all of the foregoing, is of the revolving armature type. Many of the larger machines are now built with stationary armatures and revolving fields. In such case the exciter feeds the moving element and the line currents are taken from the stationary windings.

Two three phase composite wound generators are shown connected together for parallel running in Figure 148e.

Composite wound alternators if used with inductive loads require considerable attention at the rectifier. A change in the angle of lag of the current behind the E. M. F. must be followed by a change in the adjustment of the rectifier or there will be much sparking. For this reason such machines are used mostly on lighting circuits only.

Figure 148f gives the switchboard connections of two two phase machines arranged for parallel running. Each machine is equipped with a throwover switch by which either phase may be connected to voltmeter. Each phase is also equipped with an ammeter.

E E are the rheostats by which the field strength of either machine can be adjusted. The synchronizing bus S is equipped with a throwover switch so that the synchronizing may be either dark or bright.

Whichever method is preferred should be settled upon and the switch locked so that it may not be accidentally changed. Synchronizing lamps of double the voltage capacity of the system must be provided as the two

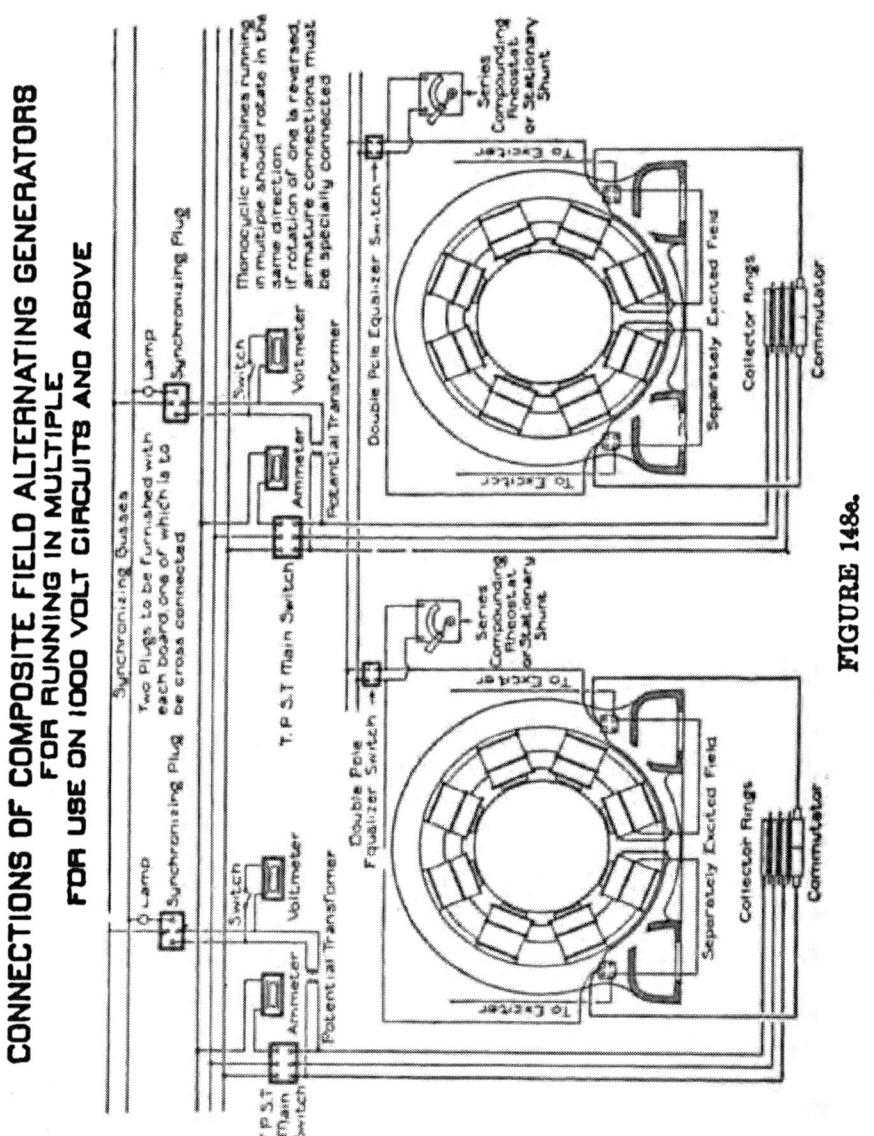

FIGURE 148e.

ALTERNATING CURRENT GENERATOR 193

machines are likely to be in series during part of the time of synchronization.

The instrument connections of a three phase 440 volt switchboard for parallel operation of two ma-

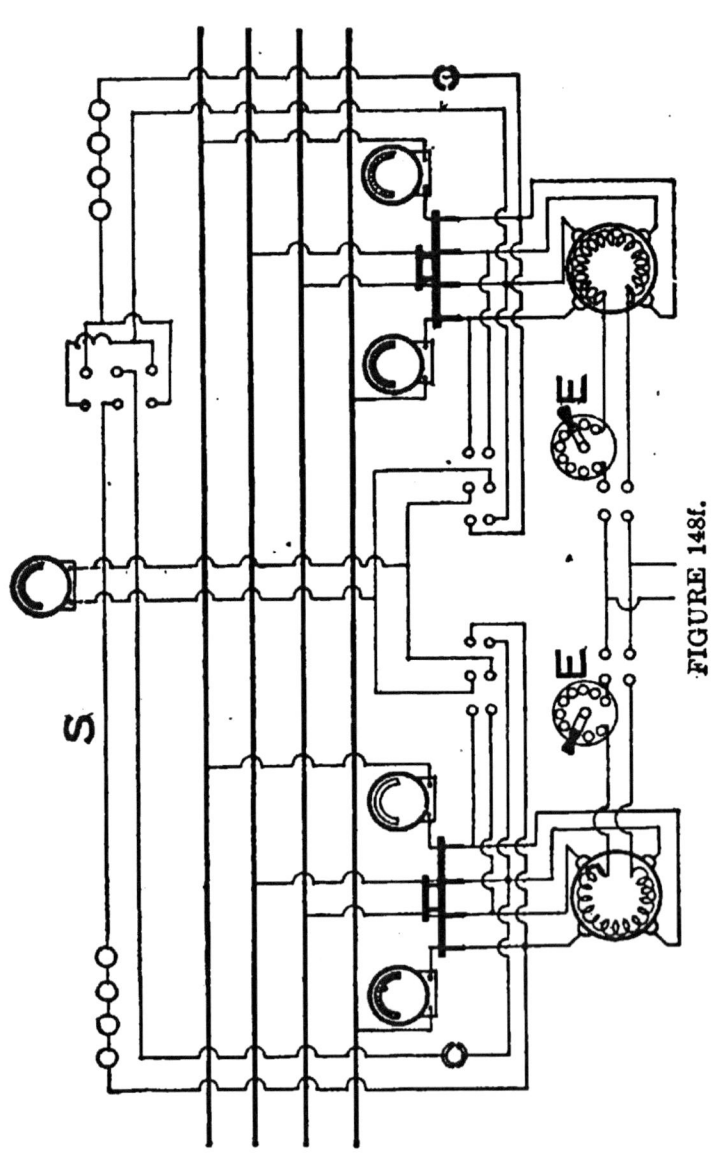

FIGURE 148f.

194 WIRING DIAGRAMS

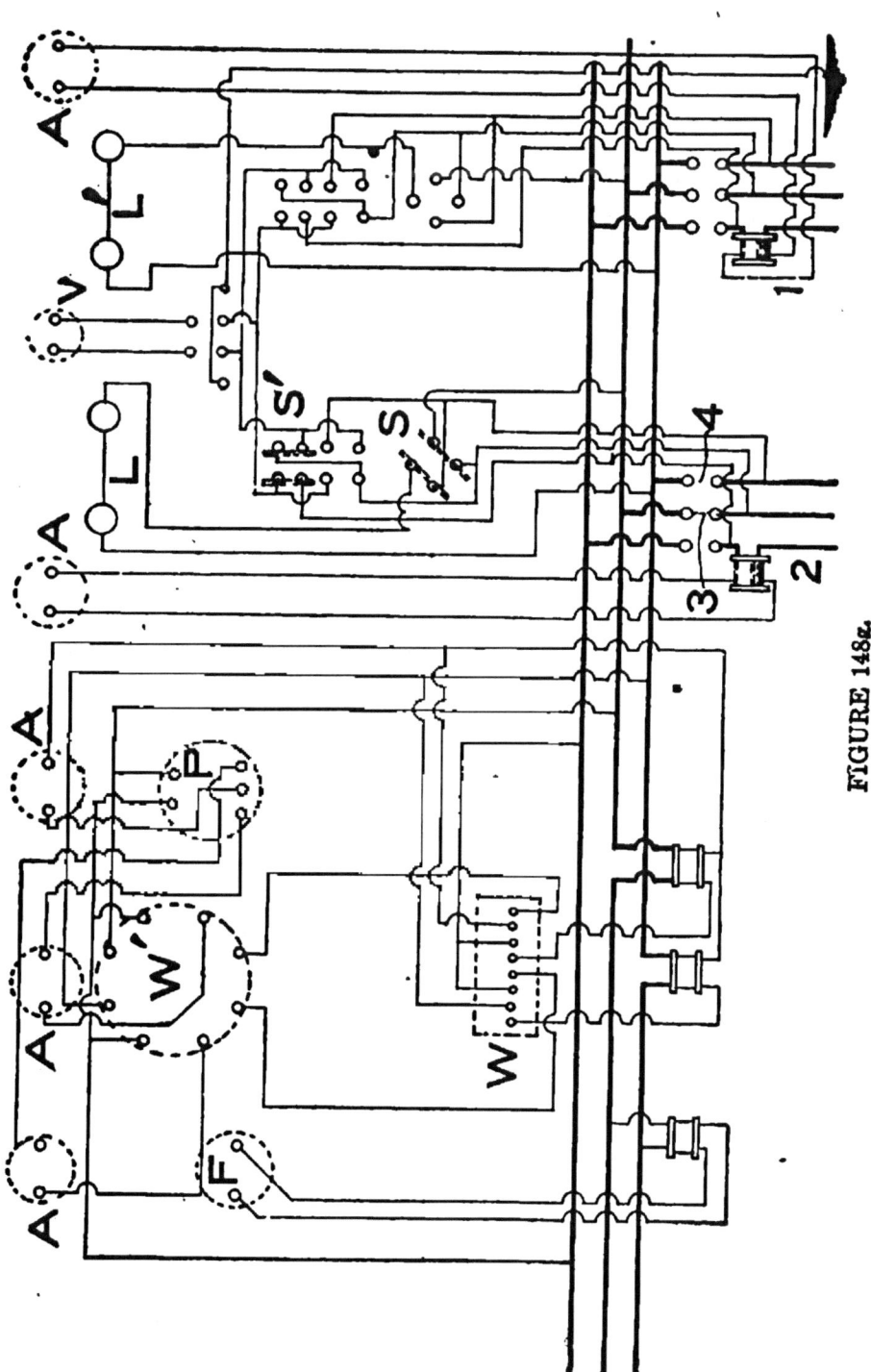

FIGURE 148a.

chines are given in Figure 148g. To avoid confusion the exciter circuits and those leading to lamps and motors are omitted.

An ammeter is provided for each machine by which it can be determined whether it is taking its share of the load. There is further an ammeter in each phase of the bus bars to indicate the balance maintained on the system.

W is a recording watt meter; W' an indicating watt meter; P a power factor meter, and F a frequency meter. (See Figure 154s.)

L and L' are the synchronizing lamps, two of which are provided for each machine. To synchronize machine 2 with 1 which is already running, the plug is inserted as at S, the lower half of the plug closes gap 3 and the upper half closes gap 4 through the lamps L. If the machines are not in synchronism the lamps will alternately be bright and dark. The speed of the incoming machine must be altered until the periods of light and darkness are of several seconds duration. During the middle of the dark period the main switch may be closed and the machines will then operate together.

By tracing out the circuits it can be seen that the plug placed as at S' by being inserted in the upper, middle, or lower set of contacts can be used to take the reading of either of the three phases on the voltmeter V. The voltmeter is also connected so as to be available as a ground detector.

195a WIRING DIAGRAMS

ARC LAMP CONTROL FOR MOTION PICTURE WORK

Arc lamps used in connection with motion picture machines have caused the construction of some special forms of generators.

Figure 148h shows the connections of an alternating-current to a direct-current motor-generator of the Fort Wayne Electric Company. The switch A is used to start it and is shown connected to a three-phase line. Aside from the field winding there are three wires leading to the generator. The wire B carries a compound winding inside of the generator which opposes the magnetization of the shunt winding. The wire C carries another compound winding which is arranged to strengthen the shunt field. D is a box containing two resistances, one for each arc lamp shown.

If only one lamp is to burn, the switch E is closed and the arc started in the usual way. When ready to change to the other arc lamp, switch E must be opened, the switch on the second arc lamp closed, and the arc struck. Then extinguish the first arc and close the switch E again. If both lamps are to be used continually, switch E must be left open.

As long as current is used through wire B, there is no loss of energy in any resistance and should the current in the arc rise, as when the electrodes are brought together, the increased current in the series winding, cut into this wire, would weaken the field and thus keep the current down. When current is used through the wire C, the series field winding strengthens the field and builds up the voltage sufficiently so that the lamps may be operated through the resistances. The field strength may be further regulated by the rheostat R.

ALTERNATING CURRENT GENERATOR 195b

Another connection of the Fort Wayne motor-generator is shown in Figure 148i. In this case the lamps may be operated either from the compensarc C or the generator. By throwing either one of the switches connected to the arc lamps up, the corresponding arc lamp is connected to the compensarc. By throwing the switch down it is fed from the generator. The lamp, by which the picture is being projected, should be fed from the generator and when nearly

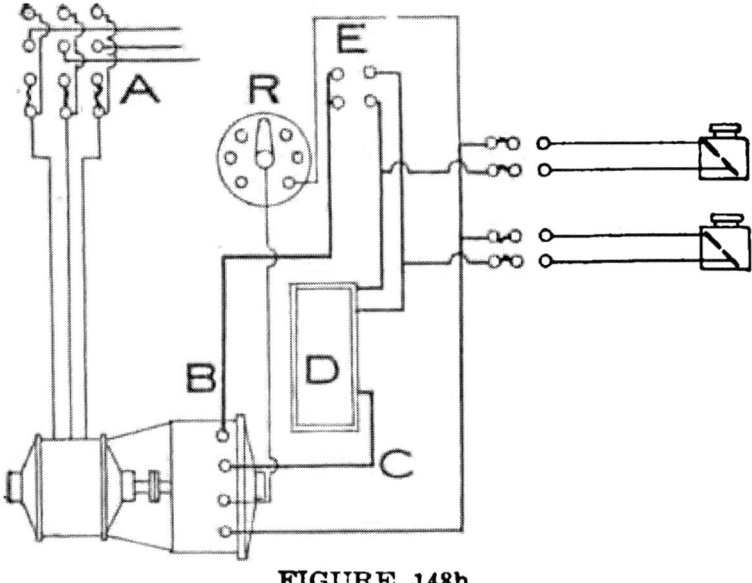

FIGURE 148h.

ready to change, the other may be started on the compensarc. This lamp will burn with a short arc and when it is connected in parallel with the one on the generator, it will immediately extinguish the latter.

Another combination of motor and generator sometimes used is shown in Figure 148j. By tracing out the circuits it will be seen that the armatures of both are in series and that the electrodes, when they come together, form a shunt about B. With the electrodes separated, if current is turned on, it must pass through both armatures in series. Thus the counter e.m.f. of both armatures opposes that of the line and they operate at a certain speed. Each motor has a natural tendency to send current in opposition to that impressed upon it by the line. If then the electrodes are brought together, they at once form a short circuit around the armature of B. The current in B

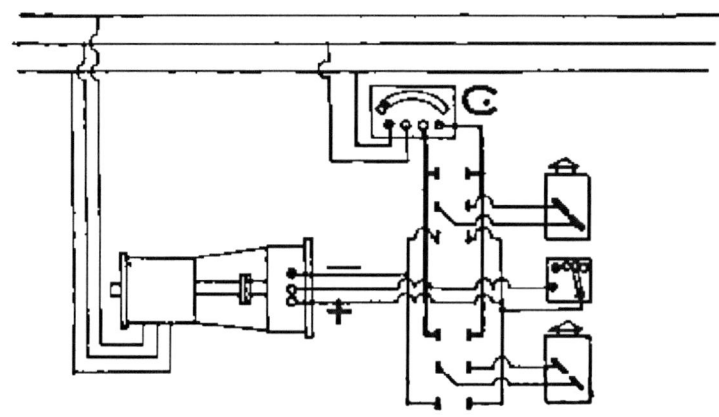

FIGURE 1481.

reverses and it then begins to act as a generator and sends current through the arc lamp. The current which passes through the armature of A also passes through the arc lamp. A is then a motor and operates B as a generator.

The voltage at the arc is less than the line voltage by as much as the counter e.m.f. of motor A amounts to, neglecting the drop in voltage due to resistance. No resistance is needed if the winding is properly arranged and there is not the loss in heat which goes with the use of resistances. This arrangement can be used with direct-current circuits only. It is not suitable where the supply voltage is very much higher

ALTERNATING CURRENT GENERATOR 195d

than the voltage used at the arc. A field rheostat is provided to adjust the field strength of *B*. *A* is equipped with the ordinary motor-starting rheostat only.

Rotary Converter Control.—This is a machine used only where the supply is alternating current. The voltage delivered to the converter must be the same as that desired at the direct-current terminals. This machine has an armature essentially similar to that of a direct-current dynamo. Alternating current is supplied to it at one set of terminals and direct cur-

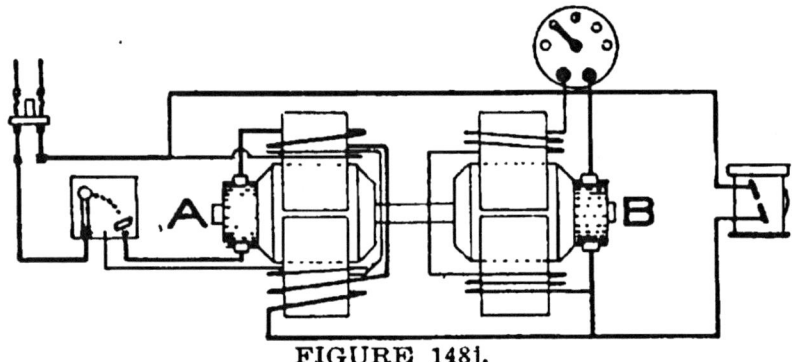

FIGURE 148J.

rent is taken from the others. This armature acts as motor and generator at the same time. Whatever voltage regulating is necessary with this machine must be done on the alternating-current side. Changing the field strength does not materially affect the voltage so that no means for regulating the field strength is provided.

The polarity of the direct-current terminals depends upon the position the armature happens to be in when the alternating current is applied to it and is very apt to come in wrong when the machine is started. It is therefore necessary to have a polarity indicating voltmeter in the circuit and to watch it when starting the machine. If the polarity is wrong, the switch must be opened and in a moment thrown in again; and if still wrong, this process must be repeated until the polarity comes right. Each arc lamp fed from a converter must be equipped with resistance.

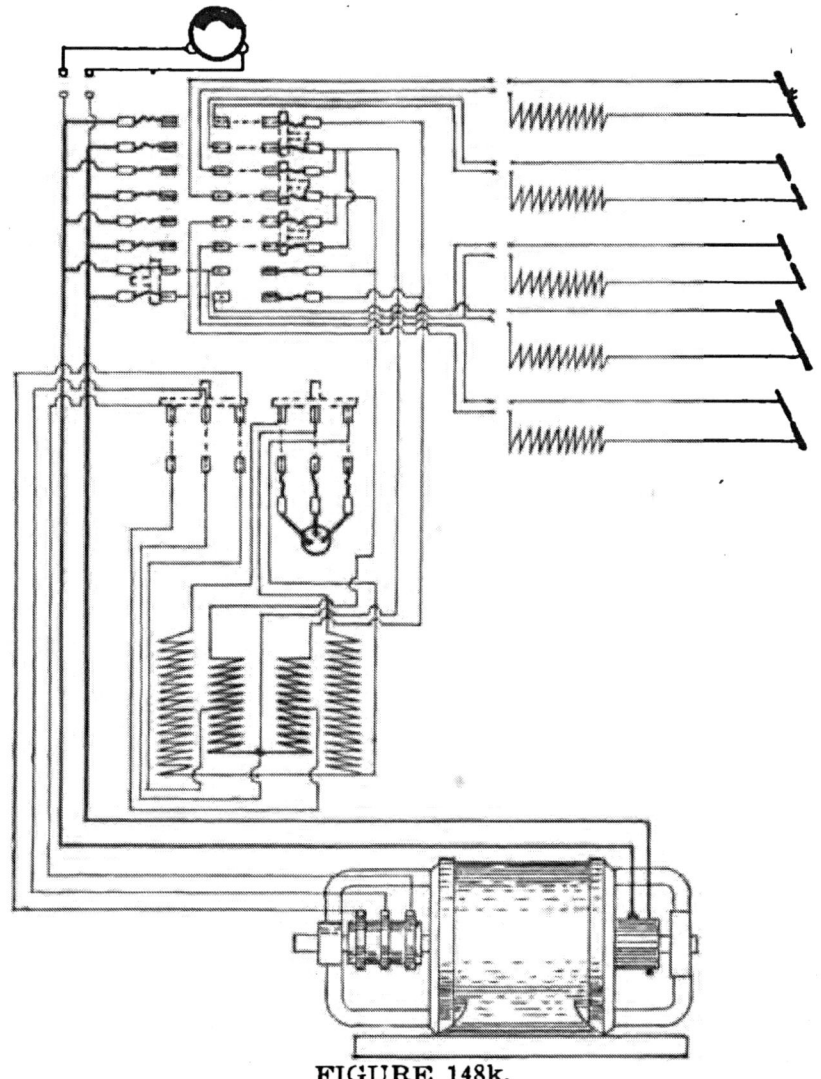

FIGURE 148k.

The Martin rotary converter is especially designed for motion-picture work and may be provided with the proper connections for either single-phase, two-phase, or three-phase work. There is a stator ring which entirely surrounds the armature. This ring is made up of laminated disks with squirrel-cage bars and slots alternating. The squirrel-cage bars are joined at the end to a copper bar and it is by the aid of this squirrel-cage that the motor may be started and brought into step. The squirrel-cage also prevents "hunting" which is one of the common troubles experienced with synchronous motors or converters. Into the slots are wound special compensating coils to balance the armature reaction and keep the neutral point in constant position from no load to full load. This prevents sparking at the brushes. On the outside of this damper ring or squirrel-cage winding is the regular shunt-field winding used with direct-current motors or generators.

Figure 148k is a diagram showing the connections of the Martin Rotary Converter as installed by the Northwestern Electric Company of Chicago. This switchboard is equipped to operate two moving-picture arcs, two dissolving stereopticon lamps, and one spot light. Each lamp is provided with a throw-over switch so that current may be used, either from the alternating-current mains direct or from the direct-current side of the converter.

Figure 148l is another panel board for moving-picture work made up by the same company. In this case resistances are provided for use when the arc lamps are operated from the converter. In case it is desired to run from the alternating-current mains, transformers or compensarcs are used. The emergency feature of these panel boards is highly to be recommended. It must be borne in mind that one may suddenly be forced to deal with an operator who has never seen a converter and knows nothing of its operation; and there is also always the possibility of some trouble with the machine.

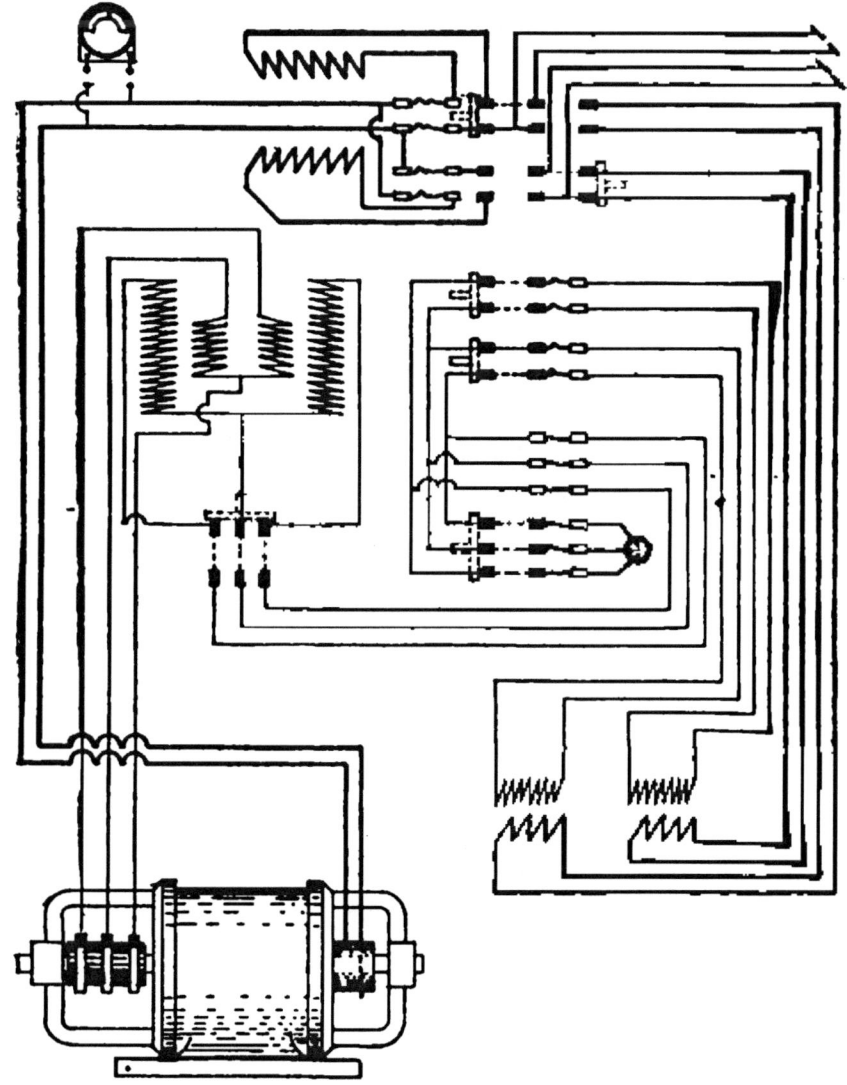

FIGURE 148l.

A Martin rotary converter to be operated from a single-phase line is shown in Figure 148m. This machine is started through the commutator side. In order to start this machine it is necessary first to close the main switch. Next throw the switch 2 to the right and leave it there for about five seconds. It may then be thrown over to the running position at the left and allowed to remain in this position. If

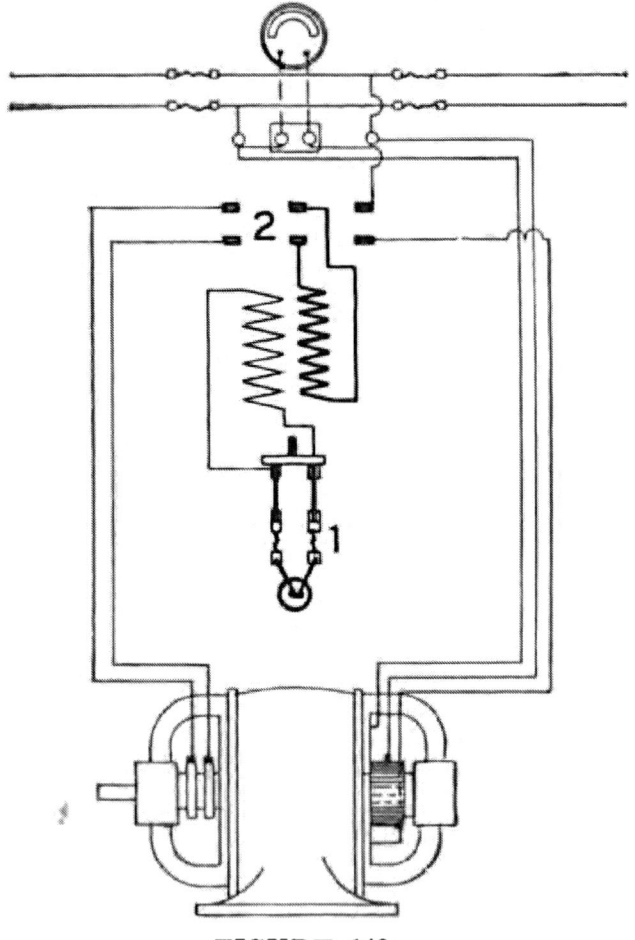

FIGURE 148m.

the polarity is not correct, the switch must be opened again for an instant and closed again; and this process must be repeated until the polarity comes in right. To stop the converter, first open the main switch and then the throw-over switch.

CHAPTER XV.

ALTERNATING CURRENT MOTORS. TRANSFORMERS.

There are two general classes of alternating-current motors, known respectively as "synchronous" and "induction" motors. As an example of the first class: If two identical alternating-current dynamos are connected together by wires, one running as a generator and the other as a motor, the driven machine would run at the same speed as the driving machine; for, at every change in the direction and strength of the current given out by the generator, like changes would be produced in the machine running as a motor. They would then run in synchronism. It may be advisable to state here that the machine running as a motor would first have to be brought up to speed, as the majority of synchronous motors are not self-starting.

When a multiphase (2 or 3-phase) alternating current is sent around the fields of an alternating current motor, a revolving field is set up in the space occupied by the armature. If now an armature of what is known as the squirrel cage type (a laminated armature in which bars of copper, running parallel to the shaft, are imbedded in slots in the periphery, the ends of all the bars being connected together,

ALTERNATING CURRENT MOTORS

(Figure 149), is placed in this field, currents will be induced in it which, acting in conjunction with the revolving field, will cause the armature to turn. These are known as induction motors, and this class is generally employed in commercial work. Such motors will start themselves from rest with a considerable torque, and will stand a reasonable amount of overload.

The direction of rotation of motors of this kind is reversed by changing the relative position of wires in any phase. It can readily be seen that this will cause the revolving field to move in the opposite direction.

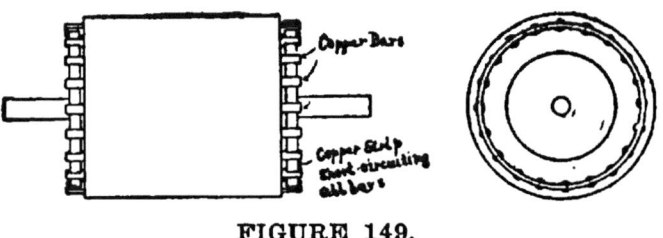

FIGURE 149.

The action of the current in the starting of induction motors is very similar to that in direct-current motors in that if, while the motor is at rest, the current was thrown directly on, it would rise to a considerable value. The smaller size motors may be directly connected to the circuit as is often done with direct current motors but with the larger size motors some device must be used to keep down the excessive current on starting.

Resistance boxes may be inserted in the motor circuits and operated in the same way as on direct current apparatus the resistance reducing the voltage at the motor terminals. On two and three-phase work resistances must be inserted in each phase and arranged to work together so that the changes in pressure at the motor terminals will be the same.

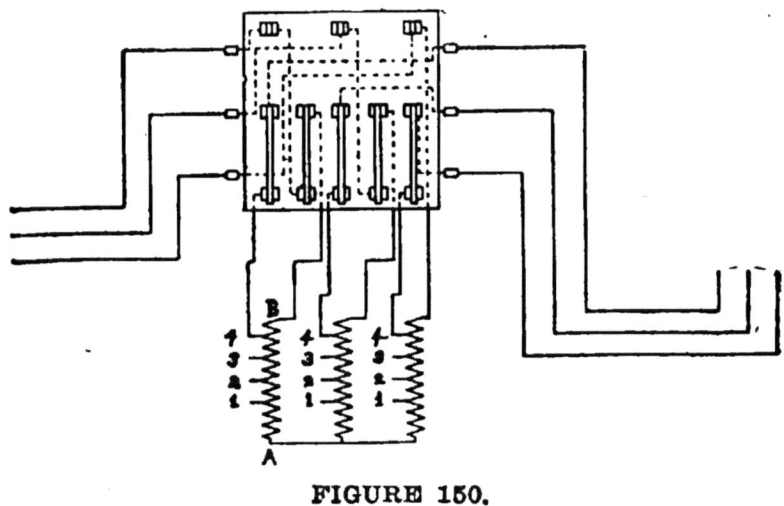

FIGURE 150.

Figure 150 shows the connections of the General Electric Company's compensator used in starting three-phase motors. This apparatus consists of three coils wound on laminated iron cores forming an autotransformer in which one wire is used for both primary and secondary, and works on the principle that, if an alternate current is sent through a coil of wire, and a tap taken from some intermediate point in the winding, the voltage between the tap and the end of the coil will be less than the full voltage sup-

ALTERNATING CURRENT MOTORS

plied, depending on the position at which the tap is taken off. In the diagram suppose that the difference of potential between the terminals A and B were 115 volts; then the difference of potential between A and 4 would be less than 115, while the difference of potential between A and 3 would be less than between A and 4. To start the motor the switch is thrown to the lower position, when the motor will receive the reduced current due to the reduced voltage between A and 4. When the motor is up to speed the switch is thrown to the "up" position, when the motor will receive the full voltage of the line. If more current is required in starting than can be obtained with the connection at 1 (this being the point of lowest voltage), connection can be made at either 2, 3 or 4 until the current required to start the motor is obtained. Were the motor, while at rest, thrown directly onto the mains without the use of the compensator, the current would rise to six or seven times that normally required; while in starting with the compensator the current varies from full load to about twice full load current according to whether connection is made at 1 or 4.

Another method used in starting alternating current motors is shown by the diagrams in Figure 151. The upper diagram shows the connections on a three-phase armature where one end of each coil is connected to a common wire, the other ends of the coils being carried to contact shoes 2, 2, 2. Between the contact shoes *2, 2, 2* and *1, 1, 1* are connected resistance wires, these wires ending in a connection common to them all. When the motor is started current flowing from the armature coils passes through the reresistances *r* and *s*. This is shown in the lower left hand diagram. As the motor speeds up the contact

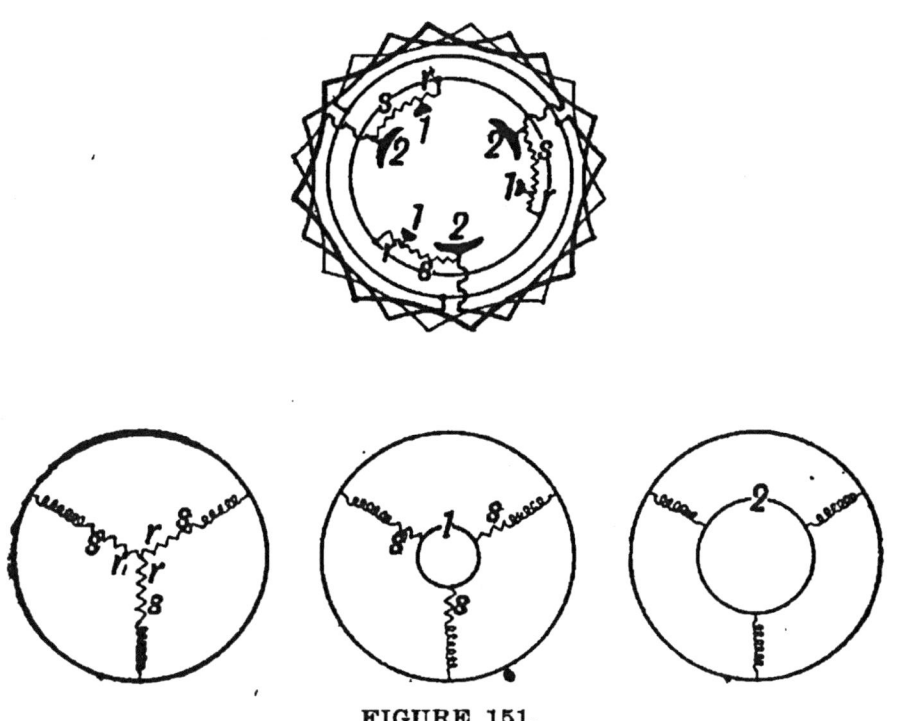

FIGURE 151.

shoes *1, 1, 1* are short-circuited, thus short-circuiting the resistances *r, r, r* as shown in the middle diagram. As the speed further increases the contact shoes *2, 2, 2* are short-circuited, this in turn short-circuiting the resistances *s, s, s*. The motor will now run with no resistance in the armature circuit as shown in the diagram at the right.

ALTERNATING CURRENT MOTORS 201

Figure 152 shows the connections for the Wagner single-phase alternating-current motor. On top of the motor are three binding posts. Posts 1 and 3 are connected to the terminals of the field winding,

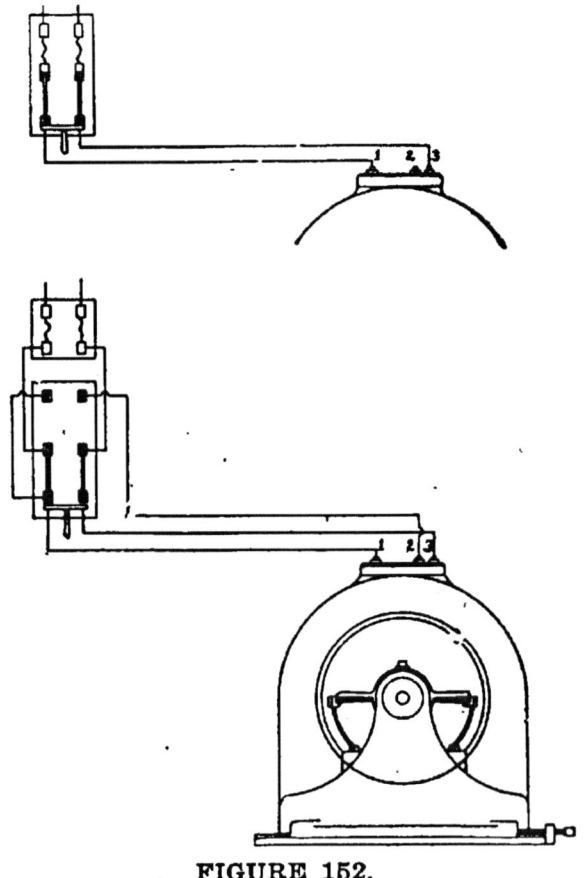

FIGURE 152.

while post 2 is connected to an intermediate point between 1 and 3. When the motor is called upon to start a heavy load, the double-throw switch shown in the lower diagram is used. With the switch thrown to the upper position connection is made to posts 1 and 2, when, on account of part of the field winding being cut out, a greater amount of current is sent through the fields and the torque increased. When the motor is up to speed the switch is thrown to the lower position, where current will be sent through the entire field winding.

The armature winding consists of a number of copper bars terminating in a commutator at one end. While running up to speed the armature is short-circuited through brushes which bear on the commutator and produce in the armature poles which, acting with the fields, cause the armature to revolve. On attaining full speed an automatic governor mounted on the shaft lifts the brushes off the commutator, and at the same time short-circuits all the commutator bars. The motor now runs as an induction motor. The upper connections are used where an ordinary load is to be started.

This motor is reversed by moving the brushes on the commutator. Note the markings on the brush holder. The starting torque can also be varied by shifting the brushes. It will be greater as the mark on the brush holder is moved farther from the center mark.

Single-phase motors, unlike the multiphase motors, will not start themselves from rest without the provision of some special means. A number of different methods are in use to make these motors self-starting. In the small fan motors made by the General Electric

ALTERNATING CURRENT MOTORS 203

Co. the ends of the pole pieces are slotted, and around one of the projecting ends is placed a band of copper (Figure 153). The effect of this band of copper is to cause two magnetic fields under each pole piece, one being slightly out of step with the other. This has an effect on the armature similar to a two-phase current, and causes it to revolve.

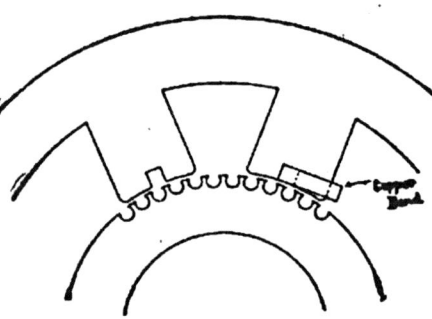

FIGURE 153.

Another method, known as the "split phase," is used for the same purpose. In some of the smaller motors made by the Holtzer-Cabot Co. the field is wound with two separate coils, one having a few turns of comparatively large wire and the other a great number of turns of fine wire. When current is turned on, owing to the difference in self-induction of the two coils, a field similar to the two-phase field is set up and the armature caused to revolve. When the motor has reached synchronism, the current to the high resistance coil is opened and the motor operated on the low resistance coil alone.

Other methods of bringing single-phase motors up to speed are described in Figures 154 and 152. Any small direct-current series motor can be used on alternating current providing the field magnets are laminated. The larger motors generally contain too much self-induction to be operated on alternating current.

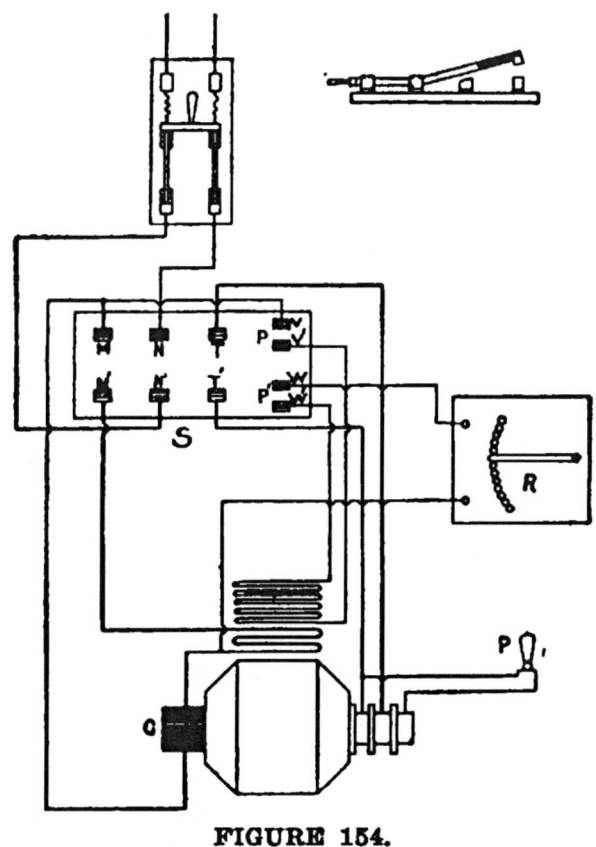

FIGURE 154.

Figure 154 shows the connections of the Fort Wayne alternating-current, single-phase motor. In order to start this motor and bring it up to speed, the armature is provided with an extra winding connected to the commutator C, shown at the left. When the motor is to be started, the switch S, which is hinged at N, N', is closed to the left. Current from the left-hand main will then pass through the contacts N', M', on the switch S to the series winding, and then to the commutator and armature and out through M, N, on switch, to other side of line. At each reversal of the current the magnetism in both fields and armature is reversed at the same time, thus causing a steady pull in one direction on the armature.

As the motor comes to speed the pilot lamp P will gradually light up, and when it has reached full candlepower the switch S is thrown to the right. Current from the left-hand main will now pass through contacts N', T', on switch, to the collector rings, through the armature, and out through points T, N, on switch to other side of line. At the same time the contacts V, V' and W, W' on switch S will be short-circuited (these points of the switch are not in electrical connection with the blades, being separated therefrom by an insulator, as shown in figure in upper right-hand corner), and the shunt field circuit closed through the commutator; the direct current from the commutator passing from the lower brush through the points V, V', on switch, to the shunt field and back to points W, W', and through the rheostat R to the upper brush on commutator. The motor will now run as a synchronous motor, the armature receiving current from the mains, while the field is energized by means of the direct current generated in the extra winding in connection with commutator C. When the motor is running with the switch to the right the series field is open.

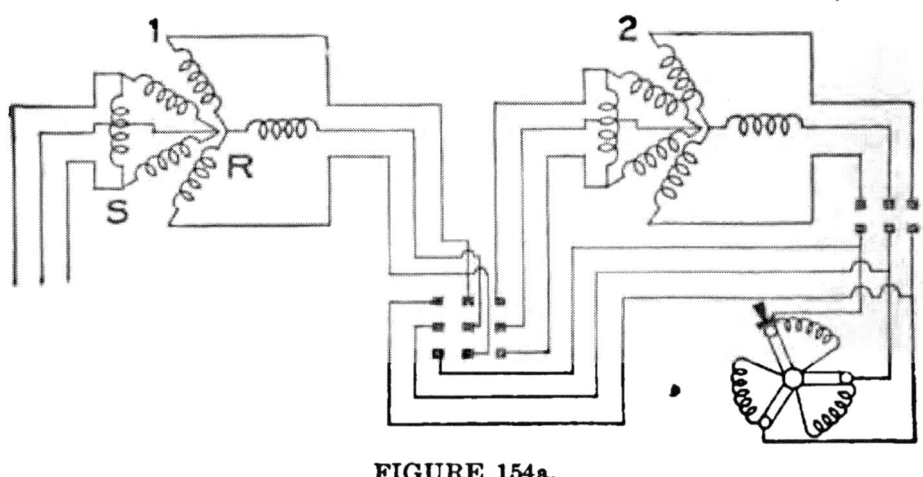

FIGURE 154a.

Figure 154a shows theoretical diagram of what is termed the cascade or tandem method of coupling induction motors for variable speeds. The rotors of the two motors are mounted on the same shaft or in other manner mechanically coupled together. The main current from the generator feeds stator S of 1. The currents induced in the rotor R of 1 traverse the stator of 2 and the controlling resistance is cut into the rotor circuit of 2 as shown.

The number of poles on two such machines may be so arranged that different changes in speed are possible. It is also possible to arrange switches so that the motors may be operated in parallel or No. 1 alone as shown.

Figure 154b shows method of operating rolling mills or other devices that require a large amount of power for a very short time. The large induction motor I

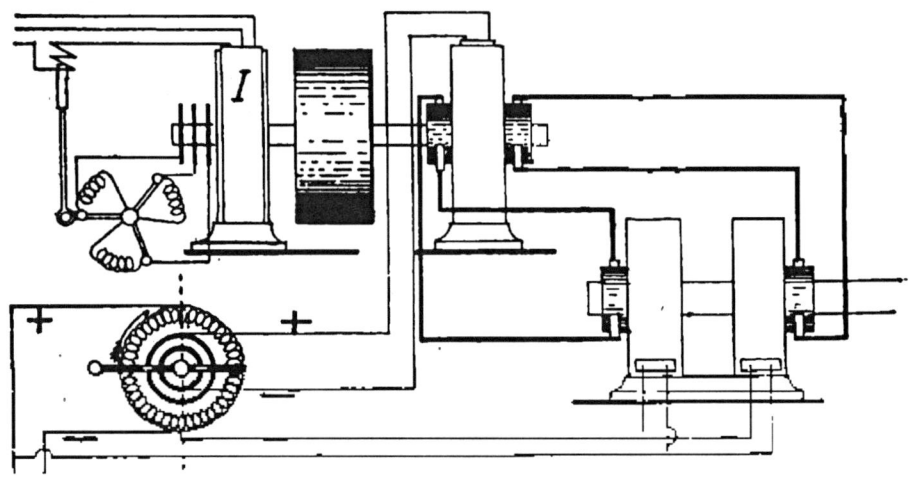

FIGURE 154b.

is supplied by a limited amount of current from the mains. The amount of current that may be drawn from the mains is governed by an automatically controlled resistance placed in the rotor circuit. Whenever the main current rises above a predetermined value the core of the solenoid is drawn up and resistance is cut into the rotor circuit, thus keeping the main current in bounds.

On the same shaft with the induction motor is a heavy balance wheel operating at a high speed and also the armature of a direct current generator. This generator carries a double wound armature which feeds two motors connected to the shaft of the rolling mill.

The only method of reversing and controlling the speed of the motors consists in changing the field strength of the generator. The fields of the generator are separately excited and controlled by resistances arranged similar to those of the well known Wheatstone bridge. With the arm in the position shown no current is passing through the fields. If the arm is moved in the direction of the arrow the polarity of the fields will be as indicated, and when the arm assumes the position indicated by broken line the current strength will be at its maximum. If it is moved in the opposite direction the current in the generator fields will be reversed.

The motors are also independently excited and the direction in which they move depends upon the direction of the armature current, which in turn is governed by the current through the fields. With this arrangement it is possible to draw 4000 or 5000 H. P. for a short time without overloading the 1000 H. P. induction motor.

Very small alternating current motors are usually connected to the line direct, and only a switch suited to the system is used. This switch does not even require to break all of the wires of the system.

As the starting current of most alternating current motors is, however, much greater than the running current (especially if the motor start under load) it is

TRANSFORMERS

advisable to place the motor under the protection of two sets of fuses. One such set of fuses is placed where the branch circuit is tapped off the mains, and the other at the motor switch.

The manner of connecting a throwover switch to two and three phase motors so as to accomplish the desired result is shown in Figures 154c and 154d.

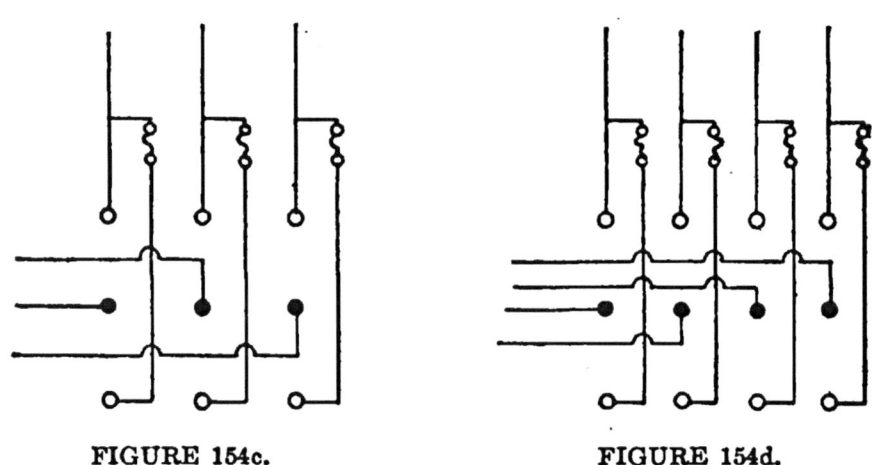

FIGURE 154c.   FIGURE 154d.

The black circles represent the centers of the switch. Thrown upward the motor feeds direct from the mains which are fused to the starting current of the motor. After the motor has acquired its proper speed the switch is thrown downward and the motor feeds through the smaller fuses shown.

In order to guard against leaving the motor without the proper fuse protection such switches are sometimes equipped with springs which will not allow the switch to remain on the upper contacts.

210 WIRING DIAGRAMS

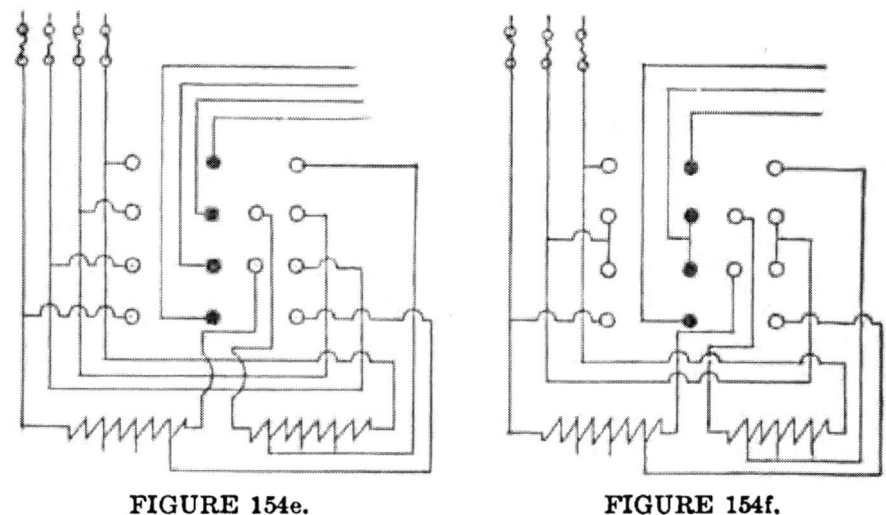

FIGURE 154e. FIGURE 154f.

Throwover switches for the starting of motors in connection with auto transformers or compensators are shown in Figures 154e and 154f.

To start, the switch is thrown to the right; this forces the current to pass through the transformers and reduces the voltage at the motor. After the motor has attained some speed the switch is thrown to the

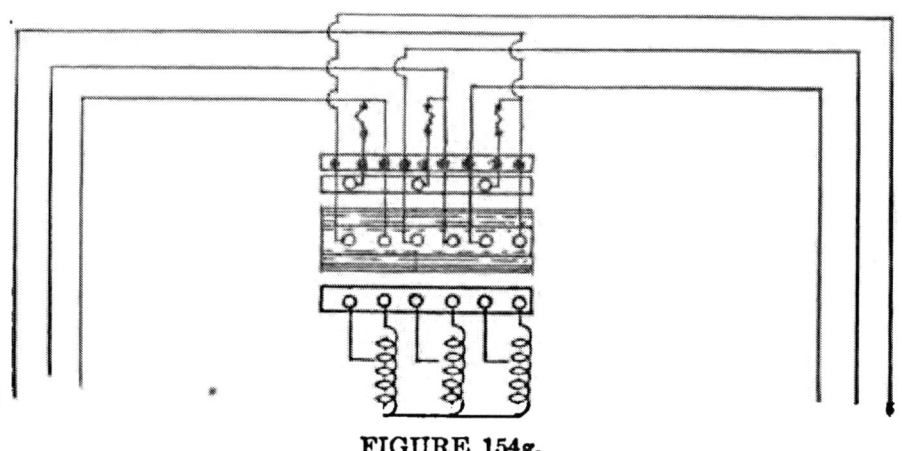

FIGURE 154g.

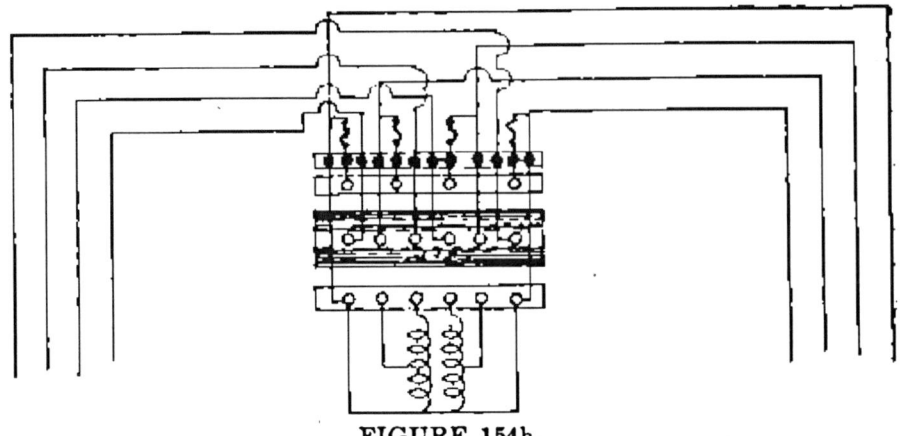

FIGURE 154h.

left and connects the motor to the mains. The starting torque of the motor may be increased by connecting the taps leading from the transformers so as to leave less of their reactance in the circuit.

The connections of General Electric controllers for three phase; two phase four wire and two phase three wire are shown respectively in Figures 154g, 154h, and 154i. The contact points on the drums in the center make connections either to the upper or lower

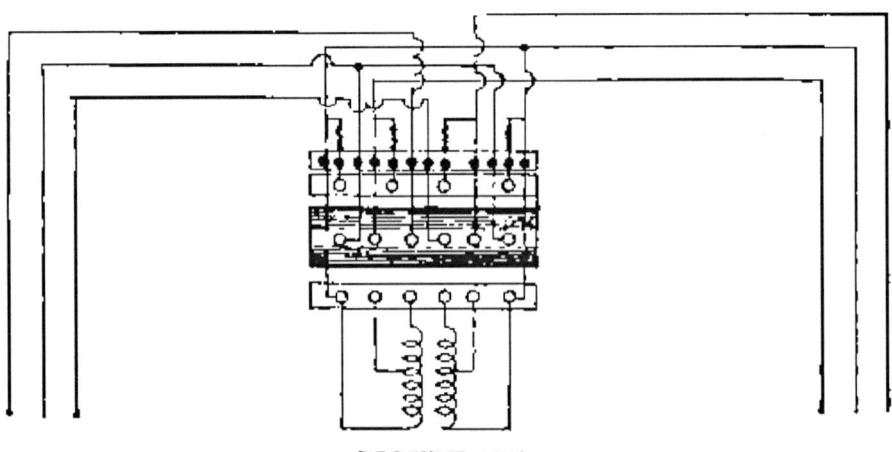

FIGURE 154i.

connections shown. The motor leads are connected to the drum. Thrown downward the current must pass through the auto transformers which reduces the voltage. Thrown upward the motor is connected direct to the mains.

Figure 154j shows diagram of a three phase auto

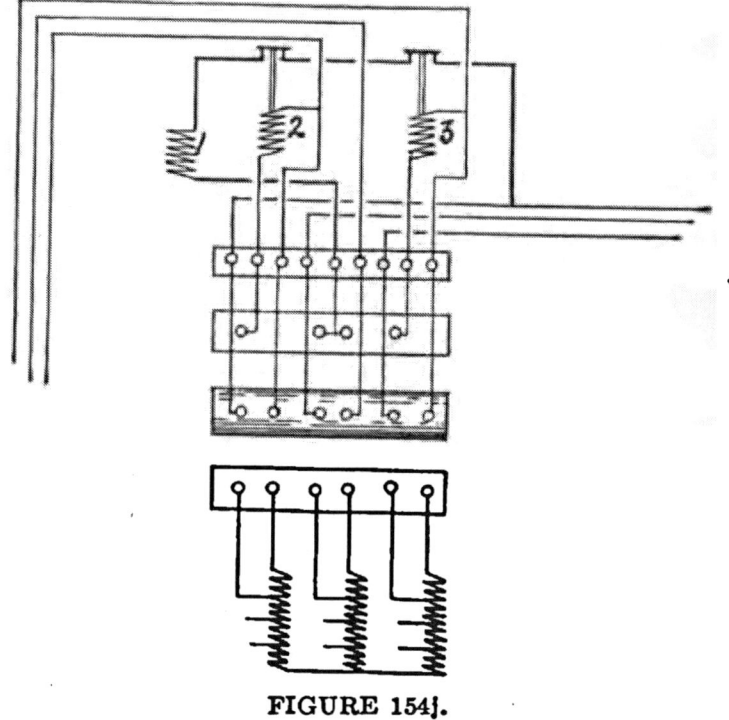

FIGURE 154J.

starter with over and under load release as made by the General Electric Co. In order that the starter may remain in circuit there must be current in coil 1. Consequently when the voltage fails the starter opens the circuit. In case the motor is taking too much current one of the coils 2 or 3 opens the circuit through 1, and trips the starter thus opening the circuit.

TRANSFORMERS

A similar arrangement is shown in Figure 154k, but is designed for high voltages and a voltage transformer is provided as shown.

With large motors the wiring is arranged as in Figure 154l.

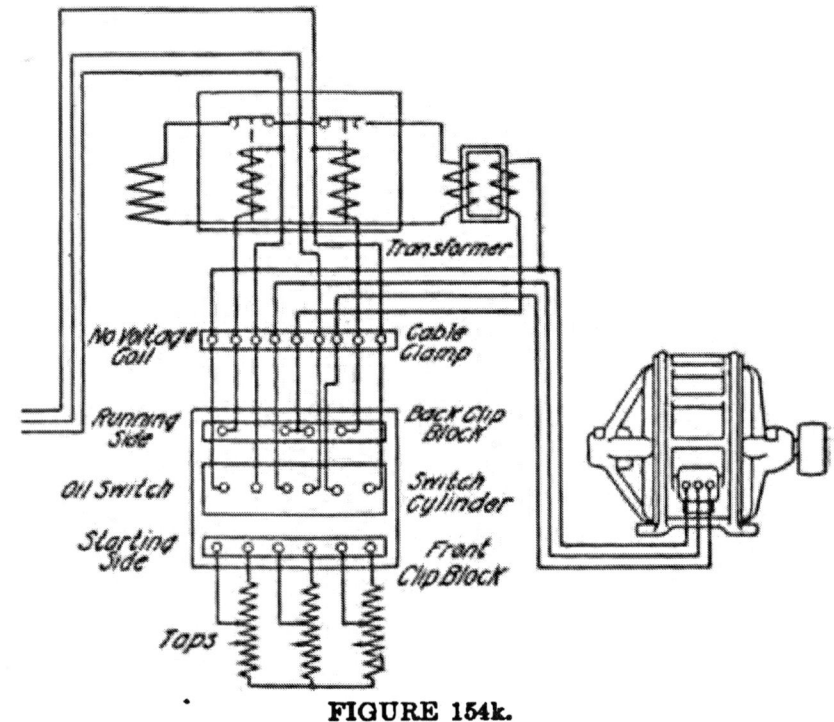

FIGURE 154k.

For motors that start under light load and require finer gradations in speed a controller as diagramatically shown in Figure 154m is often used. The compensator coils are inserted in two phases only; this results in unbalancing of the line but as long as the load is light this is not very objectionable.

The speed of a three phase motor is considerably higher when its stator is connected in "mesh" or

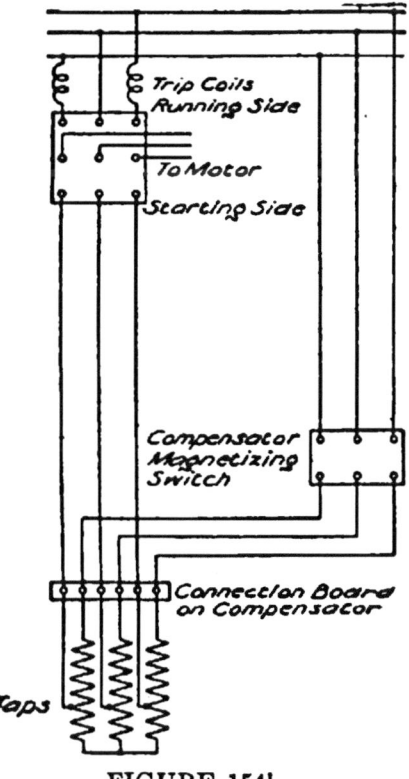

FIGURE 154l.

"delta" than when connected in Y or star. In Figure 154n the throwover switch at the left is provided to change the winding from one to the other when required. Thrown to the left the motor windings become star; thrown to the right they are delta. Motors must not be changed from star to delta unless it is known they are capable of running that way.

A method of obtaining reduced voltage for the starting of three phase motors direct from transformers is given in Figure 154n. Thrown one way the motor obtains the full voltage of the line, and thrown the other way only about one half.

TRANSFORMERS

215

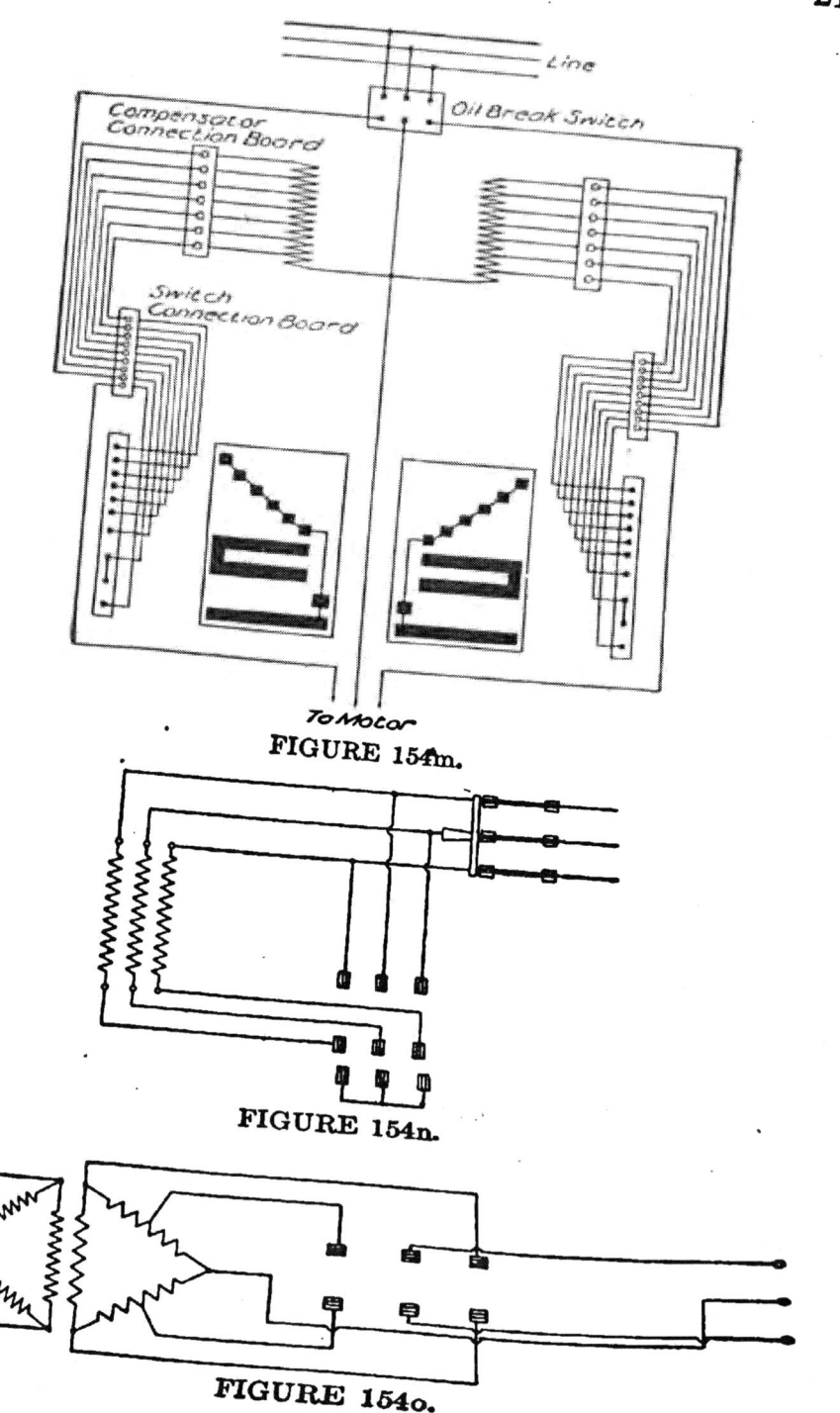

FIGURE 154m.

FIGURE 154n.

FIGURE 154o.

Two and three phase motors are often equipped with wound armatures or rotors. In such cases the starting can be controlled by resistances placed in the rotor circuit about in the same way that it is placed in the armature circuit of direct current motors. Such resistances are also made variable and are illustrated in Figure 154p for three phase and Figure 154q for two phase.

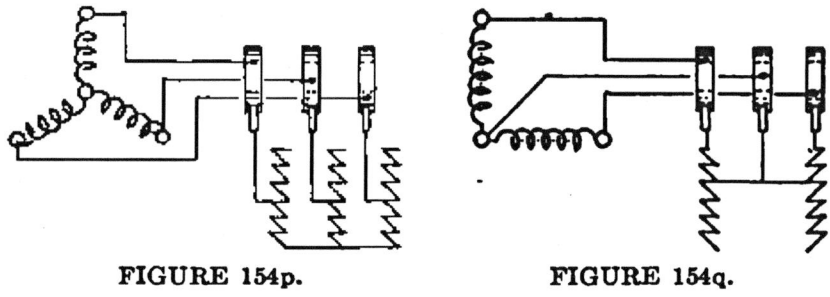

FIGURE 154p.   FIGURE 154q.

The rotor of an induction motor acts like the secondary winding of a transformer, but as the rotor comes up to its proper speed the currents in it are much reduced.

Small and medium size motors are sometimes connected to three phase systems as shown in Figure 154r. This is known as the open delta method. Only two transformers are required whereas to get the full three phase connection three would be necessary.

Figure 154s shows the diagram of an automatic controller for three phase motor as made by Cutler Hammer Co. The controller is operated by a single pole switch placed as at P, or, if the circuit be permanently closed at this point, closing of the main switch

TRANSFORMERS

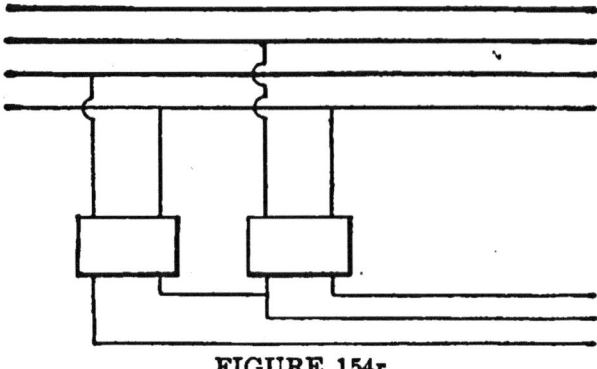

FIGURE 154r.

will automatically start the motor. 1, 2, 3 and 4 are solenoids which when energized draw up their cores and close the circuits indicated underneath.

Solenoid 1 simply closes the phase wires A and B and thereby gives current to the stator windings of the motor M. 2, 3, and 4 when energized short circuit certain parts of the resistance R which is inserted in the rotor circuit. The three small solenoids 5 must be conceived as attached to the extremity of R at 5'; 6 is attached to 6' and 7 and 8 at corresponding points of R, but only when the solenoids shown above them act. The solenoids are supposed to act in quick succession in the order 1, 2, 3, 4; 4 when it acts finally short circuits the rotor at 8' cutting all of R out.

The operation is as follows: By closing the pilot switch P circuit is established from phase wire A through solenoid 1 line C point D pilot switch and phase wire B. There is also a parallel circuit through X. Thus energizing 1 causes its core to be drawn up; this closes the stator circuit of the motor and also the fine wire circuit at E. Current in the stator at once induces currents in the rotor and these draw up the cores of 5 opening the circuit underneath until the rotor has attained some speed. As the rotor attains speed the currents in it grow weaker and the cores of 5 drop back closing the circuit underneath again.

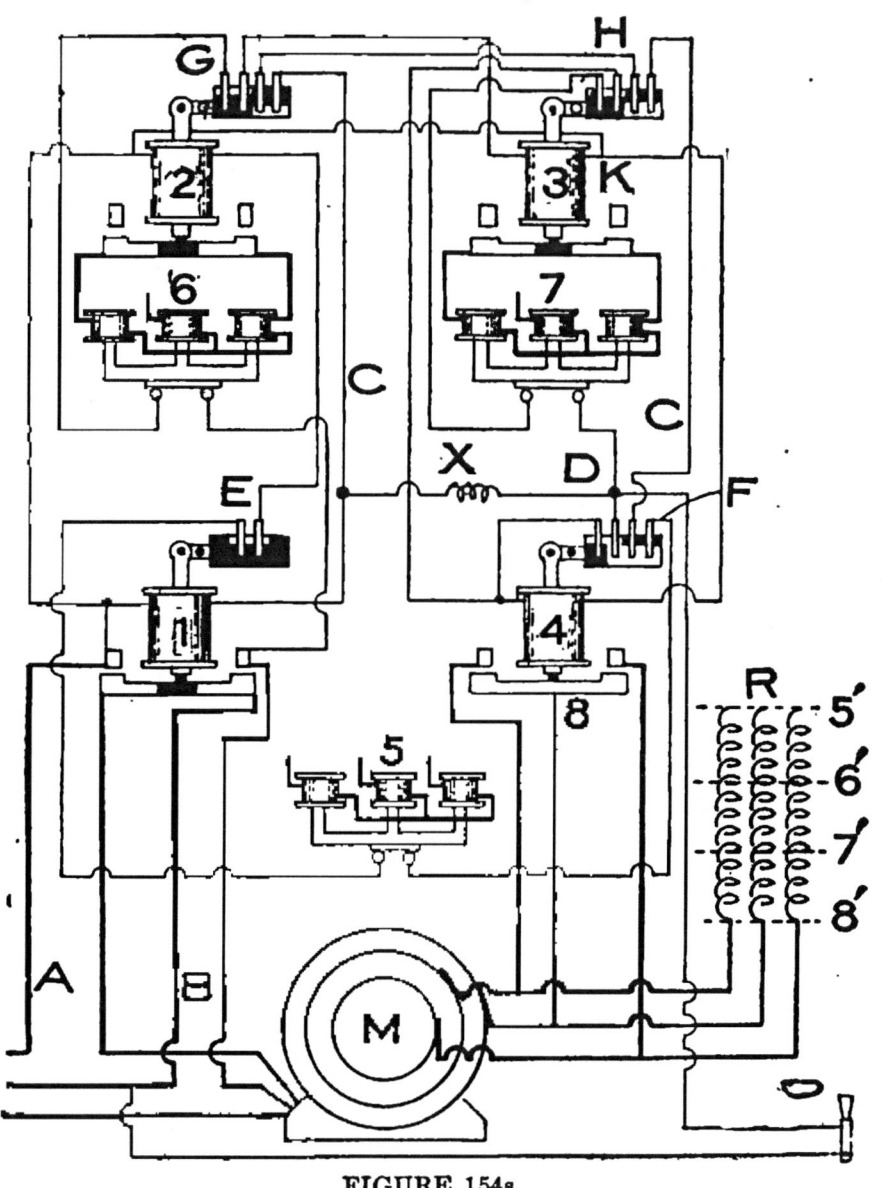

FIGURE 154s.

As the circuit is now closed at E and underneath 5, current passes from phase A through solenoid 2 to E point D and thence to pilot switch and phase B. This causes 2 to draw up its core and the rotor resistance becomes short circuited at 6'. The small solenoids act as those at 5 momentarily opening the circuit and then closing it again. Drawing up the core of 2 closes the circuit at the left of G and opens that at the right. Current now passes from the left of 2 to the right of solenoid 3 thence to G and phase wire B at 1. Line C is now open and current passes from 1 through X to the pilot switch. This reduces the current leaving only as much as is necessary to maintain the core of 1 against gravity.

Solenoid 3 now acts closing the circuit at the left of H and under 7. This sends current from point K through solenoid 4 to the left half of H point D and pilot switch.

When solenoid 4 acts it short circuits all of the resistance of the rotor and develops the full power of the motor. In its action it also closes the circuit of F at the left and opens it at the right. Closing the circuit F at the left establishes a circuit for 4 to point D, and at the same time opening of F at the right breaks the circuit of 2, and this core descending breaks the circuit of 3 at the left of G. Two circuits now remain closed, one through solenoid 1 resistance X to point D, the other around 2 and 3 to 4 left side of F and point D thence to pilot switch and phase B.

By tracing out the various circuits it can be seen that the arrangement is such that solenoid 2 cannot act unless 3 and 4 are in the off position and that 3 cannot work unless 2 has acted and 4 must in turn wait on 3. The motor can therefore not be started unless all of the resistance is inserted in the rotor circuit.

In Figure 154t a motor testing board suitable for use with two or three phase currents is shown. The

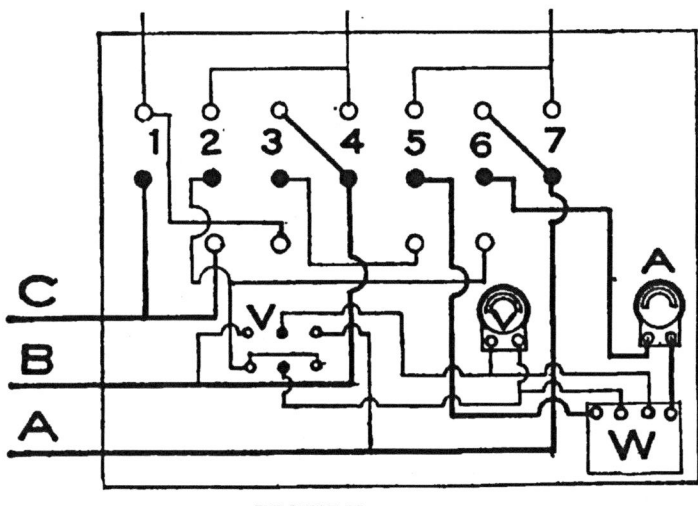

FIGURE 154t.

current in each phase may be measured and thus the degree of unbalancing of the circuit on individual motors determined. In practice it is found that very many motors are considerably out of balance electrically.

The ammeter A is shown in connection with the wattmeter so that the power factor of the motor may be determined. The power factor is found by dividing

TRANSFORMERS

the indicated watts of the wattmeter by the product of the volts and amperes existing at the same time. The power factor is always less than unity.

The switches indicated are all single pole with exception of the voltmeter switch V. If 1, 4 and 7 are thrown upward the motor feeds direct from the line A B C.

To test A for current throw 5 and 6 up and open 7; to get voltage A C throw V to right and 2 down.

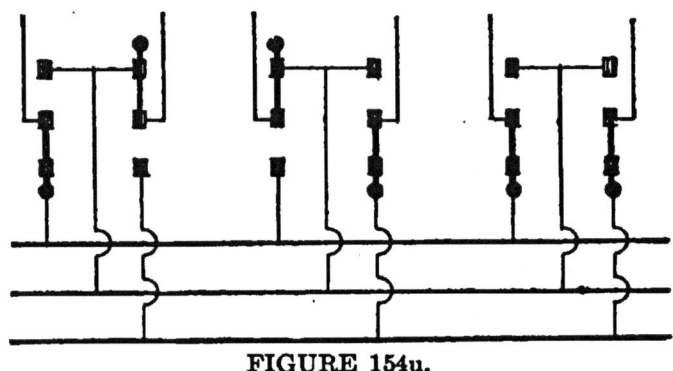

FIGURE 154u.

To test B for current throw 3 up, 5 and 6 down, and 2 up, and open 4; to get voltage A B throw V to right.

To test C for current throw 2, 6, 5, and 3 down and open 1. to get voltage C B throw V to the left.

There is often considerable trouble on three phase circuits from an unbalanced load. For the best service the current in all three wires should be the same. A simple method by which any one of the branch circuits may be transferred to any one of the phases is illustrated in Figure 154u. As shown each branch circuit is connected to a different phase.

In Figure 154v the connections of the Westinghouse frequency meter are shown. The frequency meter is simply a voltmeter with two opposing coils acting upon the pointer. Placed in the circuit this way there would be no indications.

In order to make it indicate different frequencies an inductive resistance is placed in circuit with one of the

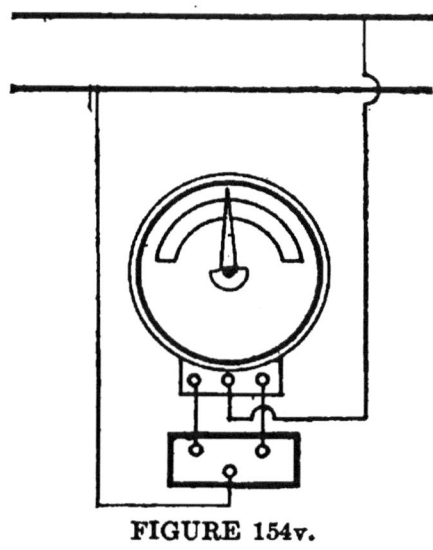

FIGURE 154v.

coils and a non inductive resistance with the other. These resistances are placed in a separate case and mounted near the instrument to which they must be connected as shown. The frequency meter in any given case is of course simply a speed indicator since the frequency of the dynamos depends upon the speed with which they revolve.

The connections of the Westinghouse portable powerfactor meter are shown for three phase circuit in Figure 154w and for two phase in Figure 154x.

TRANSFORMERS

The two phase meter has two and the three phase meter three coils which form the fields. In addition there is another coil the currents of which are in phase with the voltage. A rotating field is produced by the main coils, and this field controls the position of the pointer attached to the movable coil. The connections

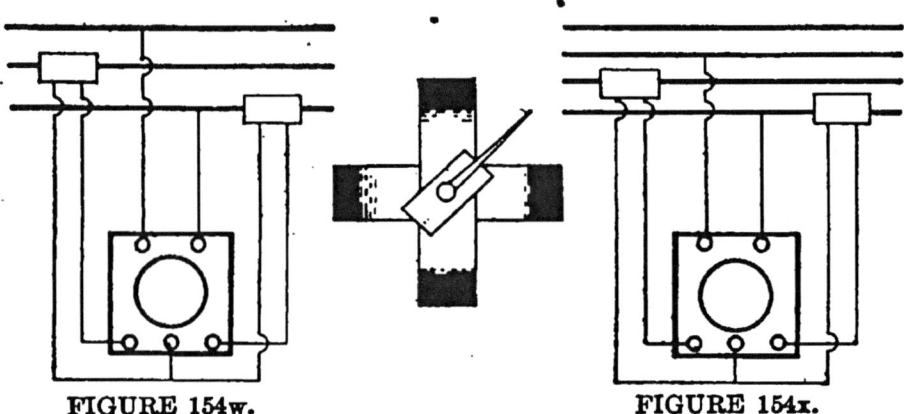

FIGURE 154w.   FIGURE 154x.

to the movable coil are shown at the top and the arrangement for two phase is shown in center.

The following instructions are quoted from publications of the Westinghouse Company: "When the top binding posts are disconnected and there is current of at least one half full load in the series transformers, the pointer should rotate in the 'lead' direction. If it rotates in the 'lag' direction reverse the leads running to the lower left hand binding posts. On a two phase circuit the reversal should be made at the series transformer shown at the left of the diagram. On a three phase circuit the leads should be reversed at the meter by connecting the common wire from the two series transformers to the left hand binding post, and the single wire from the series transformer on the left to the middle post. Then connect the shunt circuit to the upper binding posts as shown. This shunt connection should be made to the phase which is connected through the series transformer to the right hand side of the meter. Should it be necessary to reverse the series connection of the meter on three phase circuits from that shown on the diagram in order to obtain proper rotation, the shunt wire which is shown connected to the wire of the circuit having no series transformer should be changed to the wire which is connected through the series transformer to the left hand side of the meter. The upper half of the scale indicates for power delivered from alternating-current lines to the motor or rotary, and the lower half, power returned to the lines. Should the pointer indicate the reverse of that given above, the connections at the upper binding posts should be reversed.

"Move the scale by means of the projecting studs at the sides of the dial, until the 'frequency index' at the lower right hand portion of the scale points to the line marked with the number of alternations of the circuit on which the instrument is being used. The instrument will now indicate the power factor of the circuit."

Figure 154y shows the ordinary connections of Westinghouse synchroscopes for voltages between 1 and 200.

TRANSFORMERS 225

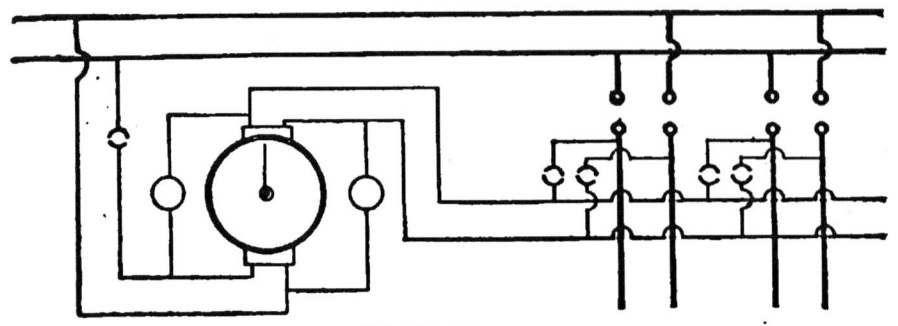

FIGURE 154y.

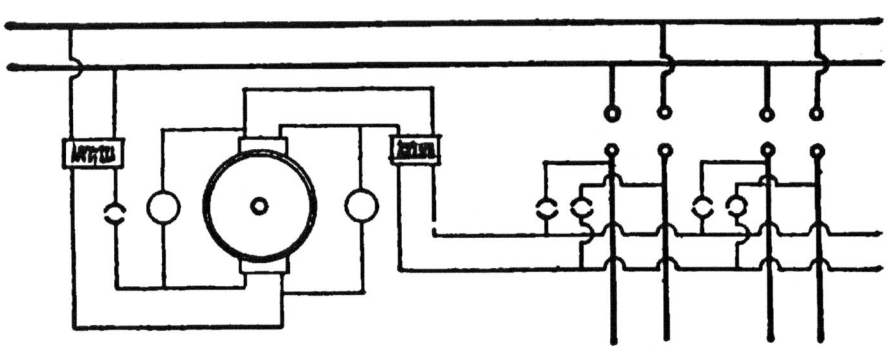

FIGURE 154z.

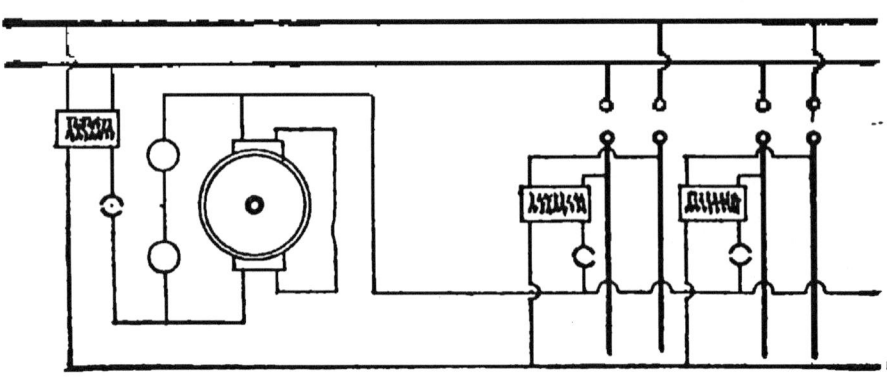

FIGURE 154'.

The connections for voltages from 200 to 500 are given in Figure 154z and those for voltages in excess of 500 in Figure 154'.

TRANSFORMERS.

Figure 155 shows the circuits in a single-phase transformer.

Figure 156 shows the circuits in a single-phase transformer with a three-wire secondary. This transformer has the advantages derived from the use

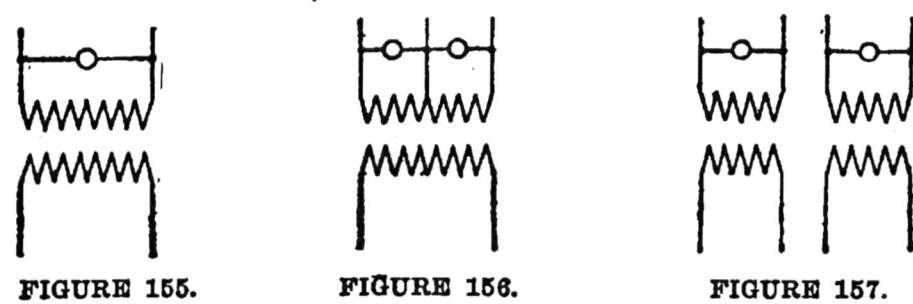

FIGURE 155.   FIGURE 156.   FIGURE 157.

of three-wire distributing circuits, and is used where a large installation is to be connected, or where one large transformer feeds a set of secondary mains supplying a number of residences.

Figure 157 shows the connections of a two-phase transformer with two separate secondaries; and Figure 158 the two-phase transformer with a common return wire for the secondaries.

TRANSFORMERS 227

Figure 159 shows a three-phase delta connection, and Figure 160 a three-phase star connection.

Figures 161 to 167 show the connections used on the Packard Mark VI. transformers. The primary windings of these transformers are made in two sec-

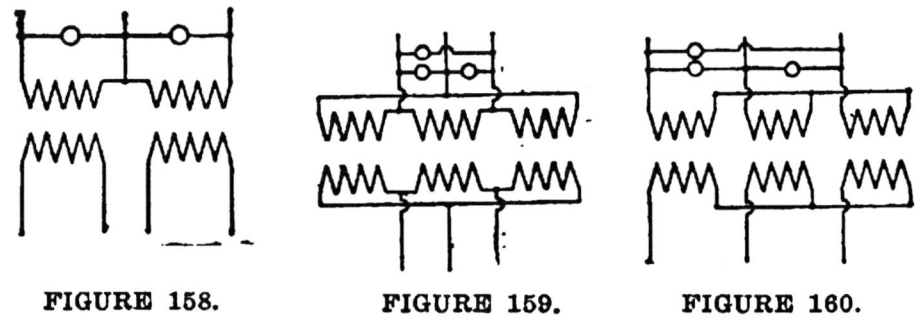

FIGURE 158.   FIGURE 159.   FIGURE 160.

tions, with leads brought out so that they may be connected either in series or parallel. When used on 2000 volt systems the two sections are connected in

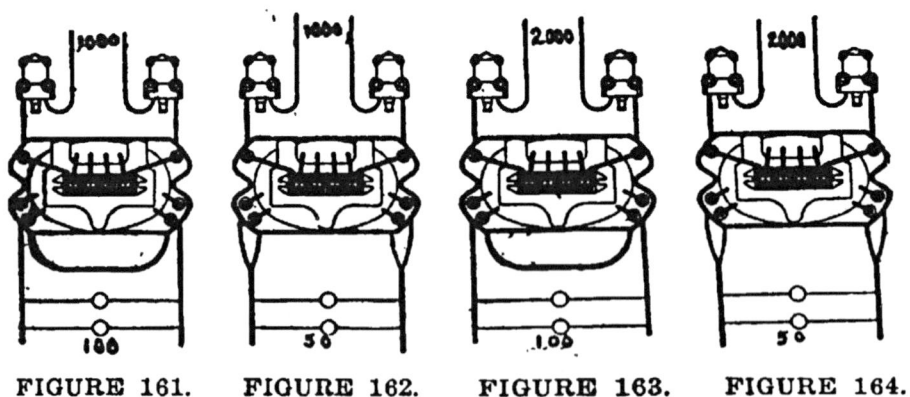

FIGURE 161.   FIGURE 162.   FIGURE 163.   FIGURE 164.

series, and when used on 1000 volt systems the two sections are connected in parallel. These connections are shown in the diagrams, where, in Figures 161 to

164, terminal blocks are used, and in Figures 165 and 168 the primaries are connected in the same way as the secondaries. The secondaries of these transformers are also wound in two sections, the same as the primaries, so that either 50 or 100 volts or 100 or 200 volts may be obtained, according to the type of the transformer used. In Figures 161, 162, 165, 166, the primary windings are connected in multiple; while in Figures 163, 164, 167, 168, the primary

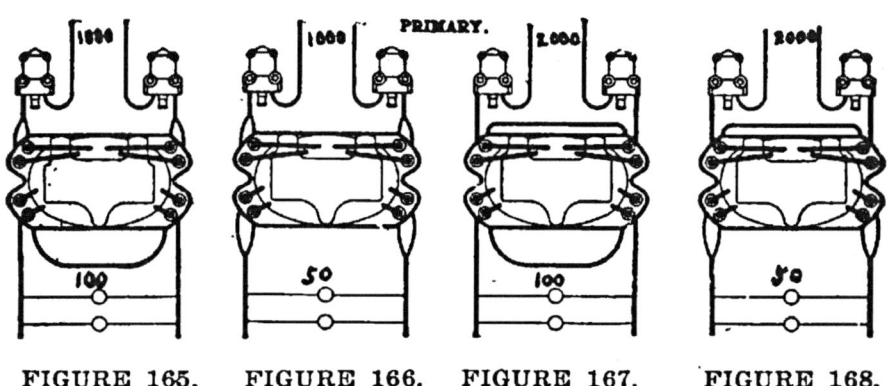

FIGURE 165.   FIGURE 166.   FIGURE 167.   FIGURE 168.

windings are connected in series. The two secondary windings are connected in series in Figures 161, 163, 165, 167, and in multiple in Figures, 162, 164, 166, 168.

When a current of electricity is sent through a wire lines of force are sent out completely encircling the wire. As long as the current in the wire remains constant these lines of force remain constant, but, if the current increases the lines of force increase, or

TRANSFORMERS

if the current decreases the lines of force decrease. If the wire is wound into a coil as the current in the wire increases the lines of force sent out from each wire of the coil will have to cut through all the other wires on the coil and in so doing they induce a counter-electromotive force which is in opposition to the impressed electromotive force. It can readily be seen that this counter-electromotive force tends to hold back the rise in current or make it lag behind the E. M. F. In the same way, when the current in

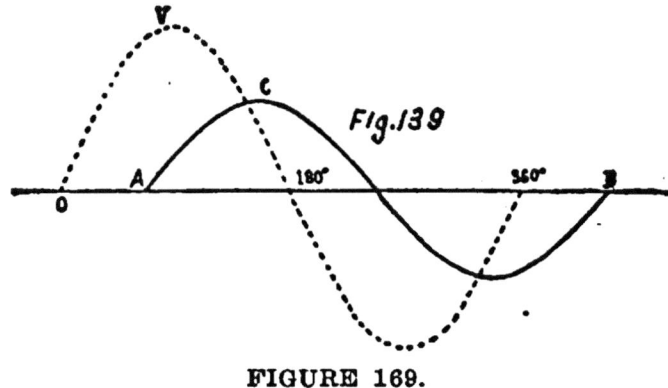

FIGURE 169.

the coil decreases in strength the lines of force closing in on the wire add their E. M. F. to that of the impressed E. M. F. and tend to prolong the current, again causing the change in the current to follow or lag behind the E. M. F. This is shown by the curve (Figure 169), where C represents the current and V the E. M. F. This action is called self-induction. Self-induction in a circuit acts in the same way as resistance: it tends to cut down the current. For an illustration: suppose the resistance of the wire in the coil just referred to was 5 ohms. A direct current of 110 volts would cause a current of 110/5=22 amperes to flow through the coil. But if we were to send an alternating current at 110 volts through the coil we would find that the resulting current would be much less than 22 amperes and if we inserted an iron core in the coil the current would be still farther reduced, because the resistance of iron to the lines of force is much less than with air so that the lines of force would be increased in number. The frequency of the current, or the rapidity of the alternations also effects the amount of current produced, the current being smaller the greater the number of alternations.

A condenser connected in a circuit acts in a way similar to an inductance except that the condenser causes the current to lead the E. M. F. in phase. When an alternating current flows along a circuit across which a condenser is connected, as the E. M. F. in the line rises the condenser is gradually charged, the charge increasing in value as long as the current is rising. As the E. M. F. in the line begins to fall the E. M. F. across the condenser terminals lowers and the condenser begins to discharge into the line continuing to discharge until the impressed E. M. F. has passed through 0 and reached a maximum negative value. At this point the current again begins to flow into the condenser. It will be seen that while the E. M. F. in the line is passing from a maximum positive value to a maximum negative value that the condenser current is negative or flowing out of the condenser and while the E. M. F. in the line passes from a maximum negative value to a maximum positive value the current in the condenser is positive. The condenser current reaches a maximum 90 degrees in advance of the E. M. F. and for this reason is known as a leading current.

In a circuit containing inductance or capacity, where the current is out of phase with the E. M. F. the current may be resolved into two currents, one of which is in phase with the E. M. F. and the other 90 degrees out of phase with the E. M. F. This latter current is known as a wattless current and is greater, the greater the inductance or capacity in the circuit.

If in a circuit containing inductance or capacity where the current is out of phase with the E. M. F., we would measure the power in watts, using a voltmeter and ammeter, W = C. E., we would get an apparent amount of power which would be greatly in excess of that actually consumed. The number of watts actually consumed could be measured by a wattmeter. The ratio of the number of watts actually consumed to the apparent watts is known as the power factor, or Power factor=Actual watts divided by apparent watts. As an example: suppose the voltmeter and ammeter showed 115 volts and 10 amperes which would be equal to 1150 watts and the wattmeter shows 920 watts. Then 920/1150=80/100 or .80 which is the power factor. The actual current doing work would amount to 8 amperes but as shown by the ammeter 10 amperes is flowing and the wire and fuses on such a circuit would have to be of sufficient size to carry 10 amperes.

CHAPTER XVI.

ARMATURES.

Figure 170 is a diagram of a Gramme ring armature. This style is often used with series arc lighting machines. It is well suited for high voltages but not for heavy currents.

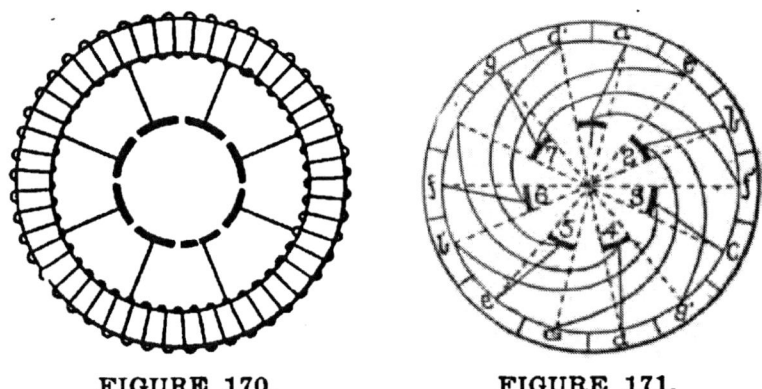

FIGURE 170.   FIGURE 171.

The winding shown in Figure 171 is that of an ordinary cylinder or drum armature. The wire wound on this armature as well as that of the preceding always forms one continuous coil or loop. This can be seen by tracing the wire beginning at commutator bar 1, thence to section a, around back of core to a' and then to commutator bar 2. From this bar to b, then to b' and commutator bar 3, etc. This is one of the simplest windings used, but many makers are using modifications of it; the principle of all, however, being the same.

Figure 172 shows a diagram of Thomson-Houston ring armature used for series arc lighting. This armature consists of three sections which terminate at three commutator segments from which current is taken off. The other terminals of all three sections terminate in a copper ring which joins all of them together.

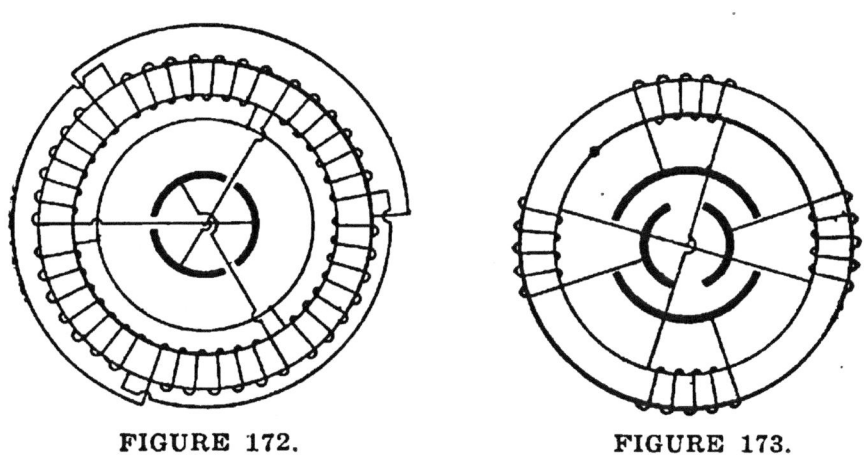

FIGURE 172.   FIGURE 173.

A diagram of the Brush armature, also for series arc lighting, is shown in Figure 173. The figure shows only two sets of coils, although in actual practice many more are used. In this style of armature some of the coils are always on open circuit and it will be seen that there is no connection whatever between the different coils except through the commutator segments and the brushes resting upon them.

Figure 174 illustrates the winding of an armature such as is used in single-phase alternating current

ARMATURES

machines. The number of coils on the armature must always be equal to the number of poles in the fields. With dynamos of this kind quite often the fields are made to revolve and the current to the outside lines flows from the stationary coils on the frame.

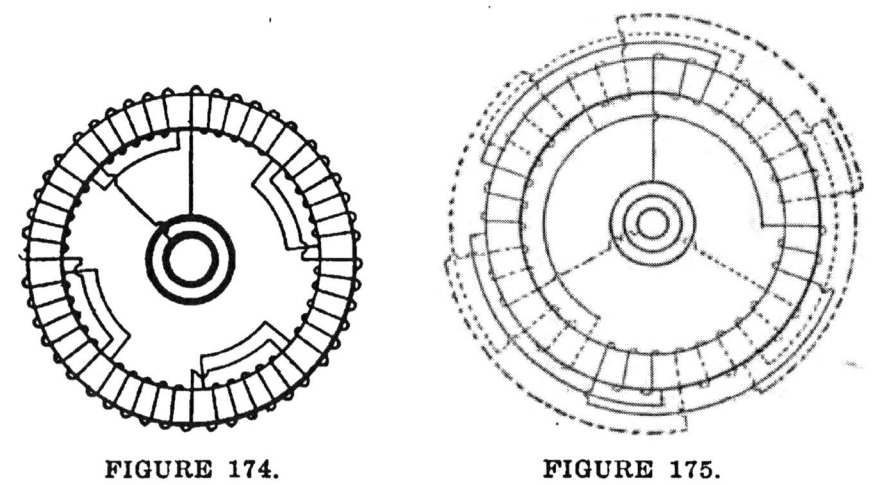

FIGURE 174.   FIGURE 175.

In Figure 175 a diagram of a three-phase, four-pole, star connected armature is shown. The winding for each separate phase is similar to that of the single-phase armature. One end of each coil terminates in a collector ring; the other ends of all the coils meeting in one common connection. It will be noticed that there are three coils (one for each phase) for every pole piece, making twelve coils in all.

CHAPTER XVII.

SWITCHBOARDS—GROUND DETECTORS.

Figure 176 shows the wiring and connections of the Western Electric Co.'s series arc switchboard. At the top of the board are mounted six ammeters, one being connected in the circuit of each machine. On

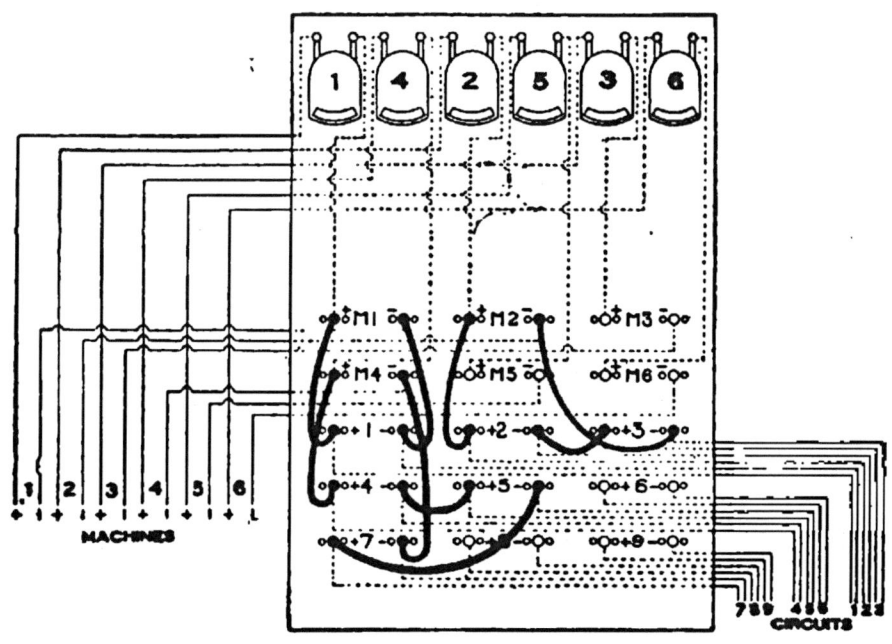

FIGURE 176.

the lower part of the board are a number of holes, under which, on the back of the board, are mounted spring jacks to which the circuit and machine terminals are connected. For making connections be-

236

tween dynamos and circuits, flexible cables terminating at each end in a plug, are used; these are commonly called "jumpers." The board shown has a capacity of six machines and nine circuits, and with the connections as shown machine 1 is furnishing current to circuit 1, machine 2 is furnishing current to circuits 2 and 3, and machine 4 is furnishing current to circuits 4, 5 and 7. In connecting together arc dynamos and circuits the positive of the machine (or that terminal from which the current is flowing) is connected to the positive of the circuit (the terminal into which the current is flowing). Likewise the negative of the machine is connected to the negative of the circuit. Where more than one circuit is to be operated from one dynamo, the — of the first circuit is connected to the + of the second. At each side of the name plate (at 3, for instance) there are three holes. The large hole is used for the permanent connection, while the smaller holes are used for transferring circuits, without shutting down the dynamo. Smaller cables and plugs are used for transferring. If it is desired to cut off circuit 5 from machine 4, a plug is inserted in one of the small holes at the right of 4, the other plug being inserted in one of the holes at the left of 7. Circuit 5 would now be short circuited, and the plug in the + of 5 can now be transferred to the permanent connection in the + of 7, and the cords running to 5 removed. If it is desired to cut in a circuit, say circuit 6 onto machine 2, insert a cord between the — of circuit 2 and the + of 6 and another between the — of 6 and the + of 3. Now pull the plug on the cord connecting — of 2 and the + of 3 and insert the permanent connections. In cutting in circuits, if they contain a great number of lights, a long arc may be drawn when the plug between 2 and 3 is pulled, and it is sometimes advisable to shut down the machine when making a change of this kind.

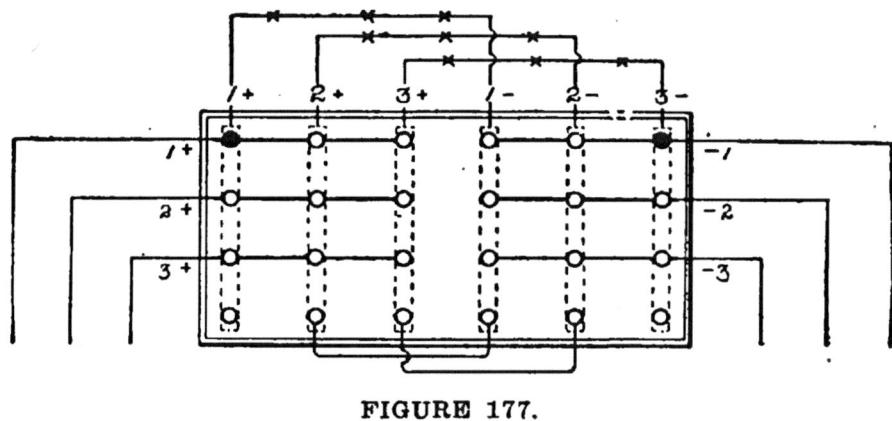

FIGURE 177.

Figure 177 is a diagram of the Thomson-Houston arc switchboard. The generators connect to horizontal brass strips fastened to the back of the board, as indicated by the heavy black lines. The circuits connect to similar strips fastened vertically to back of board but separated from the horizontal strips. These vertical strips extend below the horizontal strips and terminate in a number of plug holes shown at the bottom. Long plugs are provided suitably constructed to make connection between any of the horizontal generator strips and any of the vertical circuit strips. The lines at the bottom indicate plugs connected by short cables and by tracing out the circuits it will be seen that all three are in series with generator 1. The positive sides of all dynamos are usually run to one side of the board and the positive sides of all circuits to the same side, so that only through gross carelessness could wrong plugging, as to polarity, exist.

A, B, C, D and E, Figure 178, illustrate the successive steps necessary to change circuits 1 and 2 from dynamo 1 and 2 and connect them in series on dynamo 2. The solid black circles represent plugs.

The first step is shown in B where the positive poles of both dynamos are placed in parallel by inserting the two additional plugs.

The second step is to withdraw the two first plugs shown in A. This places the two dynamos in series, D1 connecting direct to circuit 2, as shown at C.

The voltage of dynamo D1 may now be reduced and two plugs with cable connections inserted, as shown at D. This short-circuits dynamo D1 and leaves D2 carrying the load of both circuits.

The plugs connecting D1 to the circuit may now be withdrawn, leaving the connections as at E, where dynamo D2 supplies both circuits.

In F two circuits are shown as running in series on dynamo D1 and the insertion of plug H serves to

240 WIRING DIAGRAMS

short-circuit and extinguish circuit 2. The plugs I, J and K may now be withdrawn.

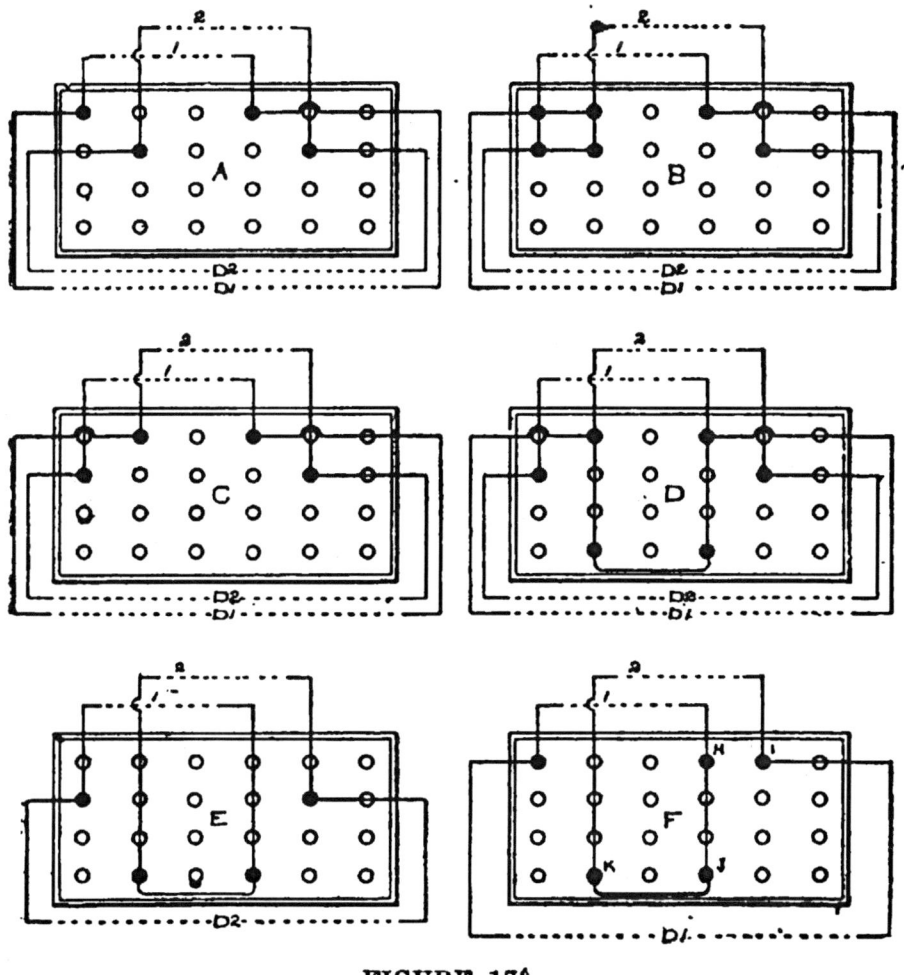

FIGURE 178.

In Figure 179 the switchboard connections and all necessary instruments for operating a single (shunt or compound) dynamo are shown. Such a board could be used on a small isolated plant. At the left a front view with the instruments is shown, while at

SWITCHBOARDS

the right is a rear view showing the connections. Referring to the view at the left, V is a voltmeter and A an ammeter with scales suitable to the voltage and current used. PL is a pilot lamp. The ground detector switch GD is used to measure the insulation resistance to ground of each side of the system. In

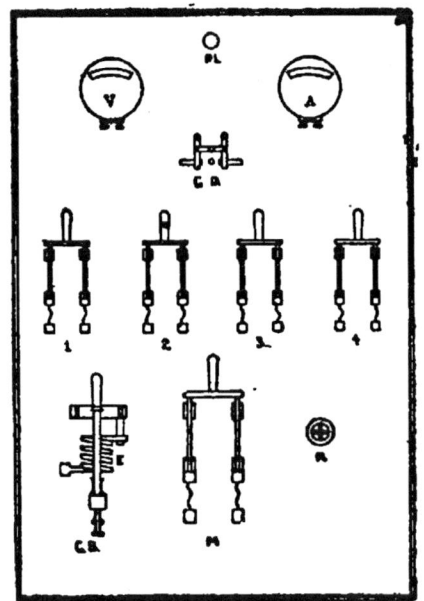 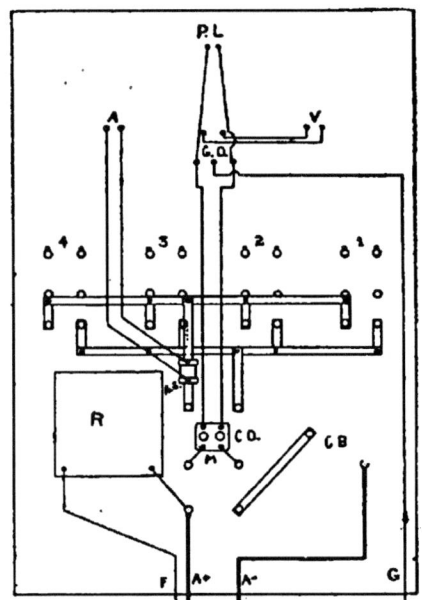

FIGURE 179.

the position shown the voltmeter is connected directly across the bus bars. If the switch is moved to the right, the + bus bar is connected through the voltmeter to ground, and, by means of the reading obtained, using the formula given under the head of testing, the insulation resistance can be determined. Moved to the left, the insulation resistance of the other side of the system can be obtained. One of the dynamo leads is carried to one terminal of the main switch M, while the other lead is carried through the circuit breaker CB to the other terminal of the switch. The circuit breaker is generally set to operate at a lower rise in current than the fuses on switch M, so that these fuses only blow in case the circuit breaker fails to operate. The circuit breaker is not absolutely necessary, but is generally installed in well designed plants. The small hand wheel R is connected to the rheostat mounted on the rear of the board. The switches 1, 2, 3 and 4 operate the feeder lines. On the rear of the board the three wires F, A + and A —, go to the dynamo, while the line marked G is connected to some good ground, such as a water pipe. The rheostat R is connected in series with the shunt field, and is used to regulate the voltage. AS is a shunt connected in series with one of the bus bars, the terminals of the shunt being connected to the ammeter. This shunt is generally furnished with the ammeter. In case an ammeter which carries the entire current is used, leads must be carried to the ammeter so that it will be connected in series with one of the mains. The feeder lines are connected to the upper terminals of switches 1, 2, 3, and 4. The ground detector, pilot lamps and voltmeter are connected to the bus bars through the cutout CO, standard No. 14 rubber covered wire being used on these circuits.

GROUND DETECTORS.

In Figure 180 a ground detector switch suitable for mounting on a switchboard is shown. Two arms A, A', pivoted at their upper ends, are connected together with an insulating bar B. These arms make contact at their lower ends with two brass strips and a contact button which are connected to the bus bars and ground respectively. When the arms are moved to the left the + bus bar is connected to ground

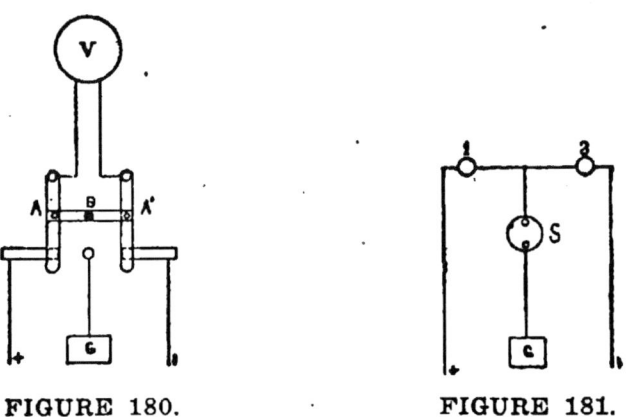

FIGURE 180.   FIGURE 181.

through the voltmeter V. By means of the reading obtained the insulation resistance to ground of the — side of the line can be calculated by using the formula given further on. By moving the arm to the right the insulation resistance of the + side of the line can be obtained.

Figure 181 shows a lamp ground detector. On a 110-volt system two ordinary 110-volt lamps are connected in series, while the line connecting the lamps is connected to ground through a snap switch S. When current is on, the two lamps will burn with equal brilliancy at a low candle-power. When the switch S is closed, if the two lines are clear the brilliancy of the lamps will not be affected; but if there is a ground on the + side of the line lamp 2 will burn brighter, the brightness depending on the resistance of the ground. If there is a dead ground the lamp will burn at full candle-power, lamp 1 not burning at all. If the ground is on the — side of the line lamp 1 will burn brighter.

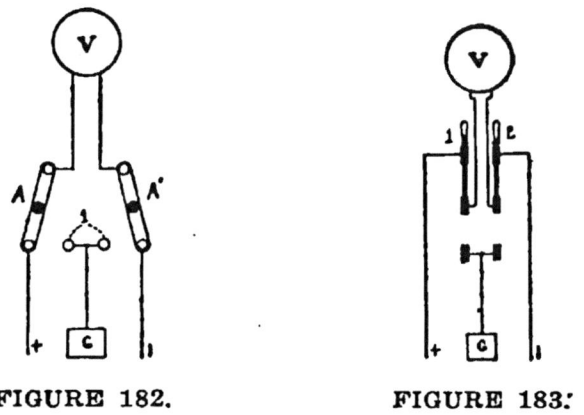

FIGURE 182.   FIGURE 183.

Figure 182 shows another method of using a voltmeter as a ground detector. The arms A A' are hinged at the upper ends and swing separately. Arm A moved to post 1 gives the reading on the + side, and arm A' moved to post 1 gives the reading on the — side of the line.

Figure 183 shows another method, using two single-pole double-throw knife switches. Throwing

GROUND DETECTORS

switch 1 to lower position connects the — bus bar to ground, and gives the insulation resistance of the + side of the line.

Another form in which two double-point push buttons are used is shown in Figure 184. In normal position contact is made to the upper points so that the voltmeter is always connected across the bus bars. Pushing button 1, the insulation resistance of the + side of the line can be obtained, and pushing button 2 the — side.

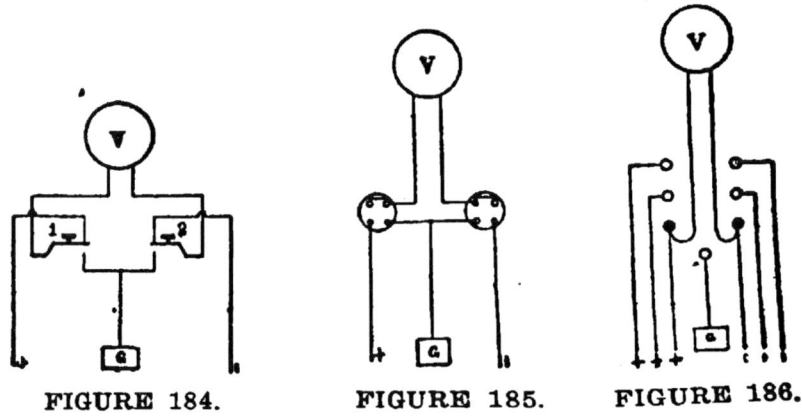

FIGURE 184.   FIGURE 185.   FIGURE 186.

Three-way snap switches are used for the same purpose in Figure 185.

When several machines are in operation the method shown in Figure 186 can be used. With this arrangement the voltage can be taken on any one of several lines or machines, and also the insulation resistance to ground. The voltmeter connection is made by means of flexible cords terminating in plugs, which fit in the jacks, which in turn are connected to the machine leads or to the various circuits.

246 WIRING DIAGRAMS

The switch shown in Figure 187 is designed for use where two dynamos are run in parallel. An arm A pivoted at the center is equipped with brass strips, which, by moving arm A, make contact between the center curved piece and the contact points 1, 2, 3 and 4. With the arm moved down the voltmeter is connected to machine No. 1, and with the arm moved up the voltmeter is connected to machine No. 2. By a slight movement of the arm the voltage of either

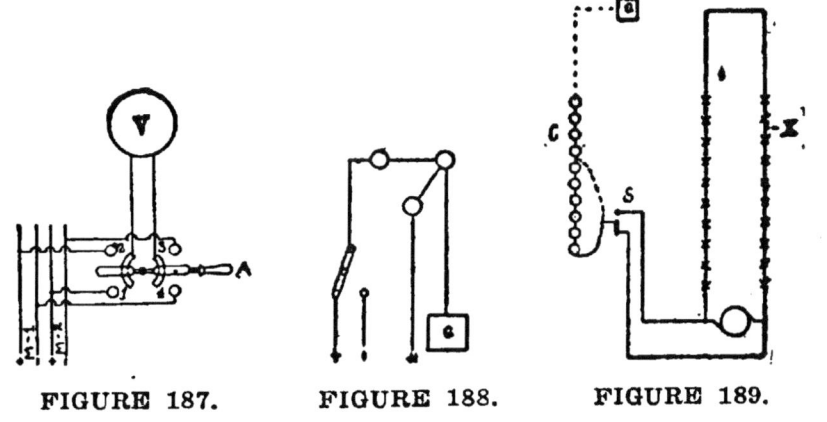

FIGURE 187.   FIGURE 188.   FIGURE 189.

machine can be taken. This is useful where a dynamo is being brought up to speed to connect on to the bus bars.

Figure 188 shows a lamp ground detector for use on a three-wire system where the neutral is not grounded. In nearly all three-wire systems the neutral is either permanently grounded or becomes grounded so that ground detectors are not used, a ground on either of the outsides blowing a fuse.

Figure 189 shows a method of locating grounds on

GROUND DETECTORS

a series arc line, where lamps are burning. A number of incandescent lamps are connected in series, the last lamp being connected to ground. Two wires are carried to the double-throw switch S, one wire being connected to each side of the circuit. From the middle of the double-throw switch a flexible connection is carried to the first lamp, and the brightness of the lamps noted. If the lamps do not burn up to full candle power, connection is made at some lamp nearer the ground, and this continued until the lamps burn at full brightness. When this point has been reached the number of lamps is counted, and if 100-volt incandescent lamps are used it will be seen that there are just twice as many arc lamps burning between that side of the machine and the ground as there are incandescents burning, for an arc lamp takes approximately 50 volts. In the diagram suppose there is a ground on the arc circuit at X; then, with the connection to the incandescent lamps as shown in the dotted lines, the lamps will burn at full brightness. Care should be taken in handling apparatus of this kind on account of the high voltages on arc circuits on which there are a number of lamps.

Figure 189a shows diagram of ground detector connections on a two phase circuit. A lamp is connected in parallel with the inductance and by connecting the lamp to different points as 1 or 4 for instance, an idea of the resistance to ground can be formed. If the lamp will burn brightly at point 4 it indicates that the insulation resistance of the line to ground is much lower than it would be if it would have to be connected at point 1 to burn brightly.

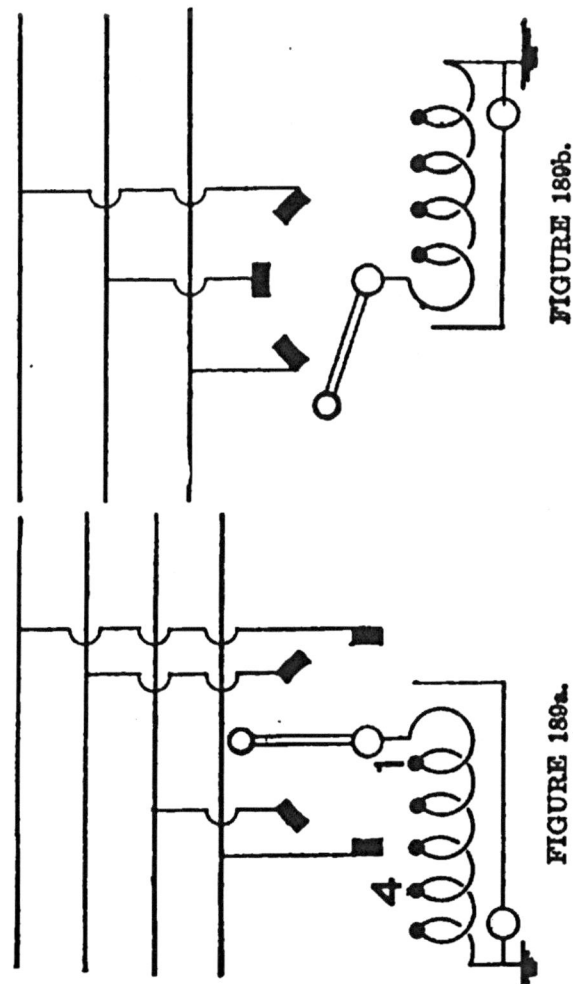

A similar plan for three phase circuits is followed in Figure 189b.

As with other ground detectors, if the ground switch is connected to the leg that is grounded the lamp will not burn at all.

GROUND DETECTORS 249

Figure 189c shows ground detector arranged for high potential service. Two voltmeters are connected through two transformers as shown. If the line is clear the two voltmeters show low readings which are equal for both instruments. With a ground coming on at A and the switch closed to guard the meter at the

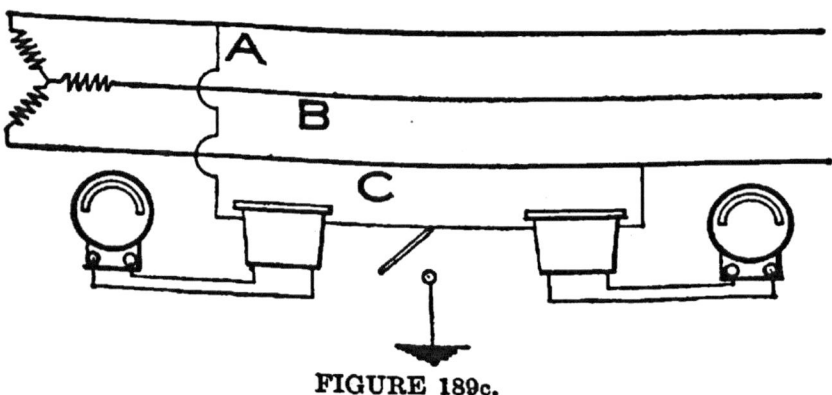

FIGURE 189c.

left will indicate lower and that on the right higher. With a ground coming on at C the indications will be the reverse, while with a ground at B both voltmeters will read higher.

CHAPTER XVIII.

STORAGE BATTERY CONNECTIONS.

Figure 190 shows a diagram of connections of a storage battery and booster suitable for an ordinary electric light installation, where it is desired to use the battery at time of heavy load to assist the generator, and to use the battery alone at time of light load. The booster B, which is driven by the motor M, the two forming a motor generator set, is connected in series with the battery circuit, and serves to raise the voltage to that necessary to charge the batteries. R is a rheostat in the field of the booster by which the E. M. F. can be regulated.

To charge, the double-throw switch S is thrown downward and the single-pole switch is closed, the end-cell switch E being placed on point 5 so that all the cells are in circuit. The motor is now started, and when it is up to speed the arm of the motor rheostat closes the charging circuit at C. To discharge, throw the end-cell switch E to point 1 and throw double-throw switch S upward. The battery is then in parallel with the generator. To run with the batteries alone open switch MS.

As the E. M. F. of the battery falls, more end-cells are switched in by moving switch E to points

STORAGE BATTERY CONNECTIONS 251

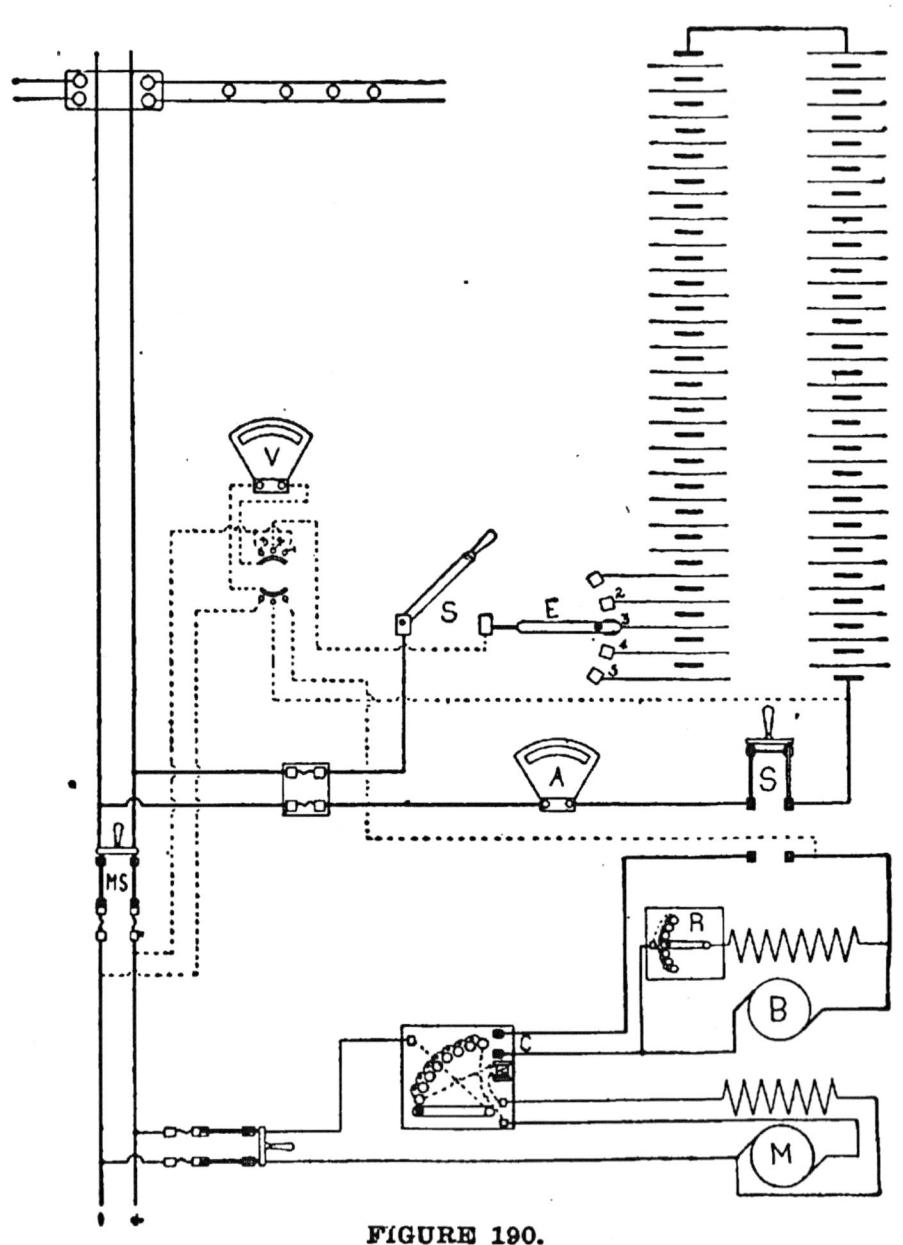

FIGURE 190.

2, 3, 4 or 5. A separate voltmeter is generally installed so that the readings of the voltage may be taken from the end-cells separately, to prevent overcharging or exhausting them.

In power work, where variations in voltage are greater and not of so much importance, storage batteries are often connected directly across the mains

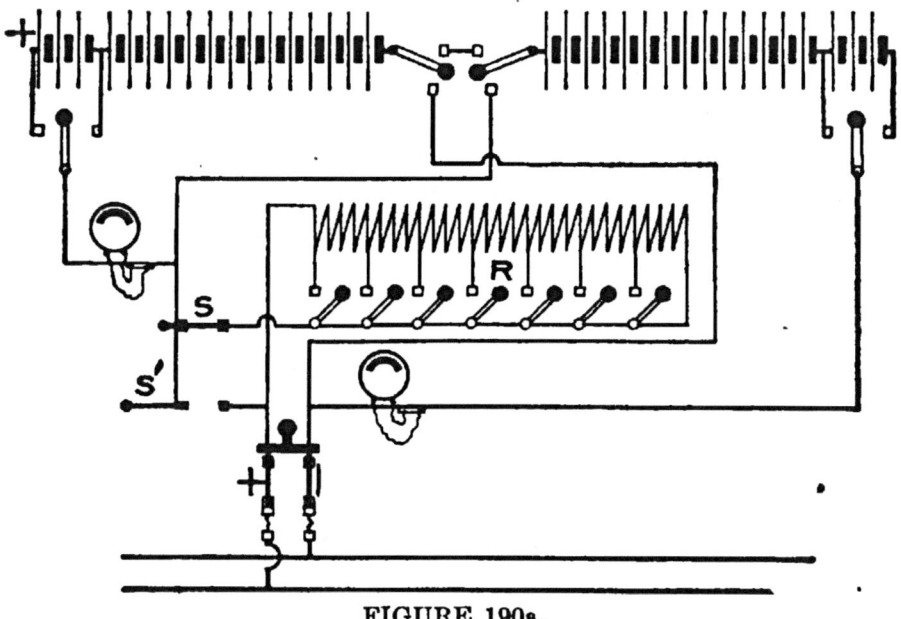

FIGURE 190a.

without a booster. In such cases the battery will take current from the mains when the load is light and the voltage correspondingly high, and give current into the line when the voltage becomes low due to heavy loads.

Figure 190a shows connections of a storage battery to be charged without the use of a booster. For charging, the battery is connected with the two halves

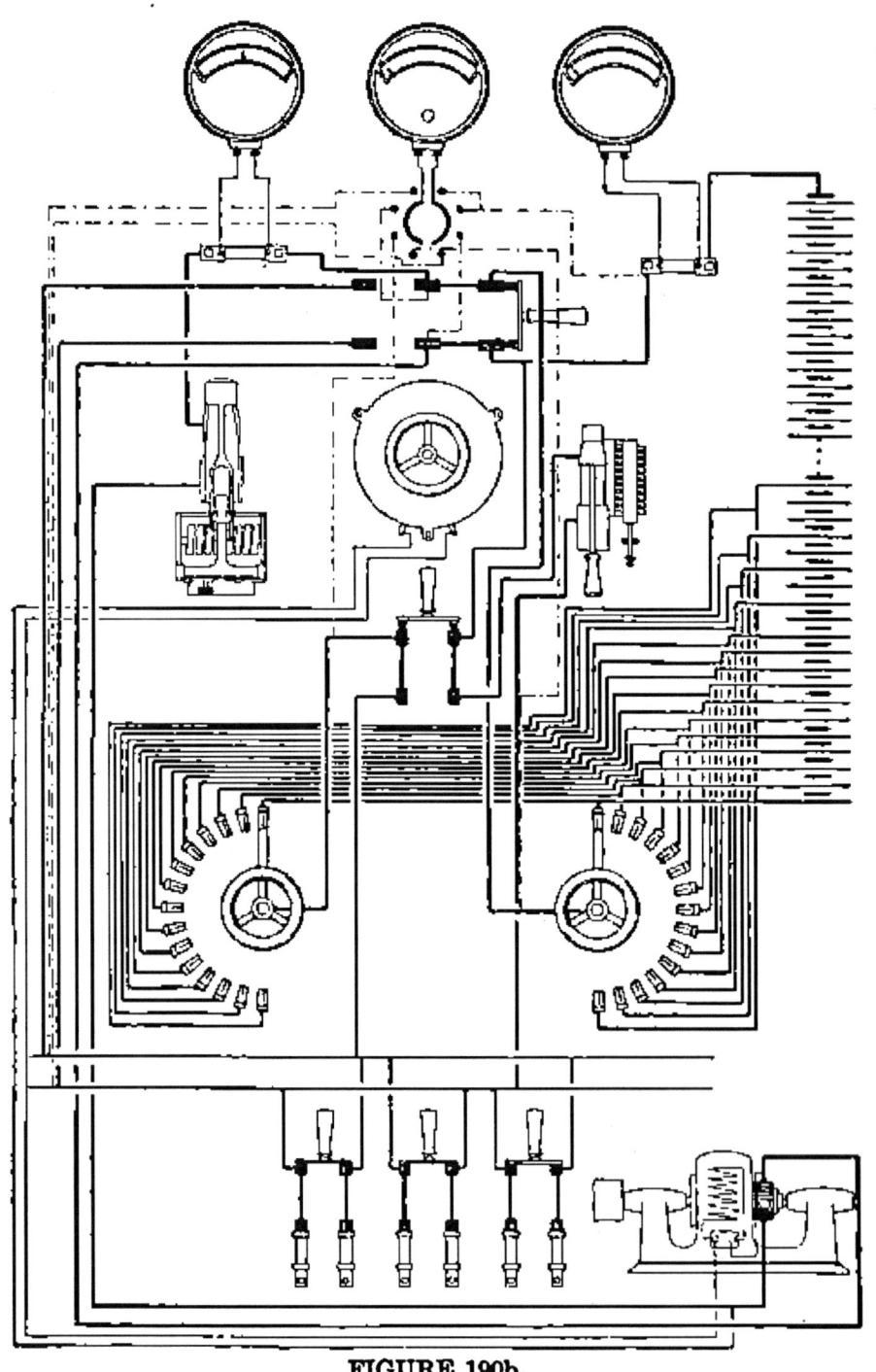

FIGURE 190b.

in parallel. As shown the battery is ready for charge if the single pole switches at the center are closed downward, and those at the right and left placed to their proper positions with the end cells in circuit. As the E. M. F. of the battery builds up sections of the resistance R, beginning at the right, are cut out. An ammeter is provided in each leg so that the rate of charge of each half of the battery may be observed. When fully charged the main switch is opened, switch S is then also opened, S' is closed and the single pole switches at the center of the battery are closed on the upper points. This places the two halves in series and fit for connection to the line. The end cells should be adjusted so that the voltage of the battery is about equal to that of the line before it is thrown in.

Figure 190b shows diagram of storage battery as arranged by the Gould Co., to be charged from a high voltage (150 volt) dynamo. A separate set of end cell switches is provided for charge and discharge so that both may be taking place at the same time. There are two circuit breakers, the one at the right is provided with a reverse current trip to protect the dynamo in case its voltage should fall so that the battery could send current through it.

In Figure 190c a large automobile charging station is shown. As a battery is connected for charge the corresponding switch S is thrown upward. This allows current to pass through the ammeter A, and the rheostat is now set so that the current flow is at

STORAGE BATTERY CONNECTIONS 255

the proper rate. When this is done the switch is thrown downward, this leaves the ammeter free for use with the next charge. By entirely opening the switch and inserting plug at P in the corresponding circuit the voltage of any battery can be taken.

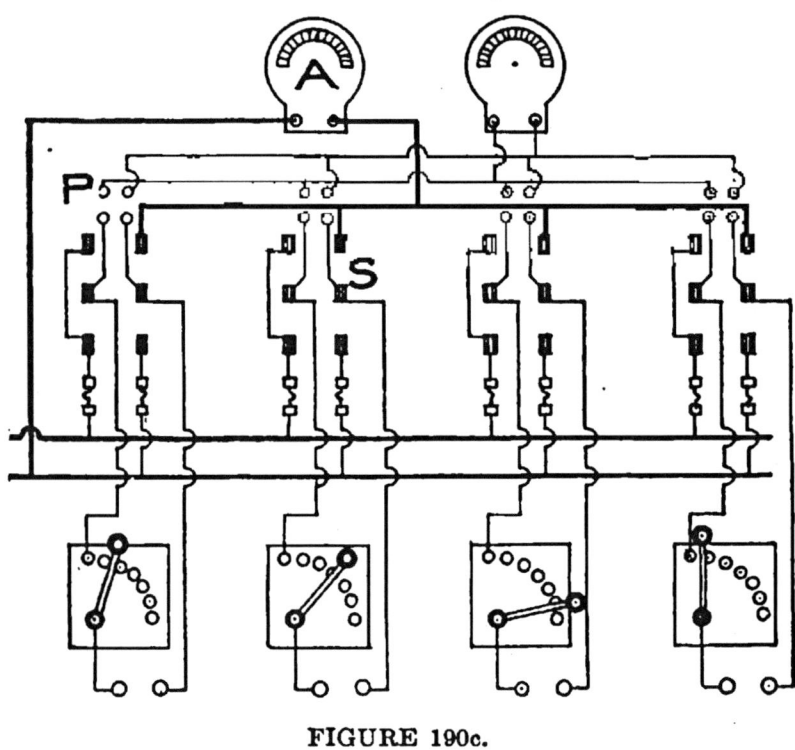

FIGURE 190c.

An end cell switch as sometimes used is shown in Figure 190d. This switch avoids short circuiting the cells while changing from one to the other, and also avoids opening the circuit entirely. The arm A makes the permanent connection, but while it is moving from one segment to the other the other arm carries the current through R.

The Cooper Hewitt Mercury Rectifier, adapted to rectifying alternating currents for the purpose of charging storage batteries, is shown diagrammatically in Figure 190e. B is a glass bulb which carries two electrodes at its upper extremity and a quantity of mercury in the bottom. The globe is further filled with mercury vapor which posseses the peculiarity

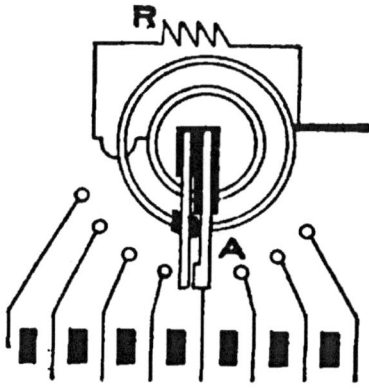

FIGURE 190d.

that it allows current flow from the upper electrodes P into the lower, but does not allow a reversal of this current.

In the bottom of the bulb there are also two electrodes, one in the mercury and the other a little above it. In order to start the operation it is necessary to tilt the bulb sufficiently so that the mercury bridges the two lower electrodes. This starts current flow through the auxiliary wires R. When the bulb is allowed to return, this circuit is interrupted and the current from whichever of the two upper electrodes happens to be positive at the time continues in its place. Should the current ever cease entirely, even for an instant, the bulb would require to be tilted again. In order to avoid this occurrence the reactance E is provided; this produces a phase difference between the impulses in the supply circuit and those

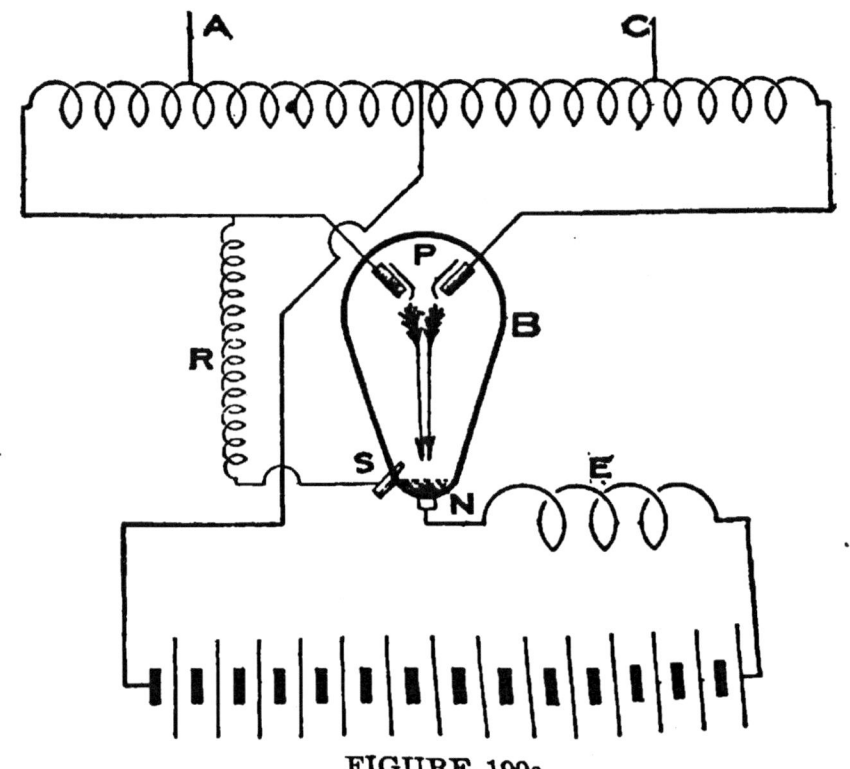

FIGURE 190e.

passing into the battery so that the currents overlap, and the current from one electrode does not cease until that from the other has been started. The alternating current supply is connected at A C.

Figure 190f shows a small storage battery connected to be charged from a series arc circuit. While the switch 1 remains in the position shown no current passes through the battery. If the switch is pulled downward part of the current passes through the resistance R and part of it through the battery. The dif-

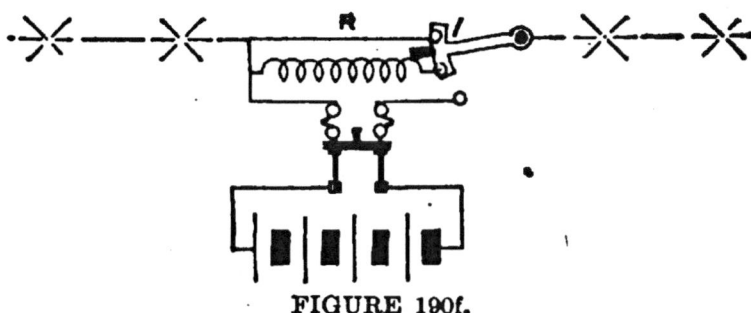

FIGURE 190f.

ference of potential existing at the terminals of R will be equal to the product of the resistance of R and the current flowing. This must always be a little greater than the E. M. F. of the battery or the battery will discharge through the resistance.

CHAPTER XIX.

TESTING.

Figure 191 is designed to illustrate a method of testing out rough wiring when lights or fixtures are to be connected. All wiring may be considered concealed except the ends at outlets, and it is assumed that nothing is known of how the wiring is run in.

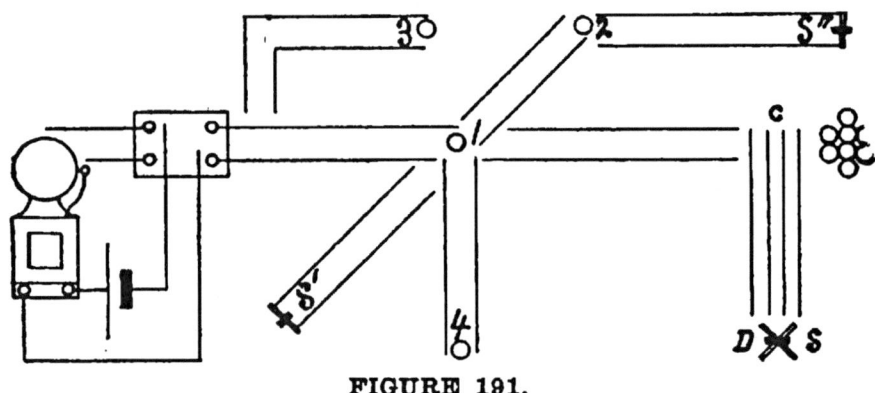

FIGURE 191.

The first step is to separate all wires at outlets, so there may be no wrong connections. Next connect an ordinary bell and battery as shown in the figure and fuse up the circuit. If the bell now rings, there must be a short-circuit in the wiring leading direct from the cutout, since we have disconnected all other wires. To locate this it will be necessary to get access to the wiring, and it may be necessary to tear off plaster or break into walls. Oftentimes it is better to abandon a circuit with such trouble as this and run in a new one. If the circuit is found clear, the next step is to temporarily bring together the bare ends of all the wires found at any of the outlets until a ring from the bell is obtained. When a ring is obtained it will indicate that the circuit feeds direct to this outlet from the cutout. Next pick out at this outlet the two wires which together produce a ring. These two wires come direct from the cutout, and may now be marked as such.

In the figure it is intended that the light 1 shall be controlled by the switch S', and the light 2 by the switch S''; the lights 3 and 4 are not provided with switches, but the large chandelier C is to be controlled by the double-pole switch DS.

The next step will be to find the two wires leading to switch S'. To accomplish this, close the switch and bring any two of the wires found at outlet 1 in contact with those coming from the cutout; when the proper wires have been thus connected the bell will ring. One of the switch wires may now be connected permanently to one of the circuit wires coming from the cutout, while the other is to be connected to one side of the lamp or fixture. The other wire coming from the cutout goes to the other side of the lamp or fixture. Lamp 1 is now completely connected and under control of switch S'. The quickest way to find the proper connections for lamp 2 and switch S'' is by bunching all the wires at 2, and then trying at 1, any two wires to those coming from the cutout until the bell rings. The two wires which cause this ringing lead direct to lamp 2, and may now be connected to the wires leading from the cutout, care being taken that they are connected so as not to come under control of switch S'. Next, separate the wires at 2, and find those which when brought together cause the bell to ring; one of these must be connected direct to the lamp or fixture, while the other is connected to one of the remaining wires. This leaves one wire, and it connects to the other side of the lamp and completes the connection of lamp 2 and switch S''. The four remaining wires at 1 may be found in a similar manner, care being taken that they are also connected behind the connections of switch S'. Two of the six wires at outlet C may now be connected direct to those coming from outlet 1. After this, go to switch DS and find the wires coming from outlet 1 and the cutout (by ringing the bell), and connect them to the proper points on the switch. The remaining wires connect to the other pole of the switch and to the chandelier. The wires leading to lamp 3 may be doubled up under the screws of the cutout terminals.

For testing of this kind the bell shown is the most convenient instrument, since it is audible at quite a distance, and a circuit as described often extends through several rooms. A magneto may also be used, with an assistant to turn the crank, or if the circuit at the cutout is short-circuited the wireman may carry it with him, making connections wherever he wishes to test. If the cutout center is "alive" a lamp may be placed instead of one of the fuses, and the wireman may carry another with him for testing. A galvanometer or telephone receiver may also be used in this way, the battery alone being connected at the cutout center.

Figure 192 shows the main and branch wiring of a two-wire incandescent system, all complete and ready for final test and connection. In the first place it is necessary to close all the switches and insert all fuses, and a test for short circuits or faulty insulation between opposite poles may then be made by placing a lamp L in circuit in place of one of the main fuses. If current is now thrown on the lamp will light in case there is any serious defect in the insulation between opposite polarities in any part of the system. In case there are any two or three-way switches controlling lights from several places, it will be necessary to turn one of these on each circuit after the first test has been made and then make another test—since one cannot well be certain whether such switches close a circuit or not unless a lamp can be seen to burn. It will also be advisable to do this with single and double pole switches, and may often be easier than removing covers from snap switches to see whether they are on or off. Snap switches will often indicate by the sound of the snap whether they are on or off, but this is not always reliable.

TESTING

If a more thorough test than that given by the lamp is required, it may be made with any one of the four instruments shown. The voltmeter may be connected in place of the lamp. If the system is perfect the voltmeter will indicate nothing, while if a short-

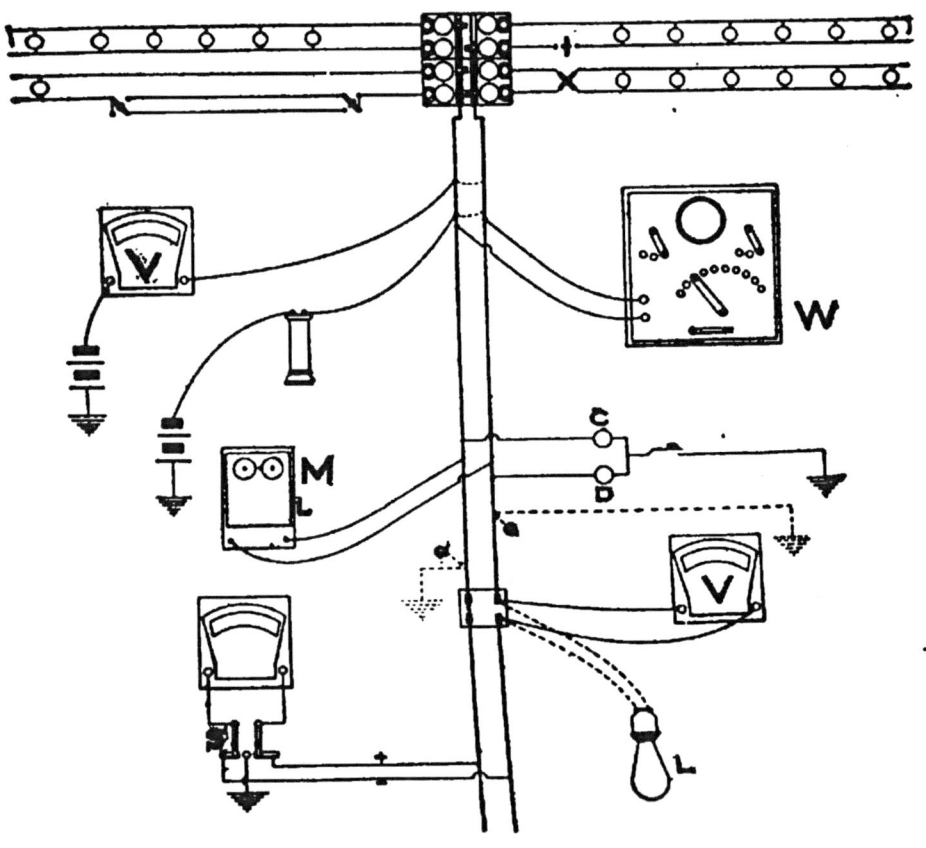

FIGURE 192.

circuit exists it will indicate the full pressure. A telephone receiver may also be used in the same way, if properly wound, and if the system contains no lead-covered wires or iron pipe and is not too large. If the Wheatstone bridge W, or magneto M is to be used for this test, both main fuses must be removed and connection made to both wires as shown with these instruments. Lead-covered wire, or wire in iron pipe, will also interfere with testing by a magneto, a ring sometimes being obtained when the insulation of the system is perfect.

The figure also shows the voltmeter V and the telephone receiver fitted up with battery to test the insulation resistance to earth of lines having no current; the same connections may be made with the magneto or Wheatstone bridge, and both main wires may be connected at once as shown by dotted lines. More detailed explanation and formulas for testing with the voltmeter and Wheatstone bridge will be given further on.

When it is desired to ascertain the current passing along the mains, an ammeter may be connected in place of voltmeter V as shown. To test the insulation resistance accurately, the system should not be alive, although approximate tests may be made with a voltmeter or ground detector lamps connected as shown in Figure 192. This method of testing live circuits is practical only on small systems, since the system cannot be subdivided, and the indications are accurate only so long as defects are confined to one side of the line. With large three-wire systems it is quite usual to have the neutral wire grounded, and these methods could not be used at all.

In Figure 192 there are shown two ground de-

TESTING

tector lamps C and D, and by means of a key or switch the wire between them may be connected to ground. As long as this key is not brought in contact with the ground wire, both lamps burn dimly in series and with equal brilliancy, and if no ground exists in any part of the system, depressing the key will not affect the lamps. Should, however, a ground exist, say at G; closing the key will establish a path through the ground and through lamp C to the opposite side of the circuit. If the ground is of very low resistance the lamp C will burn at full candle power, while D will not burn at all. Should the ground be of high resistance there will be but little difference in the brilliancy of the lamps.

The connections of the voltmeter are based on the same principle. The switch S moved one way makes connection with the positive pole through the voltmeter to the ground, and moved the other way makes connection with the negative pole through voltmeter to ground. In the position shown the switch is clear of the ground, and connects the voltmeter to the lighting mains so as to obtain full pressure. The formula for use with the voltmeter when the exact value of the resistance is to be determined is $X = R \left\{ \dfrac{E-E'}{E'} \right\}$ where E is the full voltage of the battery or other source of current as indicated on the voltmeter, E' is the reduced reading obtained through the voltmeter and the resistance to be measured, and R the resistance of the voltmeter, X being the value of the unknown resistance. This formula is based on the supposition that the voltmeter and the resistance to be measured are in series, and that all current passing through the resistance being measured also passes through the voltmeter.

Referring to Figure 192, so long as G is the only defect on the system allowing current to flow, the above formula will give us the correct resistance; as soon, however, as G' is introduced the formula becomes unreliable, since G' is a shunt around the voltmeter and robs it of current. The current passing through the voltmeter no longer depends only on the voltmeter resistance and that of G, and therefore the readings can no longer be used as a basis of calculations. As a matter of fact, if the voltmeter test on a live system as shown in the figure indicates a low ground on one side, as, for instance, G', it will usually show the other side very high. The ground detector lamps are subject to the same limitations, but although they and the voltmeter cannot be relied upon for accurate testing, both are very useful when arranged so that tests can be made several times per day, so as to give means of detecting a ground as soon as it comes on.

In Figure 193 is given a diagram of the Wheatstone bridge. This instrument is generally used where accurate measurements of resistance are to be made, and on account of its wide range it is the most

TESTING 267

useful instrument for this purpose. It will be seen that current from the battery entering at 1 has two paths open to it, one through B and X and the other through A and R, to the other pole of the battery. If the resistances A and B are equal, then an equal quantity of current will pass through each to the points 2 and 3 respectively. If the resistances R and X are also equal (though they may be much greater

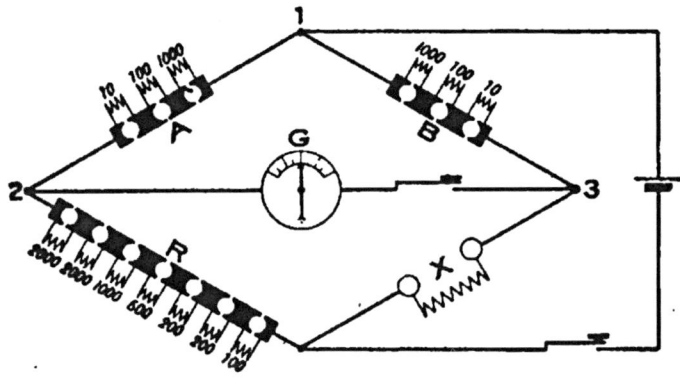

FIGURE 193.

or smaller than A and B) they will also carry away equal quantities of current. Under these conditions no current will pass through the galvanometer G.

If the resistance of A is made ten times as great as that of B, then A will carry only one-tenth as much current to 2 as B will carry to 3; and if R is made ten times as high as X, then R will carry away all the current from 2, while X takes away all current from 3, and still no current will flow through the galvanometer. So long as A is to R as B is to X, no current will pass through the galvanometer. Whenever this relation is disturbed, some current will pass through the galvanometer, either from 2 to 3 or 3 to 2. If X is entirely open, all the current flowing through B to 3 will pass through the galvanometer to 2; and, again, if R is of higher resistance than X, while A and B are equal, some current will pass from 2 through the galvanometer to 3.

To make the resistance of A, B and R variable, brass plugs are provided which may be inserted in the openings shown so as to form a shunt to the resistance bridged around the opening. In each of the proportional arms A and B two openings are always plugged, and the one unplugged is the resistance through which the current must pass. In R all plugs are removed to get the total resistance, while to get the lowest resistance all openings but the lowest are plugged.

To measure any resistance proceed as follows: If the unknown resistance connected at X is not greater than the total of R, or smaller than any one plug in R, A and B may be plugged equal; for instance, plugs inserted in the openings 1000 and 100 on each arm, leaves on each side ten ohms in circuit and leaves the greatest battery strength for the galvanometer. Now plug R so the resistance will be quite low and press the key; if this gives any deflection note whether it is to the right or left. If a decided deflection has been obtained, remove a number of plugs until the resistance of R is quite high and again press the key. If the deflection now obtained is in the opposite direction of the former, the value of the resistance is something between the first value of R, and the second, and repeated trials are necessary until no deflection is obtained. No deflection may also be caused by a weak battery. If everything is in order, increasing or lessening R should cause reverse deflections.

When balance is obtained with A and B equal, the sum of the unplugged resistances in R will give the value of X. If X is greater than R, we cannot obtain balance unless B is greater than A; and, conversely, if X is less than the smallest resistance in R, balance cannot be obtained unless B is smaller than A. Whenever balance is obtained, A is to R as B is to X. The values of A, B and R are known, and, since it is a well-known rule of arithmetic that in any proportion the product of the means equals the product of the extremes, we can find the value of X, since

$A \times X = B \times R$, $\frac{B \times R}{A} = X$, or in other words to

find the value of X we must multiply the sum of the unplugged resistances in R by B and divide by A.

If, in Figure 193, A is unplugged to equal 10 and B to 1000, when balance is obtained X will equal 100 times R. If B is unplugged to equal 10 and A at 1000, X will equal 1-100 part of R. The total range of the resistance that can be measured by the arrangement shown in this figure is from 1 ohm to **600,000** ohms.

Figure 194 shows one commercial form of the Wheatstone bridge. In this form movable arms are used to adjust the resistance instead of plugs. The

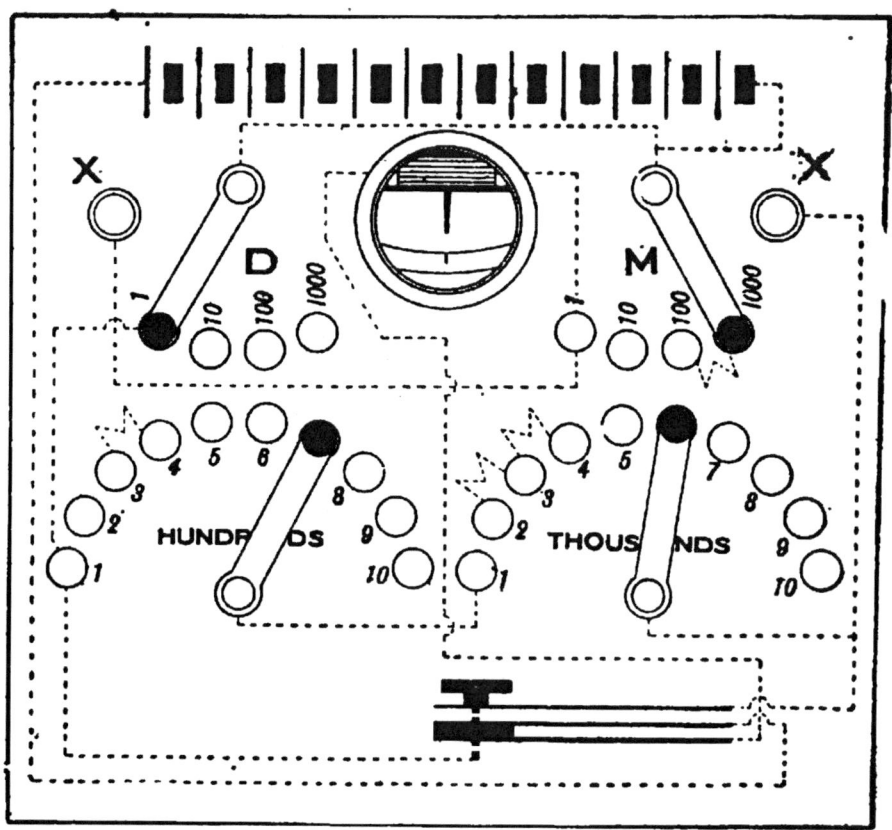

FIGURE 194.

resistance to be measured is connected to the binding posts marked X, and when balance is obtained the sum of the resistances indicated by the lower arms is divided by D and multiplied by M. The key is ar-

TESTING 271

ranged to close the battery circuit before closing the circuit through the galvanometer. This is important, especially where inductive resistances such as the coils of electro-magnets are to be measured, and prevents inductance and discharge of these magnets from disturbing the galvanometer reading.

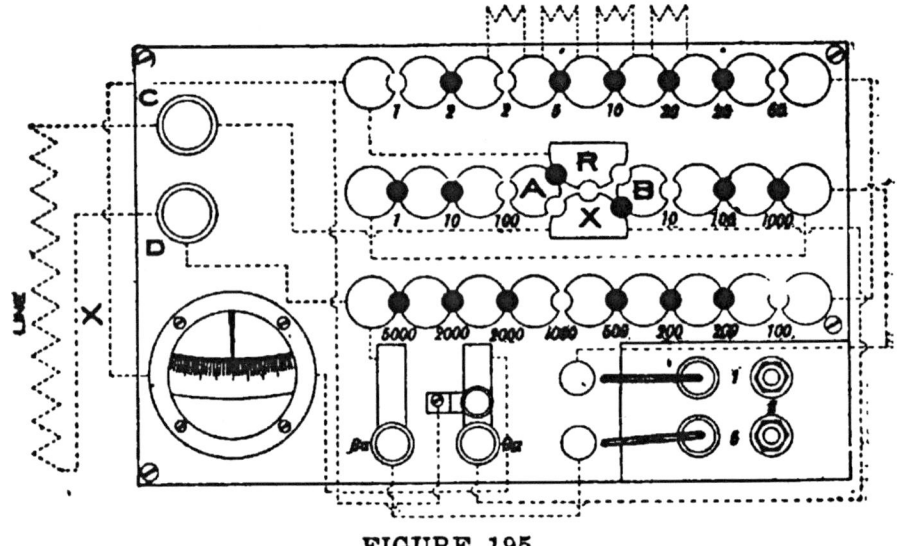

FIGURE 195.

Figure 195 shows another form of Wheatstone bridge, and Figure 196 a diagram of the connections. With this form the resistance to be measured is connected at X, and if it is greater than R the two plugs in the center are arranged as shown in black. When balance is obtained X equals the sum of the unplugged resistances in R multiplied by B and divided by A. With the plugs arranged in the opposite holes between A X and B R, X equals the unplugged resistances of R multiplied by A and divided by B.

As will be seen from Figure 193 the multiplying proportional coil is the one in series with the unknown. In this form of bridge it is possible to place either one of the coils in series with the unknown and hence we may use either one to multiply and the other to divide. This greatly increases the range of the instrument with the same amount of resistance.

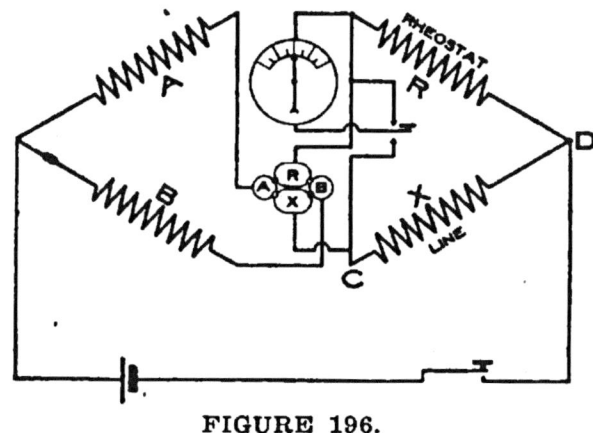

FIGURE 196.

With a plug inserted between R and X, the other two plugs being left out, the box may be used as a straight resistance box. The galvanometer key has a back contact which closes the galvanometer circuit on itself when released, and tends to stop the needle from swinging.

Oftentimes these boxes are not equipped with battery, and instead have two binding posts to which battery may be connected. If the battery in either of the above were connected at X the galvanometer needle could be made to deflect in one direction only.

CHAPTER XX.

LIGHT.

The intensity of the light varies as the square of the distance from the source. This is rigidly true only at such distances where the source of light may be considered as a mathematical point having no physical dimensions. Thus the intensity of an electric light is not four times as great at a distance of two inches as at four inches.

A 16 candle-power lamp is usually allowed for every 100 square feet in ordinary rooms, when not suspended more than seven feet from the floor. With dark colored walls, or where a very bright light is desired, more lamps should be provided.

The efficiency of lamps varies greatly with different candle-powers, a fair approximation being given below:

32 candle-power lamp requires from 100 to 110 watts
16   "   "   "   "   "   50 " 56   "
 8   "   "   "   "   "   30 " 33   "
 4   "   "   "   "   "   19 " 21   "

After lamps have been used for some time the efficiency is reduced somewhat and the current consumption increased.

The candle-power of any incandescent lamp increases much more rapidly than the current supplied to it, so that the higher efficiency demands full voltage for the lamp. If long life is desired they should be operated at low voltage. Below is given a table, taken from the General Electric Company bulletin, showing the variation in candle-power and efficiency of standard 3.1 watt lamps due to variations in voltage:

Percent of normal Voltage.	Percent of Normal Candle-Power.	Efficiency in Watts per Candle
90	53	4.68
91	57	4.46
92	61	4.26
93	65	4.1
94	69½	3.92
95	74	3.76
96	79	3.6
97	84	3.45
98	89	3.34
99	94½	3.22
100	100	3.1
101	106	2.99
102	112	2.9
103	118	2.8
104	124½	2.7
105	131¼	2.62
106	138½	2.54

Example: Lamps of 16 candle-power, 105 volts, and 3.1 watts, if burned at 98 per cent. of normal voltage, or 103 volts, will give 89 per cent. of 16 candle-power, or 14¼ candle-power, and the efficiency will be 3.34 watts per candle-power.

LIGHT

In Figure 197 the various curves show the relation between the candle-power and voltage, current and watts in an incandescent lamp, the curves having been plotted from a 100-volt, 16 c. p. lamp. Taking the curve marked Volts and C. P. it will be seen that at 70 volts the c. p. was at 2, while at 100 volts the c. p. was at 15. As the voltage rises the candle-power increases very rapidly, reaching 25 c. p. at 110 volts and 55 c. p. at about 127 volts.

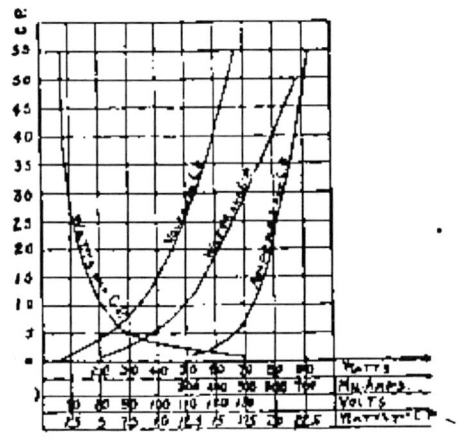

FIGURE 197.

The upper or positive carbon of an arc lamp burns away twice as fast as the negative with continuous currents, but only about 8 per cent. faster with alternating currents.

To get full benefit out of the carbons they should be protected from gusts of wind, as these often blow out the arc and cause rapid consumption of the carbons.

A very simple method of comparing the candle-powers of different lamps is that known as Bunsen's. Set up the lamps to be compared, and, taking a piece of paper with a grease spot on it, adjust it between the two lamps until the spot becomes invisible. The candle-powers of the two lamps are then in the same proportion as the squares of the distances from the paper.

The absorption of light by globes is given as follows:

Clear Glass, 10 per cent. Holophane, 12 per cent. Opaline, 20 to 40 per cent. Ground, 25 to 30 per cent. Opal, 25 to 60 per cent.

An arc light gives out from one-twentieth to one-fortieth as much heat as gas light of equal candle-power.

An incandescent light gives out from one-fifth to one-tenth as much heat as a gas jet of equal candle-power.

One 5-foot gas burner (16 c. p.) vitiates as much air as four men.

CHAPTER XXI.

WIRING TABLES.

The wiring table No. 1 is arranged in the following manner: For each size of wire and each voltage considered there is given (under the proper voltage and opposite the number of the wire under the heading B. & S.) the distance it will carry 1 ampere at a loss of 1%. The same wire will carry 2 amperes only half as far at the same percentage of loss and again will carry 1 ampere twice as far at double the percentage of loss.

From these facts we deduce the rule of this table which is: Multiply the distance in feet (one leg only) by the number of amperes to be carried and divide the result by the percentage of loss to be allowed. Take the number so obtained and under the proper voltage find the number nearest equal to it. Opposite this number under the heading B. & S. will be found the size of wire required. To illustrate: We have 22 amperes to carry a distance of 135 feet and the loss to be allowed is 3 per cent. at 110 volts.

$$22 \times 135 = \frac{2970}{3} = 990$$

We take the number 990, turn to column for 110 volts, and find 841, which is not sufficient. The next above it is 1060, which corresponds to No. 7 wire. With this wire our loss will be slightly less than 3%, while with No. 8 it would be somewhat in excess of 3%.

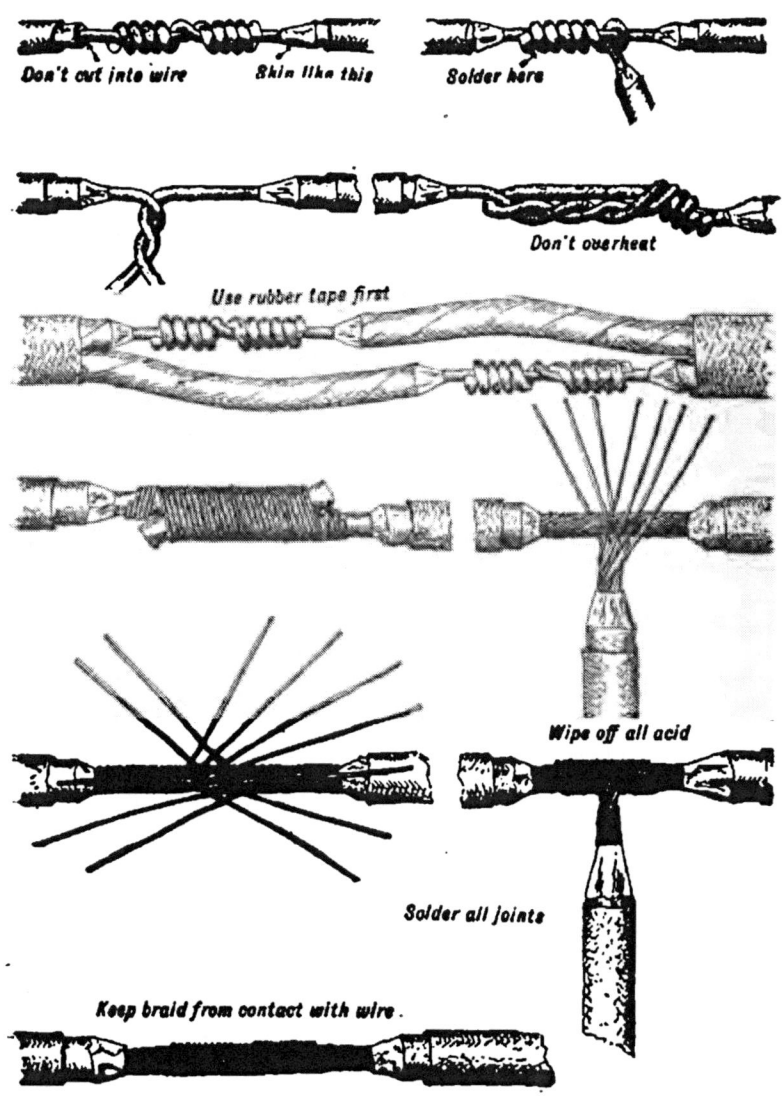

For three-wire systems using 110 volts on each side, the column marked 220 volts should be used. The column marked 440 volts is provided for three-wire systems using 220 volts on each side. The sizes determined will be correct for all three wires in both cases.

The columns at the right, marked motors, are arranged in the same way, the only difference being that, for greater convenience, they are figured in H. P. feet instead of ampere feet. For this reason we multiply the distance in feet by the number of horsepower to be transmitted and divide by the percentage of loss, all other operations remaining the same as under lights.

When any considerable current is to be carried only a short distance the wire indicated by the desired loss will very likely not have sufficient carrying capacity; it is, therefore, always necessary to consult the table of carrying capacities.

LIGHT AND MOTOR WIRING TABLE.—No. 1.

LIGHTS IN AMPERES. VOLTS.				B. & S. Gauge.	Car. Cap.	MOTORS IN HORSE POWER. VOLTS.				Resis. per foot
52	110	220	440			110	220	440	500	
98	209	418	896	14	12	28	112	448	579	.002628
124	263	526	1052	13	...	35	140	560	724	.002084
158	333	666	1332	12	17	44	176	704	910	.001653
200	420	840	1680	11	...	56	224	896	1159	.001811
250	529	1058	2116	10	24	70	280	1120	1449	.001040
314	665	1330	2660	9	...	88	352	1408	1821	.000624
397	841	1682	3364	8	38	112	448	1792	2318	.000654
501	1060	2120	4240	7	...	141	564	2256	2918	.000619
634	1338	2676	5352	6	46	178	712	2848	3684	.000411
798	1687	3374	6748	5	54	224	896	3584	4636	.000326
1000	2124	4248	8496	4	65	283	1132	4528	5858	.000259
1271	2683	5366	10782	3	76	357	1428	5712	7389	.000205
1595	3374	6748	13496	2	90	449	1796	7184	9294	.000163
2011	4264	8527	17064	1	107	568	2272	9088	11757	.000129
2543	5392	10784	21568	0	127	718	2872	11488	14762	.000102
3228	6790	13580	27160	00	150	905	3620	14480	18733	.000081
4053	8594	17188	34376	000	177	1145	4580	18320	23701	.000064
5090	10784	21568	43136	0000	210	1437	5748	22992	29745	.000051
6082	12790	25580	51160	250000	235	1696	6784	27136	35107	.0000431
7222	15277	30654	61108	300000	270	2036	8144	32576	42145	.000036
8441	17857	35714	71428	350000	300	2368	9472	37888	49017	.0000308
9629	20370	40740	81480	400000	330	2714	10856	43424	56179	.000027
10833	22916	45832	91664	450000	360	3054	12216	48864	63217	.000024
12093	25581	51162	102324	500000	390	8393	13572	54288	70235	.0000215
24074	50925	101850	203700	1000000	650	6786	27144	108576	110470	.0000108
48148	101851	203702	407404	2000000	1050	13573	54292	217168	280061	.0000054

For lights, find the ampere feet (one leg) and divide by the per cent. of loss. Under the proper voltage find the number equal to this or the next larger; opposite this number in the column marked B. & S., will be found the size of wire required.

For Motors, proceed in the same way, using H. P. feet instead of ampere feet.

It may often be desired to find the loss in an established circuit carrying a certain load. This may readily be determined from this table by observing the following rule: Find the number of ampere feet and, selecting the column headed by the proper voltage, divide by the number opposite the size of wire used. For example, we have a No. 10 wire carrying 24 amperes a distance of 90 feet at 110 volts, 24 × 90 = 2160. Opposite No. 10 in the column marked B. & S. gauge and under 110 volts we find 529, $\frac{2160}{529}$ = 4 and a very small fraction, which is the percentage of loss occurring on this line.

It is often necessary to reinforce mains which have become overloaded. It is quite usual though often very incorrect, to choose by the table of carrying capacities a wire of such size that the rated capacity of it and the wire to be re-enforced shall be equal to the load. Small wires have proportionately a much greater radiating surface than larger ones and therefore their carrying capacity is proportionally greater. In order that a wire connected in parallel with another wire shall carry a certain current, its circular mils, must be equal $\frac{C.M. \times a}{A}$ where C. M. stands for the cross-section of the larger wire in circular mils and A for the current to be carried by it, while a is the current to be carried by the extra wire. Table No. 2 is calculated from this rule and shows the size of wire necessary to re-enforce another overloaded to a certain per cent. as indicated in the top row. For instance, a 0000 wire overloaded 40% requires re-enforcement by a No. 1; a No. 3 wire overloaded 20% requires a No. 10 wire. Where large wires are re-enforced in this way by smaller ones great care must be taken that the larger wire cannot be accidentally broken or disconnected, since in such a case the whole load would be forced over the smaller wire and would likely result in a fire. The two wires should be securely soldered together.

No. 2.

Amperes.	B. & S.	10%	20	30	40	50	60	70	80	90	100
210	0000	6	4	2	1	0	00	000	000	0000	0000
177	000	8	5	3	2	1	0	00	000	000	000
150	00	9	6	4	3	2	1	0	0	00	00
127	0	10	7	5	4	3	2	1	1	0	0
107	1	10	8	6	5	4	3	2	2	1	1
90	2	11	9	7	6	5	4	3	3	2	2
76	3	12	10	8	7	6	5	4	4	3	3
65	4	14	11	9	8	7	6	5	5	4	4

No. 3.

Numbers B. & S. Gauge.	Diameters in Mils.	Areas in Circular Mils. C.M.=d^2	Weights. 1000 feet.	Weights. Mile.	Ohms per 1000 feet
0000	460.	211,600.	641.	3,382.	.051
000	410.	168,100.	509.	2,687.	.064
00	365.	133,225.	403.	2,129.	.081
0	325.	105,625.	320.	1,688.	.102
1	289.	83,521.	253.	1,335.	.129
2	258.	66,564.	202.	1,064.	.163
3	229.	52,441.	159.	838.	.205
4	204.	41,616.	126.	665.	.259
5	182.	33,124.	100.	529.	.326
6	162.	26,244.	79.	419.	.411
7	144.	20,736.	63.	331.	.519
8	128.	16,384.	50.	262.	.654
9	114.	12,996.	39.	208.	.824
10	102.	10,404.	32.	166.	1.040
11	91.	8,281.	25.	132.	1.311
12	81.	6,561.	20.	105.	1.653
13	72.	5,184.	15.7	83.	2.084
14	64.	4,096.	12.4	65.	2.628
15	57.	3,249.	9.8	52.	3.314
16	51.	2,601.	7.9	42.	4.179
17	45.	2,025.	6.1	32.	5.269
18	40.	1,600.	4.8	25.6	6.645
19	36.	1,296.	3.9	20.7	8.617
20	32.	1,024.	3.1	16.4	10.566
21	28.5	812.3	2.5	13.	13.283
22	25.3	640.1	1.9	10.2	16.85
23	22.6	510.8	1.5	8.2	21.10
24	20.1	404.	1.2	6.5	26.70
25	17.9	320.4	.97	5.1	33.67
26	15.9	252.8	.77	4.	42.68
27	14.2	201.6	.61	3.2	53.52
28	12.6	158.8	.48	2.5	67.84
29	11.3	127.7	.39	2.	84.49
30	10.	100.	.3	1.6	107.3
31	8.9	79.2	.24	1.27	136.2
32	8	64.	.19	1.02	168.5
33	7.1	50.4	.15	.81	214.0
34	6.3	39.7	.12	.63	271.7
35	5.6	31.4	.095	.5	343.6
36	5.	25.	.076	.4	431.6

No. 4.

TABLE SHOWING THE CURRENTS WHICH WILL FUSE WIRES OF DIFFERENT SUBSTANCES.

B. & S. Gauge.	Diam.	Copper.	Aluminum.	German Silver	Iron.
10	102.	333.	246.5	170.	102.8
12	81.	236.	174.4	120.5	72.6
14	64.	165.7	122.8	84.6	50.9
16	51.	117.7	87.1	60.1	36.1
18	40.	81.9	60.7	41.8	25.2
20	32.	58.5	43.4	29.9	18.
22	25.3	41.1	30.5	21.0	12.4
24	20.	28.9	21.5	14.8	8.9
26	16.	20.7	15.3	10.6	6.4
28	12.6	14.5	10.7	7.4	4.5
30	10.	10.2	7.6	5.2	3.1
32	8.	7.3	5.4	3.7	2.3
34	6.3	5.1	3.8	2.6	1.6
36	5.	3.6	2.7	1.8	1.1

CHAPTER XXII.

ELECTRIC SIGNS. FLASHERS. DISPLAY LIGHTING.

Figure 198 gives a diagrammatic view of the Reynolds Flasher for electric signs and displays. The flasher here shown is capable of controlling twelve circuits, each circuit with a single-pole switch. Only

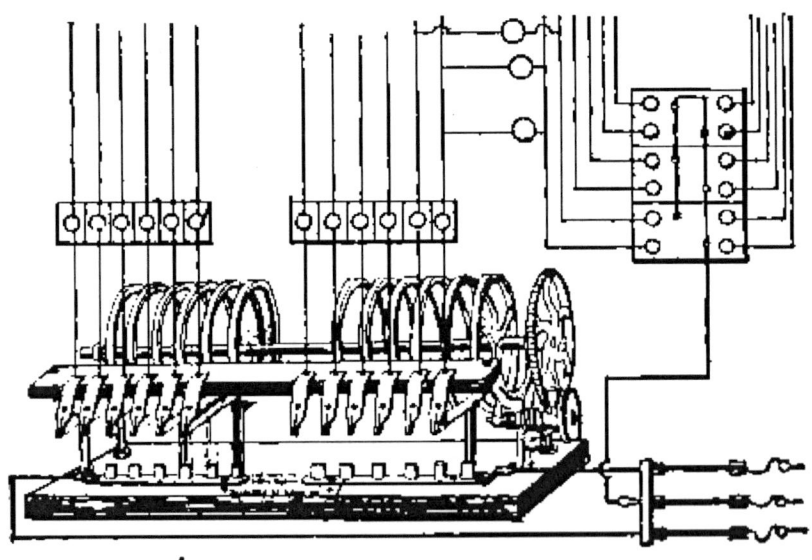

FIGURE 198.

one wire of each circuit passes through the flasher and single-pole fuses are usually installed as near as possible to the flasher. The fuses for the other sides of the circuits may be installed within signs or wherever convenient. The diagram shows flasher arranged for three-wire circuits. In case of a two-wire installation only one of the mains is led to the flasher and the two sections of the flasher are connected together.

Figures 199 to 204 show the circuits of a flasher for electric signs and displays made by Rawson & Evans of Chicago. This machine is designed to change connections from one circuit to another without ever entirely opening the circuit. From two

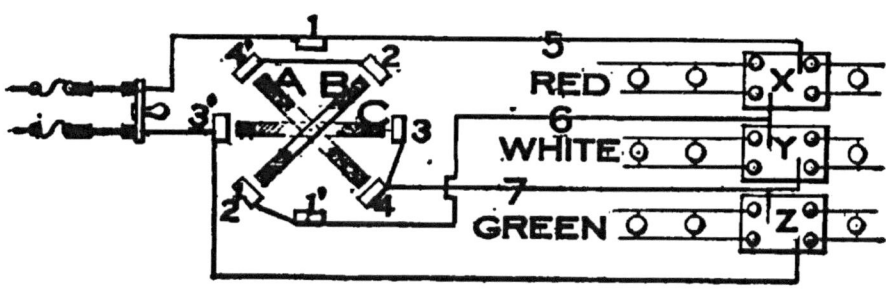

FIGURE 199.

to four groups of lamps are wired in series and the movable arms, A, B, C, Figure 199, short-circuit those groups not in use. During the time of change from one group to another all the groups are in series and most of the current which would otherwise manifest itself in the form of a spark passes through the lamps. The time of open circuit is so very short that it is impossible to hold an arc for any appreciable time. The breaking of the circuit in many places at the same time also lessens the destructive qualities of the arc which occurs.

Figure 199 is a diagram of the flasher as connected to three-color signs; the white lights being arranged to follow after the red and also after the green. Referring to Figure 199, A, B, C, are metal arms insulated from one another but firmly fastened together so as to form one movable piece. As these arms are moved from point to point they connect the diametrically opposite terminals, 1, 1'; 2, 2'; 3, 3'; and 4, 4'. In Figure 199 the current passes along wire 5 through the red lights connected to cut-out X, to wire 6, point 2', arm B to point 2, thence to point 4', arm A, points 4 and 3 to arm C, back to the other pole of dynamo. So long as the arms remain in this position the r d lights burn and all the others are short-circuited. The next position of the machine brings arm A in contact with points 1 and 1'; current now passes direct from point 1 through arm A to point 1', wire 6 and the white lights at Y; arm A now forming a short circuit around the red lights. The current passing through the white lights returns over wire 7 to point 3 and arm B (which has also moved) to the other pole of dynamo. The white lights now burn and all others are short-circuited.

The next movement brings arm A in contact with points 2 and 2' and C to 1 and 1', leaving no connection between 3 and 3'. The current now passes through arm C from point 1 to 1'; thence to point 2' arm A, point 2, 4' arm B to point 4 through the green lights and back to point 3' and to the other pole of the dynamo. The green lights now burn while the others are short-circuited.

The fourth position of the arms leaves the space between 4 and 4' open and the current again passes through one of the arms from point 1 to 1', wire 6, white lights, wire 7 to points 3, 3' and back to dynamo. An elementary diagram of those connections is shown in Figure 200. Three of the points, 1, 2, 3, 4, are always short-circuited.

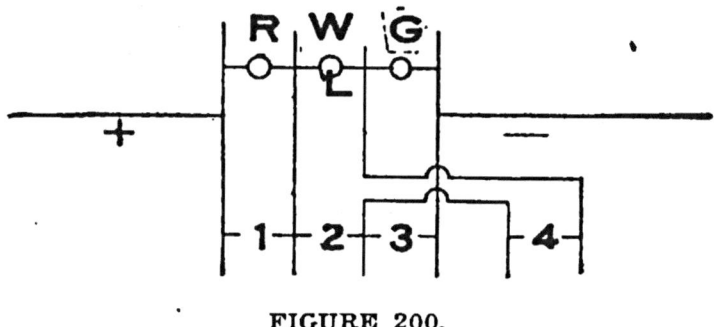

FIGURE 200.

Figure 201 shows the same machine with one of the arms removed connected to control a double-face sign, one side to burn at a time. The current in this case passes from the positive pole of the switch to the upper group of cutouts which represent one side of the sign. The current passing through these lamps continues to point 2', thence to point 1, arm A, point 1' and 3, arm B and negative pole of the switch. The next movement brings arm B in contact with point 4' and current passes along it to 4, thence to 2, arm A to 2', the lower group of cutouts representing the

ELECTRIC SIGNS 289

other side of sign and back to the negative side of the switch.

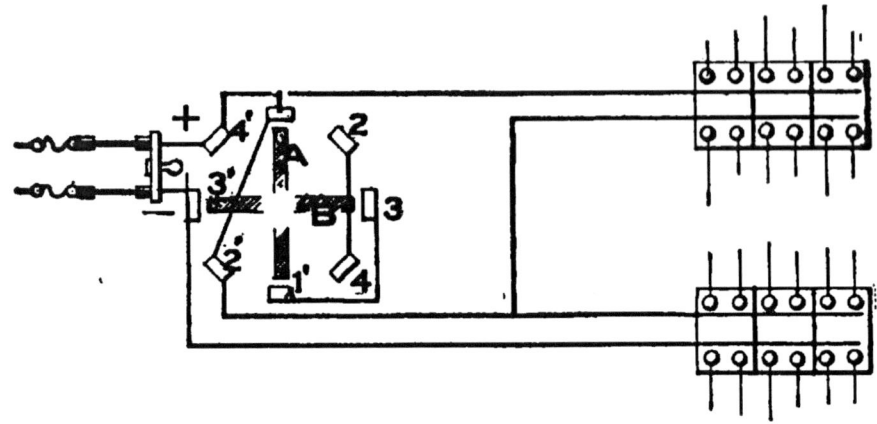

FIGURE 201.

Figure 202 shows connections for four groups of colors, one at a time being illuminated.

In Figures 203 and 204 connections for single and double-pole break are shown.

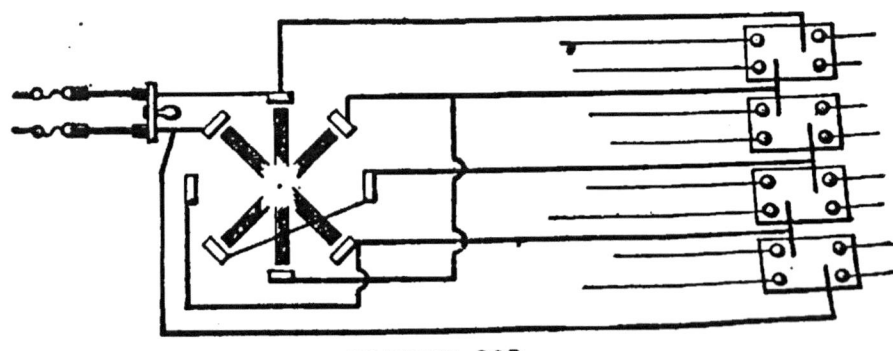

FIGURE 202.

For large installations, in connection with three-wire systems, double-disc machines are used; the positive and neutral wire connecting to one and the negative and neutral to the other.

This machine and the combination of circuits are protected by letters patent.

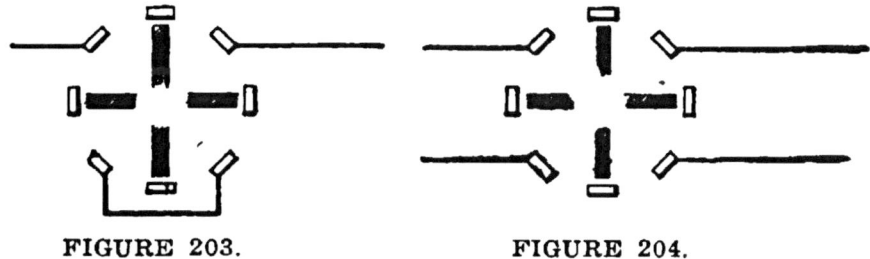

FIGURE 203.   FIGURE 204.

Figure 205 will serve to illustrate the principle of several of the monogram signs. The incandescent lamps L are each set within a metal shield which pre-

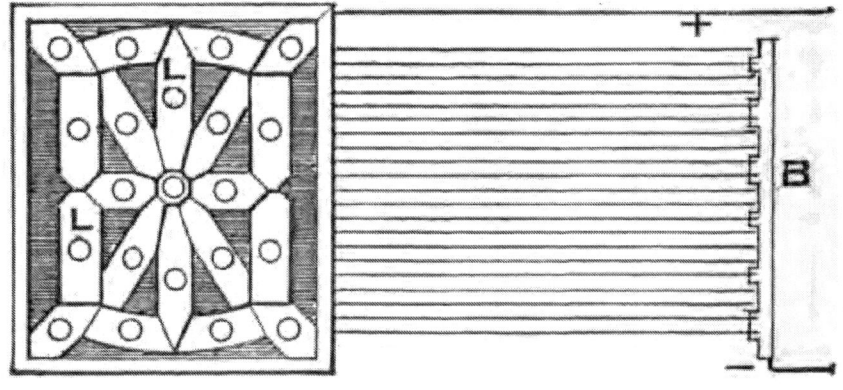

FIGURE 205.

vents the spread of light to any other part of the sign. One common feed wire leads to all of the lamps, and from each lamp a switch wire leads to the machine serving to make the proper connections. Each monogram has the lights within it so distributed that by lighting the proper lamps any letter in the alphabet can be made and a sign, consisting, say, of 10 monograms, can, therefore, be made to spell out any word or combination of words which does not exceed ten letters.

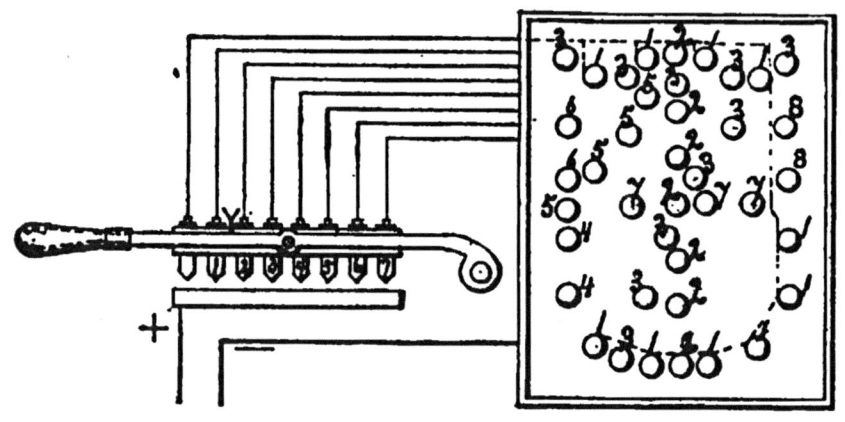

FIGURE 206.

The mechanism used for spelling out words consists of a set of discs for each monogram and these carry brass bars, as shown at B, which serve to energize

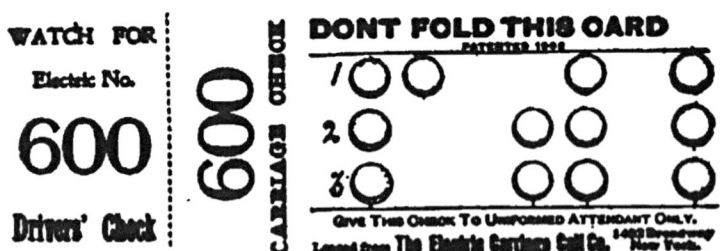

the wires leading to the lamps. These bars are cut out as shown and only those sections remaining full make contact with the switch wires.

Figure 206 is a representation of a monogram used

as a carriage call, principally for theatres. In this case only nine wires are used for each monogram and in case the sign is illuminated on both sides each of the nine wires supplies two monograms, one on each side. One wire is a common feed for all of the lamps and the other eight wires serve each to connect a small group of lamps in the monogram. These groups of lamps are so arranged that by a combination of them almost any number from 0 to 9 can be made. To accomplish this a perforated card shown at bottom of this cut is used. The card shown is arranged for a sign consisting of three monograms.

As will be seen the yoke Y carries 8 contact points each of which is capable of making contact and energizing the wire connected to it when the yoke is pressed down upon the current carrying bar beneath it. In order to allow none but the proper points to be connected the card is inserted between the current carrying bar and the yoke. Thus the figure 6 is made by allowing only the points 1, 2, 5 and 7 on the yoke to make connection with the bar below. The 0 is formed by making connection with points 1, 4, 5 and 7. In this figure all of the lamps denoted by the same number are on one circuit. The lamps marked 2, if lighted, will form the figure 1; the lamps 1, 4, 6 and 7 form the figure 6, while 0 is formed by 1, 4, 6 and 8.

A somewhat similar monogram is made by wiring the necessary number of properly distributed lamps

ELECTRIC SIGNS

on one or more circuits in the usual manner and then inserting lamps only where required to outline the letter or number wanted, the other openings being covered.

All of these devices are covered by letters patent. The information herein given is intended merely to enable wiremen to intelligently go about connecting them should occasion require.

INDEX

Absorption of light, 276.
Alternating current generator, 182.
Alternating current motor, 196.
Annunciator circuits, 21.
   telephone, 47.
Arc-circuits, 105.
   dynamo, 167.
   lamps, A. C., 117.
   lamps, D. C., 116.
   switchboard, 236.
Armatures, 233.
Arresters, lightning, 49.
Automatic cutout, gas lighting, 65.
Automobiles, 159.
Auto-starter, 212.
Auto-transformer, 198.

Battery, dry, 69.
   grouping of, 66.
   resistance of, 72.
   secondary, 71.
   test of, 84.
   wet, 68.
Bell circuits, 7.
   control of, 11.
   differential, 14.
   on dynamo circuit, 16.
   polarized, 16.
   short-circuit, 14.
   single stroke, 15.
Booster, 250.
Bridging system, telephones, 44.
Brush arc lamp, 116.
   armature, 234.
Bunsen photometer, 276.
Burglar alarms, 28.

Callow's constant ringing attachment, 34.

Candle-power, test for, 276.
Capacity, 230.
Carbons, consumption of, 275.
Cascade connection for motors, 206.
Charging circuits for automobiles, 163.
   storage batteries, 18, 250.
Circle, area of, 95.
Circular mills, 95.
Circumference of circle, 95.
Compensator, D. C., 177.
   alternating current, 198.
   in parallel, 180.
Compound wound dynamo, 170.
   motor, 134.
Condenser, 89.
   action of, 226.
Connecting bell circuits, 76.
   incandescent circuits, 231.
Continuous ringing attachments, 15.
Controller, motor, 152.
   A. C. motor, 211.
Convertible system, 98, 108.
Cooper-Hewitt lamp, 122.
Copper wire, dimensions of, 283.
   resistance of, 96.
   weight of, 95.
Counter E. M. F., 229.
Cumulative winding, 134.
Current, induced, 58.

Differential bell, 14.
   winding on motor, 134.
Direction of current, 86, 90.
Discount meter, 129.
Divided circuits, 92.
Door opener, 7.
Drum armature, 185, 233.
Dynamo current for bells, 16, 38.

INDEX

Dynamo, A. C., single-phase, 182.
   arc, 177.
   compound wound, 170.
   series wound, 167.
   shunt wound, 168.

Edward's condenser system, 63.
Electric signs, 285.
Electrolytic interrupter, 60.
Elevator controller, A. C. motor, 216.
   signals, 113.
End cell switch, 250.
Equalizer, 174.

Fire alarm system, 28.
Flashers for electric signs, 285.
Fort Wayne single-phase motor, 204.
Frequency meter, 222.
Fusing currents, 284.

Gas lighting circuits, 61.
Generator, monocyclic, 187.
   single-phase, 185.
   three-phase, 190.
   three-wire, 182.
Gramme ring armature, 229.
Ground connections, 7.
   detectors, D. C., 243.
   detectors, A. C., 247.

Incandescent light circuits, 97.
   lamps as resistance, 17, 165.
   lamps, efficiency of, 273.
   lamps, wattage of, 263.
Induction coil, 58, 89.
Induction motor, 196.
Intercommunicating telephone, 45.
Interrupter, current, 59.
Iron wire, resistance of, 96.
   weight of, 96.

Joints in wires, 278.
Jump spark, 163.

Light, intensity of, 273.
Lines of force, 86.
Long shunt, 171.
Losses, on wires, 277.
   on three-wire system, 176.

Magnetism, 94.

Magneto, testing with, 263.
Monocyclic generator, 187.
Monogram letter, 290.
Motor, compound wound, 134.
   direct current, 131.
   reversing, A. C., 197.
   reversing, D. C., 135.
   series wound, 131.
   shunt wound, 133.
   single-phase, 201.
   synchronous, 196.
   three-phase, 199.

Nernst lamp, 121.
Neutral wire, 176.

Ohm's law, 91.
Organ controller, 143.
Over-compounding, 171.
Overload starting box, 137.

Parallel wires in, 281.
   dynamos in, 171, 191.
Partrick, Carter & Wilkins annunciator system, 25.
Photometer, 276.
Polarized bell, 16.
Power factor, 231.
Power factor meter, 222.
Printing press controller, 139, 144, 152.
Pump motor controller, 141.

Rawson & Evans Flasher, 286.
Recording wattmeters, 125.
Rectifier, mercury arc, 256.
Reinforcing wires, 125.
Remote control, 107.
Repeater, telegraph, 50.
Resistance of batteries, 72.
Return call annunciators, 24.
   bell circuits, 7.

Self induction, 229.
Separate exciter, 195.
Series arc circuit, 110.
   arc dynamo, 167.
   incandescent circuit, 109.
   motors for constant current, 150.
   motors for constant potential, 131.

INDEX

Short-circuit bell, 14.
Short-circuits on bell systems, 83.
   test for, 259.
Short shunt, 171.
Shunt motor, 133.
   multiplying power of, 93.
   dynamo, 168.
Signs, electric, 285.
Single-phase armature, 234.
   dynamo, 182.
   motor, 201.
Single stroke bell, 15.
Split phase motors, 203.
Starting, A. C. motors, 198.
   box, 137.
   switch, A. C. motors, 209.
Storage batteries, 71.
   circuits for automobiles, 159.
   connections, 250.
Street car motor circuit, 147.
Switchboard, arc, 236.
   direct current, 240.
   theater, 112.
Synchronous motor, 196.
Synchroscopes, 191, 226.

Tandem connection for motors, 206.
Teaser wire, 187.
Telautograph, 52.
Telegraph circuits, 49.
   repeaters, 50.
Telephone circuits, 43.
Test for insulation resistance, 84.

Testing board, A. C., 220.
Testing incandescent circuits, 259.
T.-H. arc switchboard, 238.
   armature, 234.
Theater switchboard, 112.
Three-phase armature, 235.
   system, lights on, 100.
Three-wire generator, 182, 190.
   system, 97.
Transferring arc circuits, 236.
Transformers, 226.
Tree system, 97.
Trouble, locating on bell systems, 79.

Underload starting box, 137.

Voltmeter connections, 243.
   testing with, 263.
   formula for test, 265.

Wagner single-phase motor, 201.
Watts, definition of, 94.
Wattage of incandescent lamps, 273.
Wattless current, 231.
Wattmeter, recording, 125.
Western Electric Co. arc dynamo, 167.
Wheatstone bridge, 266, 270.
   test with, 263.
Wiring tables, 277.
Wright discount meter, 129.

X-ray, 57.

LaVergne, TN USA
07 September 2010
196099LV00003B/29/P